Zach Keele is one of my favorite preachers. In exposing
the rich terrain of the passage he has the skills of an archaeologist,
reminds us of the big picture like a master story-teller, and touches
the heart like a good pastor. This book will lead you to love and
understand God and his word more than ever before.

MICHAEL HORTON

professor, Westminster Seminary California

THE
UNFOLDING
WORD

The Story of the Bible from Creation to New Creation

THE
UNFOLDING
WORD

The Story of the Bible from Creation to New Creation

ZACH KEELE

LEXHAM PRESS

The Unfolding Word: The Story of the Bible from Creation to New Creation

Copyright 2020 Zach Keele

Lexham Press, 1313 Commercial St., Bellingham, WA 98225
LexhamPress.com

Print ISBN 9781683593805
Digital ISBN 9781683593812
Library of Congress Control Number 2020941694

Lexham Editorial: Elliot Ritzema, Danielle Thevenaz, Jessi Strong
Cover Design: Peter Park
Interior Artwork: Joshua Hunt
Design and Typesetting: Abigail Stocker

To Tovauh

אַחַת הִיא יוֹנָתִי תַמָּתִי

Song 6:9

CONTENTS

INTRODUCTION

The Bible is the best-selling book in history. For millennia, Jews, Christians, and Muslims have been drawn to the stories, prayers, hymns, and laws found within its pages. Even in twenty-first-century America, where general Bible knowledge is on the decline, references to Scripture are not uncommon in pop culture and politics. And it is more accessible than ever: while the printing press put a Bible in every house, Steve Jobs made it possible to have a Bible in every pocket, fully searchable by word or phrase.

Accessibility, though, does not necessarily correlate to understanding. The Bible, for all its popularity, is not an easy book to make sense of. It may be the greatest story ever told, but it is challenging to understand.

Without a doubt, parts of the Bible pose few difficulties. The gospel preaching of Paul is clear and powerful. The delightful stories of Daniel and David can be grasped by kids in Sunday School classes. And the preaching of Jesus is plenty approachable.

Other portions of Scripture, though, are not so user friendly. The descriptions of diseases in Leviticus 13–14 numb the mind with their endless details. Some of the sermons of the prophets seem like a labyrinth of strange imagery. The book of Revelation can scare us. There is no shortage of passages that we can read and not know what they really mean.

The Bible stretches our understanding not merely with opaque chapters, but also in how the stories are related to one another. Whether it is the classic question of how the New Testament relates to the Old Testament or how a specific story relates to the overall history, like the Levite and his concubine in Judges 19, it can be a challenge to figure out how the Bible fits together. Then there are passages where we wonder why they were even included. Why list all of Solomon's officials in 1 Kings 4? What is the point of the genealogies that open 1 Chronicles? Such chapters can be easy enough to understand, but they appear pointless. If they fell out of Scripture, would we lose anything? In reality, most of us leave such passages out by our ignoring them.

How, then, can we improve our understanding of God's word? How can we develop our appreciation for all of the vast and varied parts of Scripture?

To start off, we need to pinpoint some of the hurdles to our understanding. First there is how we read. There are two ways of reading: slow and fast. A slow read analyzes each word, phrase, and verse. It pays attention to finer details. It gazes at each tree. Most Bible studies and devotionals in the modern church employ this slower reading method. Slow reading is good and necessary, but it has certain limits. If you look only for the trees, you cannot see the forest. If you zero in on verses, you miss how whole chapters fit together. For example, moving slowly through Paul's letters makes them feel like doctrinal theses, moral guidebooks, or spiritual meditations. But if you read an entire letter in one sitting, you see what it really is: personal correspondence from a pastor to a church.

Fast reading does not fuss with the details but takes an aerial view. It has eyes for the sweeping themes of Samuel or the big picture of Israel coming out of Egypt. Fast reading aims to grasp the key points and the main story line. An example of fast reading in the Bible itself is Psalm 105, which retells the story of Israel from Abraham to Joshua in a space of 38 verses to reveal the theme of the Lord's steadfast love to his people. Like slow reading, fast reading is proper and vital but has limits. By focusing on the big picture, you can lose sight of the details. Working with a summary can lead to inaccuracies and bland generalizations.

When we read the Bible, we need to hold together both slow and fast reading. Scripture is like a large mosaic, where each tile is its own image. Put together, they form another image. We need to zoom in and out regularly; slowing down and speeding up have to work together.

That is one purpose of this book: to enable you to let slow and fast reading work in harmony. The book itself is a fast read, covering the entire Bible in thirteen chapters. Each chapter summarizes a sizeable chunk of Scripture. Yet this overview is done with an eye to detail. The chapters will explain individual stories and passages in a way that shows how they are connected to the big picture. In this way I show you how to learn more about specific passages and gauge how each story contributes to the whole. For this reason, each chapter contains a Bible reading, and it will be most helpful if you have your Bible on hand as you read.

The second hurdle to our understanding the Bible is its history. Scripture is a story, a historical one that unfolded in the lives of real people within the messiness of history. And history requires us to know facts: dates, geography, and major events. In Jonah, for example, the empire of Assyria is a major character, and we cannot appreciate Assyria without being informed about its history. Therefore, this book includes maps, pictures, and tables that lay out some of the history going on behind and within the stories of Scripture. By highlighting the history of the Bible, the humanity of the stories will come alive with greater vibrancy.

The third hurdle in developing our knowledge of Scripture is its very age. The Bible is not just history; it is *ancient* history. The men and women of Scripture lived in a very different world than the one we inhabit in the twenty-first century. Abraham not only spoke a different language, but he breathed in the ideas and assumptions of ancient cultures. One of the greatest errors we make in reading Scripture is projecting our modern selves upon its characters. The truth is that Moses and David had more in common with their pagan neighbors than they do with us. There are timeless truths in Scripture, but they are expressed in the accent and garb of ancient cultures. I hope this book will help you acclimate better to the world of Scripture, and one of the best ways to do this is to read the texts of the ancient world. Therefore, the chapters regularly engage and quote ancient literature relevant to Scripture. The archaic customs of the Hittites and Egyptians may be foreign and strange to us, but Abraham and Isaac felt quite at home in that world. The more we learn about the world surrounding the Bible, whether it concerns making wine or international treaties, the better we can appreciate its characters in their own context.

The final difficulty for our understanding comes from Scripture itself. On the road to Emmaus, Jesus preached a sermon about how the whole Old Testament was about him (Luke 24:27). He told his hearers in John 5 that Moses wrote about him (John 5:46). And Peter confesses that the Spirit of Christ testified through the prophets about the sufferings and glories of Christ (1 Pet 1:11). The Bible is about Jesus, yet it is not easy to grasp how the Old Testament looks forward to and speaks of him. Each Old Testament chapter in this book, therefore, points out how the stories lead us to Christ, and lays the foundation necessary to see Christ more clearly in the Old Testament. This foundation was mentioned by Mary and Zechariah as they praised God for remembering his holy covenant sworn to Abraham (Luke 1:55, 72–73). Christ came to fulfill the promises of the Old Testament covenants. This book, then, details the ancient covenants of Scripture so that we can more deeply recognize how all the promises are yes and amen in Jesus Christ (2 Cor 1:20).

As I address these hurdles throughout the book, my hope is that you will not only expand your knowledge of all of Scripture, but grow in your love for God and his word. The verses praising the benefits of studying God's word are manifold: "The teaching of the LORD is perfect, renewing life" (Ps 19:7, NJPS). "The words You inscribed give light and grant understanding to the simple" (Ps 119:130, NJPS).

"Sanctify them in the truth; your word is truth" (John 17:17). The study of Scripture is not easy. It takes effort, but the blessings of God's word are never ceasing, and my goal is that this book will come alongside your Bible reading to help unlock these blessings. You will see the unity running from Genesis to Revelation, even through the murky bends in the Old Testament. You will get better acquainted with the spiritual ancestors who came before us. And you will see with more clarity the bright grace of Jesus Christ showcased in the Law, Prophets, and the Psalms. In the end, we will see together how the Bible is not just a great story, but it is *your* story—how you are swept up in the drama of God's wonderful salvation throughout the ages and unto forever.

Creation | Fall | People + place promised | God so near

David (obey for the people)

Waiting for the Son | Calling Abraham | People fail to obey

Obedience for eternal life with God

↳ Promise of grace

↳ God will be with his people

Sinai = Holy God demands holiness

THEMES TO HIGHLIGHT:
1. Immanuel: lost in Eden—perfected in glory
   a. Tabernacle, incarnation
2. Promise of the Lord for the seed of the woman (gracious)
   a. Through Seth: Abraham, David, and Jesus
3. Redemption accomplished by the Son: Righteous One who paid the penalty of sin due to his love

God in
the flesh

Son's face
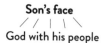
God with his people

Heralding
the gospel

Righteous One
earns new creation
by his blood

Day of the Lord
judgment

Eternal rest and glory

Chart 1: The Biblical Story

1

CREATIONAL FOUNDATION

Bible Reading: Genesis 1–3

"Who is Yahweh that I should obey him? ... I don't know Yahweh" (Exod 5:2, my translation). Pharaoh, the great king of Egypt, spat these words into the faces of Moses and Aaron. He was keenly devoted to the hundreds of gods and goddesses of Egypt and, being well versed in international diplomacy, was also knowledgeable about the deities of his allies and adversaries. Osiris, Amon-Re, Marduk, Enlil, and Taru were gods that Pharaoh could recite, but Yahweh was not a name he had ever heard before.

The situation differed little for the Hebrew slaves. They revered the God of their fathers Abraham, Isaac, and Jacob, but they were ignorant of the name Yahweh. "El Shaddai" was the name that had been published to Abraham and passed on to his descendants (Exod 6:3). And the Hebrews' devotion to El Shaddai was not exclusive. The God of their fathers was one of many gods they honored. The prophet Ezekiel frankly reports that the Israelites were polytheists when Moses showed up on their doorstep (Ezek 20:6–8).

This means the arrival of Moses enrolled the Israelites in *Who Is Yahweh? 101*. Moses began a period of cutting off old loyalties in which the Israelites had to divorce themselves from the idols of Egypt and betroth themselves exclusively to Yahweh. Moses carried with him the revelation of Yahweh, who he is and why he should be obeyed, loved, and feared. By the wonders of the exodus and the word of Genesis 1–3, Yahweh was disclosing to the ancient Hebrews (and us today) the beauties of his splendor and the majesty of his holiness.

As modern readers, we must remember that God delivered to Israel the first five books of the Old Testament, called the Torah or Pentateuch, during the forty-some years the Israelites journeyed from Egypt to the promised land. Hence, the opening chapters of Genesis were intended for the ears of the exodus Hebrews. Pharaoh's question, then, is one way to summarize the theme and goal of the Pentateuch. In the Torah, Israel is learning about Yahweh and how to love and worship him alone.

Additionally, as Pharaoh saw, God's name lies at the heart of the matter. In the ancient Near East, names and titles played an all-important role, especially for kings and gods. A name expressed a person's identity, origin, and essence. The name stood for the person himself. Moses thus asked at the burning bush, "What is your name that I should tell the people?" And the ice breaker to all of Moses' sermons was "I am Yahweh"—the Hebrew name for the Lord, which English translations render as "Lord" in small caps—or "I am Yahweh God," which in Hebrew is Yahweh-Elohim, rendered "the Lord God" in many English translations. In fact, the name that monopolizes the Sinai literature is Yahweh, in its various constructions. The covenantal name that flies like a banner over Israel's redemption from slavery, their deliverances in the desert, and the glory cloud that crowned Sinai is Yahweh, Yahweh-Elohim.

It is under the shadow of Sinai, therefore, that Genesis 1:1 sounds with the clearest notes and most profound melody. "In the beginning, God (Elohim) created heaven and earth." At Sinai, Israel beheld the glory of Yahweh-Elohim as their covenant Savior and King. In Genesis, they learn that their Redeemer is also the Creator of all. In fact, Yahweh, who is the only Elohim (God), stands as the Almighty Alpha of all things. It is best to understand "heaven" in Genesis 1:1

as referring to the invisible realm of God and his angels. Paul later echoes this verse by saying that "by him all things were created, in heaven and on earth, visible and invisible" (Col 1:16). The creation account instructed Israel about the God to whom they belonged. In it they learn that before anything existed, human or angel, Yahweh was the God of whom and through whom and to whom were all things.

Moreover, Yahweh's effortless fashioning constructed the heavens as his throne and the earth as his footstool (Isa 66:1). The tape measure in his left hand and the hammer in his right are his words. The Lord commanded and it was so. By his royal proclamation, Yahweh spoke into existence what once was not. And the miraculous products of Yahweh's voice popped into being out of nothing. Matter is not eternal in Genesis 1, but Yahweh is. As one scholar notes, "No item which God orders into being ... can be said to emerge from preexisting materials."[1] Yahweh both spoke matter into being and reshaped the chaotic into the ordered and beautiful. And the beauties of his craftsmanship are not limited to Redwoods and white marble slabs, but they include the structural order itself. God is responsible for the alternation between night and day, which is a measurement of time, and even the invention of time. Similarly, the separation of the waters above and below to form the expanse is the fabrication of space for life, while the gathering of the waters and emerging of the dry land forges the physical home for human beings. Time, space, and mass flow from the lips of Yahweh. And by building his world in the timespan of a week, Genesis shows Yahweh to be the God of history as well as creation.

The pantheons of the ancient world were like a Walmart superstore, containing every imaginable religious product. But with Genesis 1, the Hebrews were being enlightened about the splendor of the one true God and Creator of heaven and earth. Moses presented real theology to underscore their faith and devotion so that they might worship Yahweh as their God alone.

GENESIS AND OTHER ANCIENT CREATION STORIES

The theology of Genesis 1 stands out more starkly when it is compared with the general climate of pagan ideas about creation and the origins of the universe, divine and human. Numerous creation stories have survived that we can use to understand the world of Israel and to compare with Genesis. We cannot know if the biblical creation story was directly influenced by these pagan myths, but we can say that there is a general cognitive environment of creation that Genesis is interacting with. We must be familiar with the ideological climate of the ancient world since the Hebrews coming out of Egypt lived within it every day. The pastoral power of Genesis spoke to the men and women of Israel in their particular time and place. "Genesis and the ancient Near East probably have more in common with each other than either has with modern secular thought."[2]

The creational accounts of the ancient Near East can be divided into two basic categories: Egyptian and Mesopotamian. Among the Mesopotamian accounts, written in either Akkadian or Sumerian, I will summarize three that are most helpful for comparing with the Genesis account. First there is *Atrahasis*, which was likely written between 2000–1700 BC. The epic opens with the lesser gods performing burdensome and heavy labor, like digging ditches to water the land. When the drudgery and misery became too much, these gods rallied together to storm the gates of higher gods, particularly of Enlil. Upon the declaration of war, another god named Ea/Enki proposed the solution of creating another being, a man. Upon this being they would place the yoke and drudgery of the gods, so that the gods could spend their days in ease. Then the mother-goddess, Nintu, took the flesh and blood of a god, executed for rebelling, and mixed it with clay to fashion humankind. Once the heavy yoke was placed on humankind, the gods ran free of care and the revolution was over.

Atrahasis

Probably the most well-known creation myth today is *Enuma Elish*, which dates to about 1200 BC. This epic contains an account of the creation of the physical world, but its real focus is to celebrate the exaltation of Marduk to the top of the pantheon in Babylon. The *Enuma Elish* opens with a scene of the embattled gods in the primeval past. The goddess Tiamat, with her champion Qingu, rebelled against Ea. In defense, Ea summoned his champion and son Marduk, and Marduk insists on supremacy among the gods as his reward for defeating the army lead by Tiamat. After Marduk's victory, he splits open Tiamat to create heaven and earth, and with her bodily organs fabricates the stars, day, moon, and sun. As Marduk continues to make artful things, he devises a way to lighten the burden of the gods, saying,

I shall compact blood, I shall cause bones to be,
I shall make stand a human being, let "Man" be its name.
I shall create humankind,
They shall bear the gods' burden that those may rest.[3]

As punishment for leading Tiamat's forces into war, Qingu's blood is shed. From his blood, Marduk produces humans and imposes the burden of the gods on them. The Enuma Elish culminates with Marduk being acclaimed in this temple with fifty lofty names, thereby securing his kingship in the pantheon and the everlasting devotion of humankind.

A third Mesopotamian myth is Enki and Ninmah.[4] This myth is obscure in parts, and no firm date has been established for it, but it is clearly one of the earliest works dealing with the creation of humankind. Similar to the previous two myths, Enki and Ninmah commences in the days when heaven and earth were created, when gods were born and the senior gods oversaw the minor gods laboring at tilling the soil and digging canals. Yet Enki, the creator of all the senior gods, is laying upon his bed refusing to rise. The laboring gods approach with tears from their miserable work to lodge a complaint with Nammu, Enki's mother. Nammu hears their complaint and calls her son to arise from his bed and devise a solution so that the gods can relax from their toil. Arising from his couch, Enki plots a resolution. He employs Ninmah to nip off pieces of clay to generate humankind, male and female. The second half of this myth turns into a wisdom contest, where in a series of six acts, Ninmah forges different types of people (a stiffened neck, blind, crippled, and barren) as problems for Enki. Enki answers by declaring the fate for each people group to live in an honorable way. For example, in the fifth act, Ninmah shapes the barren woman and Enki decrees her fate to work in the Women's Quarter, which refers to either weaving or the royal harem. In this way, humans take up the work of the gods so that they can relax.

Turning to Egypt, it is difficult to pinpoint one creation story
or view of the cosmos. A single orthodox account did not exist that
we know of. This could be because, as John H. Walton points out,
"Egyptians focus more on divine origins while in Mesopotamia the
greater focus is on human origins."[5] Nevertheless, two Egyptian
texts will help us get a flavor for what was in the back of the ancient
Hebrews' minds when they heard Genesis for the first time.

The first text dates from the twenty-fourth century BC and was
carved inside two pyramids as dedication ritual texts.[6] By this ritual,
the god was asked to bless the pyramid just as Atum, the creator
god, brought up the primeval hillock, which was in the shape of a
pyramid. Hence, we find Atum sitting high on the primeval pyramid
that he just raised out of the waters of chaos. Then, with an explo-
sive sneeze, Atum creates Shu, the god of the air, and Tefnut, the
goddess of moisture, with his spit. Atum, as the divine source for all
matter, uses his spit and the utterance of a name as acts of creation.
In this text, the process of creation is not a material movement from
nonexistence to existence. Rather, things come into existence out of
the chaotic sea by being assigned a function and role in an ordered
cosmos. Walton says the Egyptian view of creation involves "bringing order and organization to the cosmos."[7] Additionally, this text,
and other pyramid inscriptions like it, say nothing about the formation of humanity.

Another later Egyptian account of creation comes from the temple
of Ptah in Memphis. It most likely dates to the thirteenth and twelfth
centuries BC, when the capital of Egypt was established at Memphis.
Here, Ptah is acclaimed as the supreme creator god over all other recognized gods. Significantly, Ptah first conceives of the created things
in his mind, and then speaks them into existence. Ptah is magnified as
the one who gave birth to the gods, their towns, cult-places, offerings,
and images. Ptah even enters into rest and glorification upon completion of his work: "So has Ptah come to rest after his making everything, and every divine speech as well."[8] The formation of humanity,

however, finds no place in this text. Instead, humanity's function is assumed to be building shrines and bringing offerings.

From these brief samplings, we can see six ways in which the Genesis 1 creation story is similar to creation stories in surrounding cultures:

1. There is an invisible or inaccessible world where God or the gods exist, and these gods are personally involved with and controlling human affairs. Compared to the atheistic and deistic presuppositions of our modern scientific world, this is a significant similarity.

2. The Mesopotamian myths share with Scripture a pattern of creation, rebellion, and flood.[9]

3. Like Genesis 2:7, a few of the Mesopotamian accounts include humanity being formed from clay or dust.

4. Similar to Yahweh's creative word, in Egypt Ptah conceives and speaks creation into being.

5. The myths often included the building of a temple either by the god or in dedicating one by the people. In Scripture, Yahweh's creative work is pictured in terms of construction and consecration.

6. The purpose of the myths, both in Egypt and Mesopotamia, was the exaltation of a god or gods so that the people would venerate and worship them. In Scripture, the name of Yahweh is displayed in his mighty deeds to instruct the Hebrews to love, honor, and serve him alone. The purpose was theological and historical to spur on the mind and heart in reverent godliness.

As noteworthy as the similarities are, though, the differences between Scripture and the ancient pagan creation myths are like a bright light to the eyes. Here are six of the more pronounced differences:

1. Unlike the pagan myths, there are no male and female gods in Genesis, but only Yahweh as the Almighty Alpha.

2. In the pagan myths, the gods were part of the created realities, embodied within the natural forces. The sun, moon, and stars were deities themselves. Yet in Genesis 1, God is above and beyond nature and speaks the heavenly bodies into existence, not as gods or angels, but as part of the ordered world.

3. In Mesopotamia, creation results from an uneasy balance where the gods fight and wage war, and heaven, earth, and humanity are fabricated from a dead god. But in Scripture, Yahweh is not capricious, impotent, or fickle; he does not struggle, and there are none to oppose him. Instead, as a sovereign king, he carefully builds with the words of his power.

4. No other creation story is arranged by the succession of days like the seven days of Genesis 1, which underscores Yahweh as the Lord of history.

5. In Mesopotamia, humankind is more of an afterthought to the cosmos, and humanity's purpose is to do the miserable work for the gods. Likewise, humankind was fashioned imperfect, crippled, and flawed in contrast to the holy righteousness of Adam and Eve in the garden. In fact, male and female are the crowning creation of Yahweh as his vice-regents. Genesis presents a high view of humanity as opposed to the pagan world.

6. Matter was conceived of as more or less eternal in the ancient Near East, so that creation was an ordering or

organizing of the primordial sea. In Scripture, God does perform ordering and impose function, but he does so after speaking things into existence out of nothing.

The power of these polemical differences would be invigorating to the faith of the Hebrews. At the foot of Sinai, the light of Genesis 1 would take the polytheists from the darkness of idolatry to the dazzling morning of knowing Yahweh, the one God of heaven and earth. In Egypt, the Hebrew slaves feared the god of the Nile; they paid homage to the god of the threshold and hearth. But now they know the truth: there is only One God, Yahweh-Elohim, and there is none beside him. By his word, Yahweh fashioned all things. By his right arm, God judged Egypt with hail and darkness and ushered the Hebrews through the sea to the light of his face.

COVENANTAL FOUNDATION

The opening chapters of Genesis were not only intended to correct the mistaken notions of the Hebrews about how the universe was constructed. While Genesis 1 establishes Yahweh as the sovereign Creator and enthroned King, Genesis 2–3 lays the cornerstone of how Yahweh is the covenantal Lord of the Hebrews. These chapters connect the work of God done for Israel in the exodus to God's work with Adam and Eve. They link Israel's story with that of the first humans. While the word "covenant" doesn't appear in these chapters, a concept can be present even when it is not named. For example, the cry "Go Broncos!" is more than sufficient to inform you of a football setting. Likewise, no word for "sin" appears in Genesis 2–3, but it would be irresponsible to deny that sin is present in these chapters. In the same manner, the theme of covenant dominates this story.

Remember, our starting point is Israel at Sinai. As modern readers of the Bible, our initial task is to understand the text as it was delivered to the ancient Hebrews, and covenant was hardly a minor note in their song. Yahweh brought them to his holy mountain to enter into a covenant with them. The terms and laws of the covenant covered their whole existence. Israel understood their identity as Yahweh's covenantal people. "Yahweh your God" meant he was their covenantal Lord. The Sinai covenant, though, was not the only covenantal tune to which Israel danced. The Abrahamic covenant was the bass line on which the treble of Sinai was played.

But what is a covenant? In the ancient Near East, a covenant at base was a promissory oath to do something sealed in a name of a god to ensure its fulfillment. This oath invoked the god's name to punish the one who broke her promise. And with Yahweh, since his word is unbreakable, all of his utterances were considered to have the value of an oath. "When God spoke, it was unthinkable that his word would not come to pass; it was implicit that he had sworn by himself in every promise to his people."[10] More complex covenants included commands and prohibitions, promises of reward, and warnings of punishments or sanctions.

In Genesis 2:16, Yahweh God commanded the man, "You shall eat from every tree of the garden" (my translation). This could have the sense of permission, "You may eat." Either way, the man is granted the privilege and duty to feast upon the trees. A prohibition follows the obligation: "Of the tree of the knowledge of good and evil you shall not eat." The "you shall not" of the Ten Commandments is clearly in the background. And this prohibition is wedded to a penalty for rebellion, "you shall surely die," which is the capital punishment formula of the law. Finally, the reward of the tree of life is barred from the man and woman for their disobedience, a clear curse.

The indications that this is a covenant are not exhausted with these formal features. The entire setting of Adam and Eve being in a garden with God reverberates with the sounds of covenant. As modern people, our ears are untrained to these notes because the ancient culture of Israel is foreign to us. Yet the Hebrews would not have missed the indicators. Four principles will train our listening skills.

First, "Holiness is not inherent in creation but comes by God's dictate."[11] Creation is not holy in and of itself; rather, places and objects become holy only by God's declaration or action. Yahweh must declare a place holy; he must build the shrine for it to be sacred. Hence, in Deuteronomy 12, the place where God makes his name to dwell is the holy place of his tabernacle and no other.

Second, "Holiness is a necessary ... precondition for God's presence to be manifest."[12] Yahweh only reveals himself in a holy place, and the presence of God constitutes the place as holy. The bush burned with Yahweh's splendor, and sandals had to be removed upon the holy ground. For Yahweh to plant the garden and then for him to be present in it with the man and woman constitutes the garden as a holy place, a shrine.

Third, the combination of wonderful gardens and gods invoked both the ideas of temple and the duty to maintain, which fell to the king and/or priest. Kings often planted verdant gardens next to the deity's shrine, and it was their task to maintain the fruitfulness and purity of the temple garden. Job Y. Jindo puts it this way: "In Mesopotamia, in particular, each temple city was conceived of as the manor of the patron deity, and each local ruler was divinely elected to supervise the temple estates, including its garden(s)."[13] And Jon Levenson concludes, "In sum, in the ancient Near East, gardens, especially royal gardens, are not simply decorative. They are symbolic, and their religious message is very much involved with that of the Temple in or near which they are not infrequently found."[14] Hence, Victor Hurowitz states about the temple in Jerusalem, "It seems as if the Temple was not merely YHWH's residence, but a divine garden on earth,"[15] a recreation of the garden of Eden. Likewise, Ezekiel calls Eden the garden of God and the mountain of God, and he likens the Adam figure to a guardian cherub, blameless and flawless in beauty (Ezek 28:12–14).

Finally, these temple gardens had to be cared for and protected. Impurities and detestable things were walled out. The garden had to be tended to shield it from the chaos, decay, and death of the outside world. Caring for such sacred space was a priestly duty, but this responsibility was often taken up by the kings. As such, then, Eden was a type of sacred place, and Adam was put in it as a priest-king to work it and guard it (Gen 2:15). The word here for "work" is often used of the priestly service in worship (Num 3:7-8; 8:11), and "guarding" was performed by both the priests and Levites to protect the temple from defilement (Num 3:38; 8:26). These parallels between Adam and the sanctuary further reveal the covenantal background of the garden of Eden. Just as Israel's priesthood was in covenant with Yahweh, so was Adam's in the beginning.

A COVENANT OF OBEDIENCE

Yahweh's covenant with Adam was a covenant of obedience, in which Adam and Eve had to obey for life everlasting. Being fashioned after God's image, Adam and Eve were fully capable of doing so, but it is precisely within these priestly duties where the couple failed. First, instead of being guardians, they allowed the crafty serpent in the holy garden where he did not belong. Then, he planted a profane desire within them, which sprouted into coveting and blossomed into sin—and they took and ate.

Upon the hot sands around Sinai, Israel heard from the glory cloud the demands of the covenant to be holy in obedience and to guard the tabernacle's purity, and the threat of death for disobedience shivered down their spines. The Hebrews listened to the story of Mr. and Mrs. Priest-King. It was clear to them "that Exodus echoes Eden intentionally and in significant ways."[16] Yet their first parents failed; impurity was found in Eve and rebellion was uncovered in Adam. The question of who Yahweh was had been answered, but a second question remained: Could they obey? Adam was God's son; likewise, Yahweh called Israel out of Egypt as his firstborn son (Exod 4:22). Could they fulfill his commands to preserve and attain holiness?

This question did not stay unanswered long. The Sinai covenant was ratified in Exodus 24, and while Moses remained conversing with Yahweh, Israel fashioned a golden calf idol and danced (Exod 32).

Israel committed adultery on their honeymoon. The tablets etched by the finger of God were broken. Israel flunked as Adam had. Death was theirs. These miserable sinners had no right to be in God's presence. If Yahweh remained among them, he would consume them in wrath on the way (Exod 33:3). A third question then arose: Was this the end? Would Israel perish completely?

The Eden narrative again produced fruit for the condemned Hebrews. God had said to Adam and Eve, "In the day you eat, you shall surely die." The Lord God cursed the serpent; he cursed the woman and the man, but they did not die. Sure, spiritual death infested their souls like cancer, and eventually their bodies were swallowed by the dust. But God did not execute the rebellious couple. God showed mercy; he extended grace. The Lord God even gave the naked parents a sworn promise to do them good: the woman's offspring shall bruise the serpent's head (Gen 3:15). Yahweh ensured his people a victory over the tempter, and God sealed this promise with a covering. An animal was taken; its hide was tanned as a tunic (Gen 3:21). In the shedding of blood, Yahweh became the first seamstress to clothe the nakedness of Eve and Adam. With leather and a promise, Yahweh made a new, gracious covenant with the fallen couple. He would do for his people what they could not do for themselves.

THE ALPHA AND OMEGA

Yahweh did not wipe out his idolatrous people at the foot of Sinai, but he remembered his promise to Abraham, Isaac, and Jacob and showed grace and mercy. All the nations were lost in idolatry and wickedness, and Israel was no better, but Yahweh chose Israel to be his own.

Yet Israel would play out the Eden narrative that they heard at the time of the exodus. "Just as Adam and Eve were expelled from the garden of Eden for not keeping God's command (Gen 3:11), so too the people of Israel were exiled from the Land of Promise for the same reason."[17] It is precisely this parallel between Adam and Israel that the apostle Paul will later pick up. As sin and death entered the world through the first Adam, so righteousness and life came by the last Adam, Jesus Christ (Rom 5:17).

Adam failed. Israel flunked. But by his grace, God preserved them until that son of Eve crushed the serpent to free them from sin and death. Christ prevailed and rose victorious as the righteous one. We have eternal life and justification not because we have kept a covenant of works, but through the works of another freely given to us by faith.

The opening chapters of Genesis, then, show both us and Israel who Yahweh is. Yahweh is the one God, the almighty Creator, who alone is from eternity. Yahweh is our covenantal Redeemer, who is merciful and gracious. And Yahweh is the God who became man, Jesus Christ, to bring us to that new and greater Eden, the heavenly Jerusalem. Through Isaiah, Yahweh tells us:

> I am God, and there is no other;
>   I am God, and there is none like me,
> declaring the end from the beginning
>   and from ancient times things not yet done,
> saying, "My counsel shall stand,
>   and I will accomplish all my purpose,"
> calling a bird of prey from the east,
>   the man of my counsel from a far country.
> I have spoken, and I will bring it to pass;
>   I have purposed, and I will do it. (46:9–11)

It is fitting that in Genesis 1–3 as God reveals himself as the Alpha, he also shows us how he is the Omega. The ripples of Eden echo all the way to heaven. As we commence on this survey of the story of the Bible, it is only appropriate that we let Genesis 1–3 conform us after its own image. Once we accustom our hearing, the dialect of Genesis 1–3 beautifully chants the glory of God, the Alpha and Omega, the Redeemer and Creator, for the joy of our faith and soul.

Moreover, just like the ancient Hebrews, the covenantal features and promises of these chapters whet our appetites for the rest of the story. A child of Eve will overcome. Who will be this hoped-for heir? What will be the full spectrum of his victory over the serpent?

STUDY QUESTIONS

1. What are some similarities between Genesis and the other ancient creation myths?

2. What are some differences?

3. How did the creation account help the Israelites who came out of Egypt?

4. What is a covenant?

5. What are some ways Genesis 2–3 shows itself to be covenantal?

6. How does Adam's failure in the garden showcase the success of Christ for salvation?

2

EDEN TO EGYPT

Bible Reading: Genesis 4–50

Adam and Eve faced a near-death experience when God came to them in the garden. The Lord promised sure death. The naked twosome had no other expectation. Yet mercy was given. By a new promise and a covering, the Lord made a new covenant with his sinful people. As with any promise, though, there is the issue of timing. When? When will the fallen couple receive victory over the serpent?

As the next chapter of our story opens, Adam knew his wife and she conceived. Eve names her son in praise: "I have acquired a man-child by Yahweh" (Gen 4:1, my translation). These are acts of faith by both Adam and Eve. If the Lord tells you that he will give you a child, it is faithful to start having children. With this we land upon a key principle in reading Genesis and all of Scripture: faith must be expressed as believing the Lord's promises. If the Lord promises a land, faith moves to that land. If God pledges to save you from a flood, trust builds a boat.

The primary promise within the pages of Genesis deals with children. The Lord has promised to diligently raise up covenant children, and through these offspring he will perform his redemptive deeds for his people. This theme is so important that the entire structure of Genesis is fashioned around generations. After the opening section, the book grows on a ten-part frame, where each frame opens with "These are the generations of …" As you can see from the sidebar, the generations trace the passage of time through a family line, and these family lines focus on the covenantal household: the line of promise. Indeed, the promise of Genesis 3:15 points to the warring of two houses: the woman versus the serpent. It does not take long to see how some of Adam and Eve's offspring swear allegiance to the adversary of God's people. Therefore, within each generational frame, a fissure forms that cracks apart the faithful line of those who call upon the name of the Lord

THE GENERATIONS OF GENESIS

1:1–2:4a:	Creation prologue
2:4a–4:26:	Generation of heaven and earth
5:1–6:8:	Generations of Adam
6:9–9:29:	Generations of Noah
10:1–11:9:	Generation of Noah's sons (lines rejected)
11:10–11:26:	Generations of Shem
11:27–25:11:	Generations of Terah/ Abraham
25:12–25:18:	Generations of Ishmael (line rejected)
25:19–35:29:	Generations of Isaac
36:1–37:1:	Generations of Esau (line rejected)
37:2–50:26:	Generations of Jacob

from the wicked, unbelieving heirs. This separation unfolds the twofold theme of the promise: animosity between the two lineages, and God's faithfulness to preserve Eve's promised progeny. Enmity and fidelity wrestle throughout the halls of history.

CAIN AND ABEL

When Eve gave birth to Cain, she thought surely this man-child would smash that vile snake who tricked her into eating the fruit. Eve, though, had more to learn. It was not just any son of hers who will march in the victory parade; instead, it must be the right son—the believing,

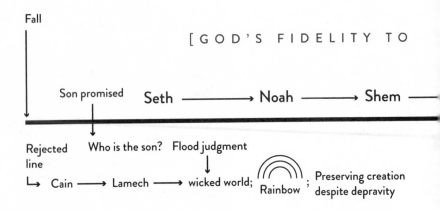

obedient son. Cain did not develop such virtues. He brought an offering to the Lord in worship, but his heart was not right. Insincerity and
ingratitude salted his gifts; he did not offer the best of his produce. His
brother Abel, though, was pure of heart; he sacrificed the best of his
flock to the Lord in love and faith, so that the Lord regarded Abel's
gift with favor but did not regard Cain's. The Lord then gave Cain
a second chance to prove he would serve with heart-felt devotion.
Cain then had to rule over sin and not open the door to sin's desire.

Cain, however, did not take advantage of the Lord's second chance.
Why be like your good younger brother, he thought, when you can
beat him down? Feigning love, Cain lured Abel to an unpopulated
place and murdered him. Bone of his bone, Cain poured the blood
of his own brother upon the soil, and so he became the world's first
murderer.

The dust cried out to God for justice, and the Lord heard—at
least to a certain extent. Justice had to be done, a life for a life. Cain
killed, so Cain must die. Yet the Lord lets the murderer live. Rather
than kill Cain, he banishes Cain from the covenant family. Cain

PRESERVE THE PROMISED LINE]

——→ Abraham ——————→ Isaac ————→ Jacob with 12 sons

Chart 2: Genesis

even protests this mercy: "My punishment is too great to bear! I will wander as a vagabond, and when people find me they will kill me. I will not last a day banished from the community of God" (Gen 3:13–14, my paraphrase).

Who are these people Cain is afraid of? The text did not clarify in the opening of chapter 4 that Cain was Adam and Eve's firstborn, so this is not a presumption that we should make. Hence, those who would find Cain are fellow extended family members who would want to avenge the blood of Abel. Later, in Israel, murder was avenged by the victim's next of kin (called the "blood redeemer," Num 35). The force of Cain's grievance is that while the Lord showed him mercy, others will not. What good is the Lord's clemency if it is not upheld by those Cain may meet on the road?

The Lord extends his assurance to preserve the life of Cain: "If anyone kills Cain, vengeance shall be taken on him sevenfold" (Gen 4:15). Then he puts on Cain what many English translations render as a "mark," but it would be better translated "sign." This sign is a commemorative token to confirm the truth of an earlier statement, that is, the promise made in the first half of verse 15—the sevenfold vengeance.[1] This sign guarantees God's justice to protect Cain's life with the penalty of capital punishment. Therefore, while God mercifully sustained the life of the first murderer, from now on murder will be punished with execution. In this way, God graciously provides for two communities, one believing and the other unbelieving. Cain moves away, founds a city, and in a matter of five generations the city is thriving with shepherds, blacksmiths, and musicians. The culture of the arts and sciences flourishes in the city of Enoch (Gen 4:17).

But where faith must be expressed according to the promises, wickedness is manifest in contradiction to God's law and order. Cain's descendant Lamech typifies the rebellion of Cain's city. First, he takes two wives, when God had ordained man and woman to become one flesh. By committing polygamy, Lamech redefines the sovereign good order of the Lord and acts like a god. Second, Lamech perverts perfect justice into oppression: "If Cain's revenge is sevenfold, then Lamech's is seventy-sevenfold" (Gen 4:24). Lamech has exacted disproportionate vengeance by killing a young man for striking him (4:23). Slap Lamech and he will slice your throat. The balanced life-for-a-life decreed by God is distorted into the oppressive imbalance of injustice.

TWO FAMILY LINES

God's mercy, then, creates a place on earth for two communities: those of Eve and of Cain. Within this first generational frame, the unbelieving, wicked line is separated from the faithful descendants of Eve. Hence, this frame closes with Eve bearing another son, a gift from God. Eve has learned that the chosen son is the one who is upright; Seth replaces not Cain, but Abel (4:25). It is in the family of Seth that people began invoking the name of Yahweh. Even though the name "Yahweh" is not revealed until Exodus 3, the text of Genesis applies the name to his previous dealings with his people.

With the faithful heir highlighted, the second generational frame opens "the generations of Adam," who begot Seth in his likeness. The genealogy of Genesis 5, then, follows the covenant family of Genesis 3 from Adam to Noah and the flood. In Scripture, genealogies are compressed theological history. A genealogy's interest lies not in empires, events, or even ages of world history, but in God's faithfulness to preserve his people from father to son.

In fact, biblical genealogies have gaps and an elasticity to them. That is, we cannot add up the life-spans to figure how many years passed from beginning to end. Rather, when Scripture says so-and-so begot so-and-so, this child could be a son, grandson, or a grandson ten or more generations removed. For example, in the priestly genealogy of Ezra, the text says Azariah was the son of Meraioth (Ezra 7:3). The same line of Aaron in 1 Chronicles lists five generations between Meraioth and Azariah (6:6–9). Similarly, Matthew puts forty-two generations between Jesus and Abraham, while Luke gives fifty-seven. A relationship could be any number of generations removed; the important thing is that they belong to the same family line. Therefore, the text of Genesis 5 does not allow us to add up the years from Adam to Noah; that is not its intent. Instead, the genealogy maps out God's faithfulness through the death-torn realities of miscarriages and diseases to protect his own.

Additionally, the breaks in the pattern of biblical genealogies highlight special theological themes. Here in Genesis 5, the pattern is obvious: "When Enosh had lived 90 years, he fathered Kenan. Enosh lived after he fathered Kenan 815 years and had other sons and daughters. Thus all the days of Enosh came to 905 years, and he died" (5:9–11). Each generation closes with "he died." When this pattern is broken with new or different information, it signals us to pay attention. These breaks are called annotations, and the ten generations of Genesis 5 include two. The first comes with Enoch, who walked with God and was no more. In a special way, the Lord delivered Enoch from the curse of death. The second annotation comes with Lamech (not the same Lamech who descended from Cain) naming Noah, through whom the Lord would provide relief from the cursed soil and toil. These two annotations highlight the piety and uprightness of these sons and fathers. This is the genealogy of the faithful, of God's people. Indeed, it is the piety seen in this genealogy that contrasts so sharply with the business of the city of Cain found in Genesis 6:1–8.

As we saw with the first generational frame, there is divergence and opposition between the two family lines. While the family of Seth are calling on the name of Yahweh, what is the world doing? They are multiplying wickedness after the image of Lamech. In Genesis 6:2, it is best to take "sons of god" not as referring to angelic, demonic, or divine beings, but as human kings. "Son of god" was a title that kings took for themselves in arrogance. These proud kings, who took wives for themselves, are amassing large harems. From this selective breeding, mighty war heroes and giants are born—the Nephilim, who were famous for their violence and bloodshed. The sons of Cain are building their expansive empires with the bricks of sexual immorality and the mortar of blood. The quiet piety of the saints is drowned out by the world's noisy depravity. Therefore, no longer will the Lord abide with the degeneracy of humanity. By a terrible deluge, God will put an end to the world that once was.

THE GENERATIONS OF NOAH

The third generational frame again opens by focusing on the covenant family (Gen 6:9). The Lord will send the world to a watery grave, but he will sail the upright Noah and his family safely through in an ark. As the just fury of the Almighty demolishes the world city, the Lord magnifies his mercy as the Savior of his covenant people. The line of Eve is preserved; the road of fulfillment is wide open for the promise. Furthermore, the flood account closes by touching on the two lines in its depiction of a covenant (8:21–9:17).

This covenantal account begins with God in heaven talking to himself. God promises never to destroy the world again with an inundation, and he makes this promise despite humanity's ingrained evil. Cold and heat, day and night shall maintain the undeserved life of every living thing. Yet this resolution is only heard in heaven; no one on earth has this information until the Lord creates a covenant with Noah. The heavenly promise is confirmed, even with all flesh that is on earth (9:17).

The parties of this covenant are not limited to Noah and his offspring but include all creation. The covenant blessing spares creation from judgment by waters, and the covenant sign is the rainbow as a reminder for the Lord not to judge. As oppression infests the ground, a rainstorm will come, and God may be tempted to fling open the gates of heaven. But the bow of many colors will span the horizon, and the Lord "will see it and remember the everlasting covenant between God and every living creature" (9:16). This covenant, then, is unconditional. Duties are included in the first part of chapter 9—to be fruitful in childbearing, to work and eat, and to do justice when a person's blood is shed—but they are not required for God to keep his promise. Rather, this covenant is unilateral and gracious for all living things, and it lays the foundation for the unfolding of the rest of human history. This covenant is the arena where the battle will be fought between the evil one and God's people, and where God's promise of salvation will come to fruition.

But without delay, the covenant family is again fractured and divided in 9:18–27. Noah's son Ham turns out to be of the line of Cain, and he passed his genes on to Canaan. Whatever the exact nature of Ham's sin, he dishonored his dad and broadcasted Noah's shame to his brothers. Noah thus curses Canaan the son of Ham, but he blesses his other sons, Shem and Japheth. This prophetic blessing and curse is the lead-in for the next generational frame for the sons of Noah, which lists how humanity spreads out into nations. Genesis 10, called the Table of Nations, records the repopulation of the earth after the flood. The inclusion of the rebellion at Babel further makes clear that the gene pool of Cain and Lamech survived the flood waters. In fact, in the population explosion of Japheth, Ham, Canaan, and Shem, the line of faith is not easy to spot. Therefore, to contrast the many sons and peoples in the Table of Nations, we are given the single genealogy of Seth through Arpachshad (11:10). The family line follows only one son of the blessed Shem, but this genealogy is without annotation. The pattern resembles the one found in Genesis 5, but it lacks any highlight of family behavior. We are left wondering if anyone is calling upon the name of the Lord, and this doubt leads us to Abram, son of Terah.

THE GENERATIONS OF ABRAM

With the introduction of Abram, the story of Genesis slows from a sprint to a walk. It begins with the Lord appearing to Abram with a call and a promise (Gen 12:1–3). The call is to go, to leave his kin and journey to a far-off land. This separation hints that his parents did not call on the Lord's name but Abram will. The call is paired with a promise: "I will make of you a great nation … I will bless you … in you all the families of the earth shall be blessed." This series of promises focus on two points: a people and a place. The Lord guarantees Abram a land, and a great people will come from Abram's loins that will honor his name and through whom the nations will be blessed or cursed. The promise is given here in skeletal form. As the drama of Abram unfolds, muscle, tendon, and skin will grow on the bones until it is fully developed. This burgeoning body of promises becomes the main theme for the rest of the book of Genesis. The Lord has made his promise; how then will his people respond: with faith or with disbelief?

Abram passes his first pop quiz with a gold star. Out of the blue, the Lord tells him to leave his family. He has to move to a foreign land, where he does not know the language. Yet Abram does it. He treks nearly four hundred miles with his wife, Sarai, and his nephew, Lot, to Shechem. Once under the oak of Moreh, the Lord appears to Abram and confirms his promise, "To your offspring I will give this land" (12:7). The faith of Abram is enlivened as he constructs an altar to worship. Then, as he moves on to Bethel, he raises another altar and calls on the name of the Lord. The covenant family has been found; the faithful line of Eve continues, and the Lord is keeping his promises. Moreover, the Lord lavished on Abram a rich land. As one ancient Egyptian described Palestine, "Figs were in it and grapes. It had more wine than water. Abundant was its honey, plentiful its oil. All kinds of fruit were on its trees. Barley was there and emmer, and no end of cattle of all kinds."[2]

Yet faith is meant to be tested. When the sun roasts the green hills of Bethel bare and dry, Abram flees south to Egypt, which is not the safest neighborhood. Sarai is attractive, and Abram is afraid the Egyptians will kill him to get their hands on her. To protect himself, Abram weaves a lie that exposes Sarai to sexual predation, and he attempts to justify the lie as a half-truth. Out of his desire for self-preservation, Abram stumbles. He should have defended the purity and honor of his bride. He should have trusted the Lord to protect him in a foreign land instead of taking matters into his own feeble hands. Pharaoh, the ruler of Egypt, takes Sarai into his house (12:15), and admits that "I took her for my wife" (v. 19). It is unclear whether the relationship was consummated, though the plagues that followed may indicate that it was. Still, the Lord ends up enriching Abram in spite of his disgusting cowardice. He leaves Egypt with more wealth than he came with. The Lord is faithful, even when his people are unfaithful.

And the blessings of the Lord just keep rolling in. In a matter of literary moments, the herds of Lot and Abram are bursting at the seams. To keep family peace, they split up. Lot chooses the lush Jordan Valley that is like the garden of the Lord, which leaves Abram with the rugged hill country. But this is no hindrance for the Lord, as he now expands on the grandeur of his promise: "I will make your offspring as the dust of the earth," such that no one will be able to count them (13:16). The Lord also bestows military victory on Abram after Lot was carried off as plunder by a confederation of four kings. With a battalion of 318 men, Abram rescues every last possession of Lot and more. He then tithes (gives ten percent) to a Canaanite king, Melchizedek, and is blessed by the God Most High, who delivered him from his enemies.

In another vision, the Lord confirms, "I am your shield; your reward shall be very great" (15:1). Abram, though, has a counter-point: "I continue childless." How can his reward be great without a son? The Lord reiterates his promise with an oath: "One from your body, he will be your heir" (my translation). The son of inheritance will not be adopted; Abram will sire this son himself. Abram believes the incredible word of God, and it is credited to him as righteousness (15:6), which Paul refers to in Romans 4 as the gospel goes to the nations. Pharaoh's rebuke undressed Abram as unrighteous, but here as a gift, the Lord grants Abram a righteous status. The Lord grants his people what they lack when they trust in him. The Lord wants to give a double assurance to Abram's faith, so he moves to ratify his promise with a riveting covenant ritual.

The usual Hebrew idiom for making a covenant is literally "to cut a covenant." It comes from a ceremony that is found widely in the ancient world in one form or another. In this ceremony, a dead animal would be cut into pieces, and the parties would walk between the pieces that lay on the ground. In texts discovered in 1933 from the kingdom of Mari in northern Syria, "to kill a donkey foal" concludes a covenant. A Sefire treaty from the eighth century BC reads, "As this calf is cut up, thus Matti'el and his nobles shall be cut up."[3] As Menahem Haran writes, "This gesture seems to have become so widespread and common that it may have turned into a kind of prevalent supplement to a covenant ceremony."[4]

One of the symbolic values of the ceremony was to enact the curse for violation. If either party broke his commitment, he would become like the dead animals. This was a ritual of self-imprecation. Therefore, the Lord directs Abram to cut in half a three-year-old heifer, billy goat, and ram, as well as two birds, whose halves were lined up opposite each other to create a path down the middle. But while Abram is asleep, the Lord alone passes through the severed animals in the form of smoke and fire. Hence, the Lord takes upon himself a self-imprecation if he breaks his promise—an impossibility.

This makes this covenant unconditional and irrevocable. The Lord himself will perform these promises, which again build on and add detail to promises of the previous chapters. The Lord restates his land promise ("To your offspring I give this land," v. 18), clarifies the borders of the land by listing off ten tribes (vv. 19–20), and places the fulfillment in the future (vv. 13–15). Abram will be laid to rest, and the Lord will bring Abram's descendants back into the land after four hundred years of affliction as sojourners. This is the gracious covenant of God where Abram and his offspring are the beneficiaries of the Lord's unilateral obligation.

The comforting splendor of this covenant ratification ceremony, however, does not have a lasting effect on Abram's faith. Ten years have passed since they arrived in the land with a promise of a child (Gen 16:3), yet Sarai is still barren. As many couples know, trying to get pregnant for a decade can be quite discouraging. Impatiently, Sarai turns to alternative methods: "Here is my handmaid, Hagar. Go in to her so that I may have a son through her" (16:2, my translation). She thinks surrogacy by concubine surely will work as a way to accomplish God's promise.

When God seems slow, our faith stumbles and we look to our own ways, but these human attempts have a way of backfiring. After the birth of her son Ishmael, Hagar no longer respects Sarai. In anger, Sarai blames Abram and abuses Hagar. Abram goes along with whatever Sarai says. Sin and dysfunction again threaten the covenant family, but in the end the Lord preserves the life of Ishmael, and Abram ends up with a son at age eighty-six.

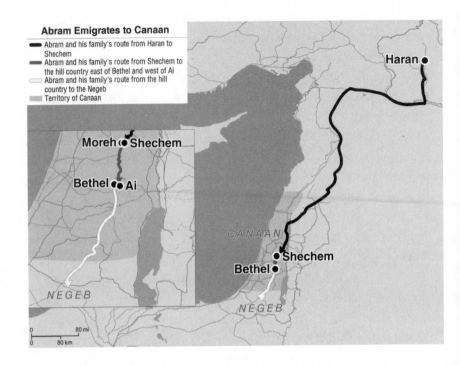

After another thirteen years, Abram's faith needs a refresher. The Lord appears to him to reaffirm his covenant and add assurances by bestowing on Abram a new name, Abraham, meaning "father of many nations," which embodies the destiny God promised (17:5). Moreover, from the fertility of Abraham, kings will rise up according to the eternal covenant of the Lord. God even adds a sign to the covenant with Abraham: circumcision. Circumcision is an obligation for Abraham and all his future sons, but it is also a token of consecration and assurance that one belongs to God and is an heir of his promise. The Lord also blesses Sarai with a new name, Sarah, which confirms that she will bear the son of promise. Muscle and ligaments are growing on the bony promises of chapter 12.

Abraham, however, struggles to take these assurances seriously, for he breaks out in laughter (17:17). Can a centenarian become a father? Can a post-menopausal old lady get pregnant? Abraham doubts God, and he pleads that his lovely Ishmael would be accepted. Why should he wait for the impossible when he has a perfectly good son at his right hand? The Lord's mind, however, will not be changed. Ishmael is not the heir; the son must come from Sarah. Despite his impious laughter, Abraham submits in faith to be circumcised along with his household.

Yet Abraham is not the only one who gets to laugh. Shortly after the circumcision party, the Lord comes to Abraham by a visit of three men. During supper, the Lord tells Abraham that in one year's time, Sarah will become a mother. Sarah is eavesdropping, and it is her turn to laugh in doubt. The Lord hears her laughing and calls her on it, but she tries to lie her way out. Both Abraham and Sarah take the promise of a son within a year as a joke.

The intervening year brings its ups and downs. Abraham is on his good behavior as he intercedes for Sodom (Gen 18). Like a stubborn mule, Lot drags his feet getting out of Sodom. Then, during a trip to Gerar, Abraham again lies about Sarah (Gen 20). As he did in Egypt, Abraham protects himself by only saying Sarah was his sister. Sarah could become pregnant at any time, and Abraham lets her be taken into the house of another man. Abraham is not respecting the promises, but God ensures the safety of Sarah, so that no one touched her (20:6). Once again, the weakness of Abraham is contrasted with the faithfulness of God.

And then, after twenty-five long years in the land, Sarah conceives—the ninety-year-old becomes an expecting mother. The due date arrives and the labor is smooth—a miracle in itself. With a baby on her breast, Sarah's laughter of doubt and skepticism has transformed into the laughter of joy and gratitude. Abraham names the boy "Isaac," meaning "laughter," and Sarah says, "God has made laughter for me" (Gen 21:6). Abraham's and Sarah's faith has been up and down, but the Lord has remained constant.

However, the next test for Abraham's faith makes him wonder about the Lord. When Isaac is a young boy, God calls Abraham to go to Mount Moriah and sacrifice his beloved son (Gen 22:2). The

Lord wants Abraham to sacrifice the son it took so long to get? What is going on? Yet Abraham obeys immediately. He saddles up a donkey, reaches Moriah, straps the firewood on Isaac, and sets off for the summit. Stone after stone, Abraham keeps thinking "the Lord will provide" as he puts together the altar. He arranges the firewood and ties Isaac on top. Strapped on the pyre, Isaac's eyes are locked on the blade as it is lifted over him by his father's hand. The knife is about to go into his neck when the Lord speaks: "Abraham. ... Do not lay your hand on the boy ... for I know you fear God" (22:12). A rustle is heard in the bushes, and Abraham turns to see a ram trapped in the thorns. The Lord did provide a lamb for the burnt offering.

After this test, the Lord reiterates his covenant promises in a way that is both similar to previous ones and builds on them. In 22:16–19, as reward for not withholding Isaac, the Lord swears again to Abraham, "I will surely bless you" (so 12:2 and 17:16). "I will surely multiply your offspring [so 17:2] as the stars of heaven" (so 15:5) and "as the sand" (similar to 13:16). The Lord adds, "Your offspring shall possess the gate of his enemies," which is a new development, though this could be implicit with kings from 17:6. Finally he says that "in your offspring shall all the nations of the earth be blessed" (so 12:3). This is the same covenant of God growing and being reiterated again and again for the benefit of Abraham's seasonal faith.

With this successful test, the generation of Abraham starts winding down. Sarah dies, and Abraham buys a burial plot. Isaac reaches marrying age and a new theme sprouts in our story. Abraham makes his servant swear, "You must not take a wife for my son from the daughters of the Canaanites" (24:3, my translation). The Lord's promises applied to covenant children that come from marriage, so marriage cannot be with the Canaanites. This requirement will be an ever-increasing issue in the narrative. For the moment, the Lord gives Abraham's servant success on his trip back to see the family. We meet Rebekah and her brother Laban, who has eyes for shiny things, and without delay the servant brings Rebekah home to Isaac and she becomes his wife. A few decades pass and Abraham is gathered to his fathers at 175 years old. The curtain is drawn on the long generational frame that opened in 11:27. This is the generation of Abraham.

THE GENERATIONS OF ISAAC

A short generational frame is squeezed in for Ishmael (Gen 25:12–18), which reveals that the Lord blessed him in accordance with his promise, but also that he is of the rejected line. Ishmael was not the covenant heir, and so the story returns to the generations of Isaac (25:19). Isaac's episode opens with a dilemma: to continue the covenant family requires having kids, but Rebekah cannot get pregnant. To overcome this obstacle, Isaac's first step is taken with faith. He prays for his wife. The Lord hears his plea and Rebekah conceives.

Rebekah's pregnancy has complications. Twins develop in her womb, but the fetuses jostle and wrestle in a prenatal war. Rebekah is beside herself, so she inquires of the Lord. The answer shapes the destiny of our story: "Two nations … two peoples from within you shall be divided" (25:23). As with Isaac and Ishmael, these twins are the progenitors of nations. These brothers will be hostile competitors, striving against each other for supremacy, and the outcome of this animosity will be that the younger boy wins: "The older shall serve the younger." This was a cultural taboo; it was not how things were done. The firstborn should retain the honor of superiority. But as we have seen, God has a way of doing what is unexpected and countercultural. The striving between two descendants has been center stage since the woman and the serpent. One child belongs to the faithful line; the other does not.

The promise of God has been the litmus test for the faith and life of the covenant family, but here we find a family in disarray. Isaac loved Esau, the hairy man's man who hunts and loves the wild outdoors. With bow or javelin, he can bring home his dad's favorite meal. The heel-grabbing Jacob was a different story. Sensitive, polite, and civilized, he stayed indoors. Jacob could not suffer dirt under his fingernails, so he found a place in Rebekah's heart. Parental favoritism is never pretty, but it becomes repulsive when opposing the promises of God.

The dysfunctionality of the parents is visited upon the children. Hunting is Esau's first love; he thinks with his stomach. On an occasion when he was particularly peckish, a bowl of stew became more precious than his birthright. Esau happily exchanged his God-given status as firstborn heir for some lentils swimming in a red broth. Esau despised the covenant gift of God, and Jacob had no scruples in taking advantage of his brother.

This distorted family does not stop the Lord from showing kindness. Amid the family strife, the Lord comes to Isaac and confirms the covenant of his father with him (Gen 26:3–5). Again the promises line up with what we have seen before: "I will bless you ... I will give all these lands and I will establish the oath that I swore to Abraham." This is the same covenant being passed down to another generation. The Lord's confirmation of his fidelity, however, does not seem to have many positive influences on the family. After a while, Esau gets strike number two. By age forty, he has married two women, and both of them are Hittites. He has married outside the covenant, which gives life a bitter taste for his parents (Gen 26:34–35).

The acidity of his son's marriages does not hinder Isaac's favoritism. Old and blind Isaac insists on blessing Esau. Rebekah, though, thinks the blessing should go to Jacob. So as Esau is out on a hunting expedition to bag game for his father, she—like Jacob earlier—takes advantage of the situation. After braising a lamb, Rebekah disguises her gentle Jacob with a hairy manliness like Esau's and sends him in to steal the blessing from Isaac, whose eyesight is failing. Jacob is not just a passive actor; he resourcefully contributes wine to rob clarity from Isaac's mind. Of course, the plan works. Isaac blesses Jacob with plenty, supremacy, and protection, which seals Jacob's destiny (Gen 27:27–29). The seeming victory for Rebekah and Jacob, though, does not bear immediate rewards. With Esau angry at the deception, the life of Jacob hangs by a thread. Therefore, mom and dad send Jacob back to live with the extended family, with an explicit command not to marry one of those Canaanite girls (28:1). Jacob must marry within Abraham's extended family back in Paddan-aram.

So far in this generational frame, none of the characters has remained unblemished. Esau married Hittites, sold his birthright, and hated his brother with the jealousy of Cain. Isaac wanted to pick his heir instead of God. He allows his senses of smell, taste, and touch to dominate him instead of listening to God's word. The primary actor is Rebekah, who cheats, deceives, and steals. Jacob walks with an opportunistic and unprincipled gait. Stealing from his brother and lying to his father does not smart his conscience in the slightest. Nevertheless, there are small glimmers of faith. Rebekah acts according to God's word she received when she was pregnant. Jacob values the covenantal birthright and blessing, even if only for selfish reasons. After the con, Isaac mandates that Jacob not marry a Canaanite. The Lord uses these crooked people and their weak faith to carry out his good plan and to establish his covenant with Abraham.

Once Jacob is on the road, he experiences an event that shapes the drama of the story for many chapters to come, if not all the way to the end of the book. Jacob camps for the night at the city of Luz, which he renames Bethel. As Jacob sleeps with a rock for a pillow, the Lord appears to him in a dream to confirm the covenant of Abraham and Isaac (28:13–15). Importantly, Jacob responds to God's promise with a vow (v. 20). In the Old Testament, a vow is a conditional promise made to God, which means that if God does not meet the condition, the other party is not required to complete his promise. The condition of Jacob's vow includes God remaining with him, protecting him, giving him food and clothing, and allowing him to return safely. This is what God promised in verse 15. The avowed promise begins in verse 21, "then the Lord shall be my God. This stone ... shall be God's house. ... I will give a full tenth to you." Jacob promises exclusive loyalty to the Lord if he is with him for good. Like his grandfather Abraham, Jacob is part of a polytheistic culture; he has not made his father's God his only God yet. The developing piety of Jacob and the fidelity of the Lord are in the background as the story unfolds.

When Jacob arrives in Paddan-aram to visit family, the impression Laban gave earlier as a lover of money proves to be true. At first, Laban agrees to give his daughter Rachel in marriage to Jacob for seven years of labor, but when the time comes Laban tricks him into marrying his older and less desirable daughter Leah. It costs another seven years for Rachel. The trickster Jacob is outfoxed by Laban. Then, over the next six years, with a growing family, Laban changed his wages ten times (31:41). Laban threatened that if Jacob left, he would seize Rachel and Leah. Jacob was a hired shepherd of Laban, but this job felt more like slavery. Nevertheless, the Lord was with Jacob. Amid the arduous labor, eleven sons and a daughter were born to Jacob. Laban attempted to take advantage of Jacob, but the Lord increased his herds and flocks greatly. When Jacob finally journeyed home and was afraid of Esau charging him in battle on the way, he found that the Lord had softened Esau's heart, so that he met his brother with a kiss and an embrace.

This protection was not lost on Jacob. In faith, he gives credit to whom it is due: "If the God of my father ... had not been on my side, surely now you would have sent me away empty-handed" (31:42). Jacob prayed earnestly to God to deliver him from Esau (32:9–12); he wrestles with God and will not let go (32:26). At the city of Shechem, where the Lord first appeared to Abram in the promised land (Gen 12:6), Jacob builds an altar as did Abram, calling it "El-Elohe-Israel." And coming full circle to Bethel, the place of his vow, Jacob orders his whole house to put away all their foreign gods before he builds another altar to worship the Lord alone. The Lord had been a God to Jacob, so Jacob becomes exclusively devoted to the Lord. The Lord even reconfirms the covenant of Abraham with Jacob at Bethel (35:11–12). The selfish trickster has been transformed into a trusting child of God. Even though Rachel dies in giving birth to Jacob's youngest son, Benjamin, this generational frame closes with a list of the twelve sons of Jacob, who get to kiss Isaac before he is gathered to his fathers. All seems well.

Yet any family with thirteen kids has to have some drama, and Jacob's is no exception. Amid the noble acts of Jacob, a tragedy occurs. His lone daughter, Dinah, gets raped by the good-for-nothing Shechem, the son of Hamor. Enraged, two of her brothers, Simeon and Levi, decide to avenge Dinah by feigning an offer of marriage: "Become circumcised like us and Dinah can be your wife." As Hamor, Shechem, and the men of the city are convalescing from their surgery, Levi and Simeon slaughter every last male in the town, and the others plunder all the wealth, wives, and little ones (Gen 34:25–29). The sons repay rape with genocide. Jacob is furious, but his sons' retort carries weight: "Should he treat our sister like a prostitute?" (34:31). Jacob had not pursued justice for Dinah, so it fell to his sons to exact disproportionate vengeance. "Jacob shows no moral outrage, and the sons justify their slaughter as just punishment."[5] Jacob's failure as a father forced the boys to take matters into their own hands.

THE GENERATIONS OF JACOB

The family drama continues into the next generational frame, which opens in 37:1. Just as Isaac's generational frame gave much of its attention to Jacob, so Jacob's frame is mostly devoted to his son Joseph. When we are introduced to him, Joseph is a mere seventeen years old, and Jacob suffers from the same favoritism ailment as did Isaac—signified by the many-colored coat he gives Joseph. Joseph's brothers are jealous of him, and Joseph's haughty tone when he relays his dreams aggravates their jealousy into hatred. Tragically, but all too commonly in Genesis, hatred grows within the covenant family. The brothers plot to murder Joseph, but his brother Judah comes up with a way to get money instead. Why kill the boy for nothing when you can sell him to a slave trader and make a profit? With the sale of Joseph, the pattern of separation within families re-emerges. In the rest of the Joseph story, however, the themes of God's faithfulness and Joseph's piety intermingle.

Semitic traders bringing their wares to Egypt

Joseph's growth from a young, pompous teenager into maturity is steady and unmistakable. He will not sin against God by sleeping with the wife of his employer, Potiphar (39:9). Though put in prison unjustly, his good behavior makes him the warden's pet. When he interprets the dreams of his fellow prisoners, Pharaoh's former baker and cupbearer, he credits the Lord for the interpretation (40:8). For two years, Joseph waits patiently on the Lord as he is forgotten in prison. When he finally stands before the mighty Pharaoh, Joseph again testifies that the Lord alone interprets dreams. At age thirty, when he enters the service of Pharaoh, Joseph is wise and impeccable. His shrewd preparations rescue the whole world from an unrelenting famine. One sign of how much he has grown is the names he gives to his two sons. Manasseh means "God has made me forget all my hardship and all my father's house," and Ephraim "God has made me fruitful in the land of my affliction" (41:51–52). The growth of Joseph has the fingerprints of God's steadfast love all over it. Throughout, it is true that "whatever he did, the Lord made it succeed" (39:23).

The name of Joseph's firstborn, however, injects tension within the story. Does "God has made me forget ... all my father's house" mean he has forgotten his family? Is Joseph moving beyond his childhood strife, or is he disowning his family? The ambiguity is raised but not resolved, and soon ten of Joseph's brothers show up needing grain. Joseph recognizes them, but they don't recognize him. He speaks to them harshly, remembering his dreams of chapter 37, but he is torn (Gen 42:8–17). "The instinctive desire for revenge is tempered by the knowledge of his father and brother back in Canaan. ... Above all, he feels he must find out conclusively whether or not his brothers regret their actions and have truly reformed themselves. He decides upon a series of tests."[6] Joseph has changed; he must determine if the brothers have, too.

As the story unfolds, the themes of repentance and reconciliation focus on the brothers. When Joseph detains Simeon, the brothers immediately acknowledge their guilt toward Joseph (42:21). Then, when Jacob refuses to let his youngest son (and Joseph's only full brother) Benjamin go to Egypt, it is Judah's turn to grow up. In chapter 38, Judah had moved away from the family to marry a Canaanite woman. He acted horribly toward his daughter-in-law Tamar until he was forced to acknowledge that she was more upright than him (Gen 38:26). It had been Judah's vision to sell Joseph into slavery. Up to this point, Judah has been a fornicator and slave trader. But in the face of Jacob's stubbornness, Judah shows virtue by pledging his life for Benjamin's. Joseph demands the return of Benjamin upon pain of death, and Judah both swears to be Benjamin's guarantor and to be held fully responsible for him (42:20). Judah, therefore, puts his life on the line both for Benjamin and to get Simeon back. The man who sold Joseph is now willing to die for Benjamin. This is the turning point in the story.

Judah's pledge convinces Jacob to send Benjamin to Egypt. The brothers return to Joseph with a present—double the money—and Benjamin (Gen 43:15). Joseph sees Benjamin and he quietly prepares a feast for his brothers. At the meal, compassion swells within Joseph, but one more test is needed. As he sends his brothers away, Joseph hides his silver cup in Benjamin's sack. After sending servants to stop them on the road, Joseph demands the life of the man with the silver cup. Finally, in a long speech, Judah confesses their sin and guilt toward Joseph; he expresses concern for his grieved father and he makes good on his pledge. He gives his life in the place of Benjamin's for the sake of Jacob. The emotion and self-sacrifice of Judah breaks Joseph's act. He reveals himself to his brothers and confesses that he put his trust in the Lord's providence in it all: "God sent me before you to preserve you a remnant on the earth" (Gen 45:7).

In short order, seventy persons make the journey to the fertile land of Goshen, which lies in the north of Egypt. Jacob is reunited with his long-lost son. The Lord assures Jacob that he will be with him in Egypt (46:4). The Lord's gracious blessing has the last word. The covenant family is restored and reunited. Before Joseph closes Jacob's eyes in death, Jacob punctuates the end of his life with a grand blessing. The blessing of Jacob in Genesis 49 is one of the great poems of Scripture, and it both recalls the past history and prophetically forecasts the things to come.

First, it makes clear that Reuben, Jacob's firstborn, has been demoted and replaced by Joseph's sons. Reuben had slept with Bilhah, Rachel's servant (Gen 35:22), and for this he will not have preeminence (49:4). Instead, the double portion of the firstborn goes to the two sons of Joseph, Manasseh and Ephraim (Gen 48:5–6). This is why in later lists of the twelve tribes of Israel, Manasseh and Ephraim are named, and not Joseph.

Second, while the firstborn honor goes to Joseph, Judah is also honored with kingship (Gen 49:8–12). "The scepter shall not depart from Judah." The promises of kings and victory made to Abraham will be realized through Judah. In fact, this crushing of foes echoes the promise of Genesis 3 to bruise the head of the serpent. The Lord's fidelity extends backward not just to Isaac and Abraham, but even to Noah and before him to Eve.

How did Judah earn this royal honor? He did it by giving his life as pledge to save another. Judah's sacrifice passed Joseph's test so that the whole covenant family was reunited and saved. Here our eyes can see a foretaste of the Lion of the Tribe of Judah, the Lamb who was slain, Jesus Christ (Rev 5:5–6)! Since the death of Abel, sin has grown to cover the face of the earth, and the covenant family has hardly been immune to this sin. But amid the lies, infidelity, and hatred, the Lord has been faithful to his covenant. The Lord even used the weakness and perverseness of his people to work his blessing in and for them. Or as Joseph said, what others meant for evil, God meant for good (50:20).

STUDY QUESTIONS

1. How does the structure of Genesis show God's faithfulness to his promise?

2. How did Lamech express his rebellion against God?

3. Who are the parties of the covenant found in Genesis 8:21–9:17?

4. What is the significance of the Lord alone passing through the carcasses in the covenant ceremony in Genesis 15?

5. What are some of the ways Abraham showed faith? How did he show lack of faith?

6. How were Isaac and his family dysfunctional?

7. List some of the ways the Lord showed his faithfulness in spite of the unfaithfulness of his people.

3

EXODUS AND SETTLEMENT

Bible Reading: Exodus, Joshua, Judges

Time erodes memory. Monuments decay with each passing year. Photos give us the false security that we will always remember. But sometimes when you dust off an old photo, you cannot remember the person next to you. We lose memory more often than we preserve it.

Forgetfulness marks the opening of Exodus—with great consequence. The new Pharaoh is not at all aware of Joseph and his wise rescue of Egypt. The Hebrews are no longer family to Pharaoh, but a strange people to be exploited. When a later Pharaoh orders the newborn boys of the Hebrews to be killed, the midwives fear God and preserve the Hebrew babies, but it is unclear if their memories link this God back to Abraham.

Likewise, four hundred years in Goshen have erased the memory of the Hebrews. Oppressive toil has rusted the Hebrews' piety into polytheism. Their agonized wailings ascend to God, but these are not targeted prayers to the God of their fathers (2:23). Even Moses, when he arrives at the uncanny burning bush, does not know which God is speaking; Yahweh has to identify himself (3:6). True, the God of their fathers is one of the gods the Hebrews revere, and he may be the chief deity for some, but exclusive loyalty to El Shaddai of the covenant promises has been buried in Egyptian sands.

Yet where humans forget, Yahweh remembers. His memory stands out from the very opening of this book, as the people of Israel are fruitfully multiplying and increasing in strength (1:7). This record fulfills most specifically the promise given to Jacob in Genesis 46:3, but the language reverberates through the promises from Genesis 1:28; 9:7; 28:3; and 35:11. The fruitful seed planted in Adam, Noah, Isaac, and Jacob has blossomed within the Hebrews even as they are parched and sagging with burdens. The Egyptian taskmasters were cruel, demanding more work with less rest and fewer resources. As the moaning of the slaves ascended to heaven, Yahweh "remembered his covenant with Abraham, with Isaac, and with Jacob" (Exod 2:24), and he already had a redeemer on deck in Moses. As the people forgot and collected for themselves more gods, Yahweh continued to bless, faithful to his oath.

YAHWEH CALLS MOSES

As God converses with Moses on holy ground (Exod 3-4), five themes arise that are crucial to the exodus drama. First, there is the link between the past and the future. Yahweh is about to bring his people into a land flowing with milk and honey, which links back to Genesis 15 (Exod 3:8, 17). The past promise is becoming the present and future reality for Israel. Second is the identity of God, who reveals his name to Moses and the people: Yahweh (3:14). This name was not revealed to the patriarchs, but it is the name to be remembered through all generations (3:15). Third is the power of Yahweh. Pharaoh will not let the Hebrews go willingly; he will have to be compelled, and Yahweh will do this by his strong arm smiting Egypt with wonders and plagues (3:19-20). Fourth, when the Hebrews are finally liberated, they are to ask their Egyptian neighbors for treasure and so plunder the Egyptians (3:22).

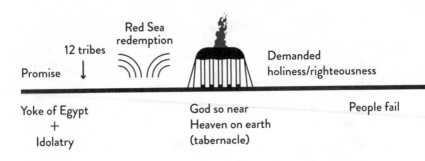

Finally, the theme of protest and hesitancy pops up in Moses. He does not want to be the deliverer of Israel. The progression of demurral grows in boldness from "Who am I?" (3:11), to "What name shall I say to them?" (3:13), to "But ... they will not believe me or listen to my voice" (4:1), to "I am not eloquent ... but I am slow of speech and of tongue" (4:10), and finally, "Please send someone else" (4:13, my paraphrase). Moses struggles to believe and obey Yahweh. God is handing Moses a glorious victory, but Moses would rather sit on the bench. His excuses are exposed as groundless when God piles up encouragements: "I will be with you" (3:12); "I AM WHO I AM" (3:14); "I will ... strike Egypt with all the wonders that I will do in it" (3:20); he provides three signs for the people to believe Moses' word (staff, leprous hand, water into blood, 4:2–9); "Who has made man's mouth? ... I will be with your mouth" (4:11–12); and finally he says that Aaron will go with Moses as his mouthpiece (4:15–16). Yahweh will take care of every single anxiety of Moses, and this theme of floundering to believe and obey will continue not only in Moses but especially in the people.

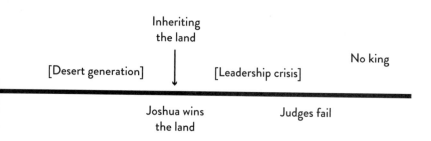

Chart 3: Exodus to Judges

With these five themes, the story is set in motion. Moses and his brother Aaron summon the elders of Israel, they preach all the words Yahweh gives them, and the people believe. Faith and worship are the first fruits of the Israelites. So far so good.

Yet the true test of character comes when times are not so smooth. The road turns rough as soon as Moses opens with his famous icebreaker, "Let my people go!" (5:1). Pharaoh parries with scorn: "Who is Yahweh?" Pharaoh does not know Yahweh and has no reason to obey him. Not only is this question foundational to the book of Genesis, as we have seen, but it also sets the course for upcoming events. Pharaoh wanted to know about Yahweh. Well, Yahweh is going to give him a thorough introduction, one that Pharaoh will never forget.

BATTLE OF THE GODS

Pharaoh's first reaction to Yahweh's name and demand is to charge the Israelites with laziness. They want time off for a religious retreat? Let them gather their own straw. The added workload and beatings quickly turn the Israelites sour, and they blame Moses for it all (5:21). Moses turns around to blame Yahweh: "Why did you ever send me? ... You have not delivered your people at all" (5:22–23). In the face of hardship, leader and people fail to trust in Yahweh's word, and so the time comes for him to show his strength. Aaron and Moses march into Pharaoh's presence to commence the plagues; Yahweh is about to flex his mighty arm.

In the plagues, the ancient motif of divine combat (theomachy) surfaces. A common belief in the ancient Near East held that as armies battled on the field, the nations' respective deities waged war above the firmament. Pharaoh's scornful question (Who is Yahweh?) taunted the God of the Israelites; it implied that Pharaoh's gods were mightier. Hence, in the plagues Yahweh drops bombs on the gods of Egypt to vaporize any reverence paid to them. As Old Testament scholar K. A. Kitchen writes, "The impact of various plagues can be understood as devaluing or denying Egyptian beliefs."[1] Here Yahweh reveals himself as the Divine Warrior, who fights for his people. The ten plagues progressively intensify to underscore the supremacy of Yahweh. At first, the Egyptian magicians could replicate the signs of Moses: they turn their staffs into snakes, turn water to blood, and summon frogs. This gave Pharaoh a reason to harden his heart, even though the scale of Yahweh's wonders dwarfed the puny arts of the magicians. The third plague, though, bests the magicians and prompts them to testify to Pharaoh, "This is the finger of God" (8:19). With the fourth plague, Yahweh steps up his game again by sparing his people in the land of Goshen. This seems to last for the rest of the plagues, even though it is not mentioned with the boils and locusts.

The plagues also become increasingly lethal for the Egyptians. The frogs, gnats, and flies drive the people crazy and harm the land. The plague on livestock kills animals. The boils inflame the bodies of humans and beasts; the hail smashes the skulls of all who are outside. The locusts devour every green thing—tree and plant. Finally, just before the pinnacle, Yahweh kills the sun, which was identified with the chief god and father of Pharaoh, Re. The Egyptians considered the setting and rising of the sun to be an endless cycle of decay and regeneration, death and resurrection. The failure of the sun to rise was the death of Re. Yahweh had just slayed the hero god of Pharaoh.

If this defeat was not enough, Yahweh finishes it with a final plague. The angel of the Lord, called "the Destroyer" in the narrative, tromps through the land to swallow every firstborn, from the goat to the son of the king himself. Only the blood of the lamb painted on the doors of the Hebrews kept death away.

With his son dead, Pharaoh's hard heart finally relents and he lets the people go free, which brings us to a season of fulfilled promises. Just as Yahweh promised in Exodus 3, the people plunder the Egyptians of their precious jewelry. The Hebrews have multiplied into a great host (Exod 12:37). Israel exits their prison 430 years after arriving (Exod 12:40), and Moses takes Joseph's bones (Exod 13:19). With his muscular arm, Yahweh laid waste to Egypt and poured out judgments on all the gods of Egypt (Exod 12:12). Lastly, Yahweh himself joins his people as the pillar of cloud and fire on their journey from Succoth to Etham (Exod 13:20–21).

The crushing judgment on Egypt, the sweet mercy and amazing redemption of Israel, and the surpassing grandeur of Yahweh's might— all of these are more than enough to dry the last drop of unbelief and disobedience from the Israelites and to replace it with a strong faith and fealty. Yahweh's word and wonders expunge any excuse for distrusting or defying him. Sadly, though, this does not stop the Israelites. The theme of insubordination first seen in Moses becomes full blown in the people.

Israel had only been on the road for a few days when regret fueled Pharaoh and his six hundred chariots in hot pursuit of his runaway slaves. Squeezed between a mountain and the sea, death appeared to be inevitable. In fury, the Israelites ripped into Moses and Yahweh: "What have you done to us in bringing us out of Egypt? ... It would have been better for us to serve the Egyptians than to die in the wilderness" (Exod 14:11–12). The people labeled the wonderful redemption of Yahweh as an evil. They preferred slavery with their idols to liberty with the living God. This was an act of apostasy. But Moses was not crippled with doubt; rather, in a burst of righteous anger, he said, "Fear not, stand firm and see the salvation of Yahweh. ... Yahweh will fight for you; as for you, be quiet!" (Exod 14:13–14, my translation). He tells them to shut up and watch Yahweh's salvation. The sea is unzipped like a coat; its floor becomes smooth pavement, and every last foot and hoof passes safely across. Yet when Egypt attempts to follow, the ground melts into mud and the waters rush back into place. On the eastern shore, Moses lifts up his voice to sing a grand Song of the sea: "I will sing to Yahweh, for he has triumphed gloriously; horse and rider he has hurled into the sea" (Exod 15:1, my translation). Once again, Yahweh has done what he said he would.

This drama at the sea in many ways becomes the reoccurring pattern for Israel's time in the wilderness. The people's disbelief and disobedience engage in a tug-of-war with Yahweh's wonders and provisions. The water is bitter; the people bellyache and Yahweh sweetens the water (Exod 15:22–25). Israel complains about hunger and Yahweh gives them manna (Exod 16). They grouse about thirst and water pours forth from the rock (Exod 17). The Amalekites swoop in for the attack, but Yahweh gives Israel victory and the eternal oath to blot out the memory of Amalek from under heaven. And so it is by these fits and starts that Yahweh brings Israel to Mount Sinai in Exodus 19.

Once Israel is at Sinai, the historical narrative retreats into the background for the law and the tabernacle to take center stage. The rest of Exodus through the beginning of Numbers all takes place at Sinai. We will drill down into the contents of these laws in the next chapter; here, our story picks back up in Numbers 10 as Israel gets back on the road again with their eyes fixed on the promised land.

As the desert trek begins, the mood seems cheery and positive. Since the census in Numbers 1, Israel has been on its best behavior. The camp structure has been set, the marching order lined up. The chieftains joyfully gave a superlative offering. The Passover was celebrated. Moses kicked things off with the Song of the ark: "Arise, O Yahweh! May your enemies be scattered, let your haters flee before you!" (Num 10:35, my translation). Israel marched straight like an arrow, and the sharp arrowhead was Judah. The ark, along with the other holy furniture of the tabernacle, was nestled in the middle on the Levites' shoulders. The Divine Warrior and his covenant army advanced with banners flying toward a victorious conquest. Terror fell on the inhabitants of the promised land, and the

EXODUS TIMELINE

Year 1

First Month

    14—First Passover (Exod 12)

    15—Departure from Egypt

Third Month: Arrival at Sinai (Exod 19)

Year 2

First Month

    1—Tabernacle set up (Exod 40:2–3)

    2–8—Priestly ordination (Lev 8)

    9—Inaugural worship (Lev 9:1)

    14—Keeping of the Passover (Num 9:1)

Second Month

    1—Census (Num 1:1)

    2–13—Chieftains' offerings (Num 7)

    14—Second Passover (Num 9:11)

    20—Cloud ascends and tabernacle sets out (Num 10:11)

Israelites were confident Yahweh would soon plant them on his own mountain, where he will reign forever and ever (Exod 15:16–18). Yet the higher hopes fly, the more terrifically they can crash.

The first crash happens at the first campsite. Israel complained bitterly, and a fire from Yahweh ravaged the outskirts of the camp. Then, a gluttonous craving erupted in their bellies: "If only we had meat. Why did we ever come out to this desert?" Yahweh gorges them with quail, and while the meat is stuck in their teeth, an epidemic slays a large crowd. The place is named Kibroth-hattaavah, "Graves of Craving." Camp number two is Hazeroth, where Moses' sister and brother, Miriam and Aaron, complain against Moses. Yahweh confirms Moses as his servant and strikes Miriam with leprosy. Two camps, and already Israel has failed twice.

Will the third time be the charm? Israel sets up camp in the wilderness of Paran (Num 12:16), the ideal staging area to investigate the promised land. Twelve spies were selected, one from each tribe, and their objectives were clear: check out the people and the land and bring back some fruit (Num 13:17–20). There and back again hiked the chosen dozen. The land was good, gushing with milk and honey, and they returned with a single cluster of grapes so big two men had to carry it together. However, the Nephilim, the sons of Anak who grew seven, eight, and nine feet tall, dwelled in the land. They were like grizzly bears with swords who would devour the little ones of Israel.

This report stirred up a riot, and the riot became a rebellion: Away with Moses! Back to Egypt with a new leader! (Num 14:1–4). They called God's lush, holy land evil, and they chose the slavery of Egypt over milk and honey. Yet amid the clamor of rebellion, one voice rang with obedience. One of the spies, Caleb, stood against the insurgency: "Let us go up at once!" (Num 13:30). Joshua, Moses' assistant, joined him. Twelve spies journeyed forth, but only two came home faithful.

This insubordination is strike number three. Yahweh will disinherit and massacre the entire congregation of Israel, who are rotten to the core. Then, he will sprout an entirely new nation from Moses alone (Num 14:11–12). Yahweh has opened the gate of judgment on Israel; here comes the fury. Moses, however, stands between Yahweh and the people; and his intercession succeeds, at least in part. Yahweh will not put an end to Israel; rather, he will be reconciled with the people and continue the covenant. Yet this mercy will fall only on the

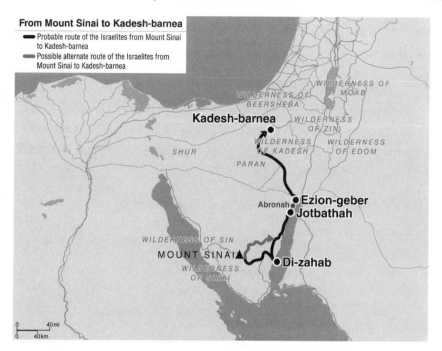

From Mount Sinai to Kadesh-barnea
- Probable route of the Israelites from Mount Sinai to Kadesh-barnea
- Possible alternate route of the Israelites from Mount Sinai to Kadesh-barnea

little ones, whom the people thought would be eaten by the Nephilim. All the Israelites twenty years old and up will perish in the wild desert, while those under twenty will inherit. Joshua and Caleb are the only exceptions. In forty years, the wilderness graveyard will be filled up with the older generation.

With this judgment, the road trip is put on hold. For the next forty years and five chapters of Numbers, Israel dwells somewhere around Kadesh-barnea, which is in the wilderness of Paran. The narrative of these years is occupied mainly with extra laws and regulations. At the end of the long, funeral-filled years, Miriam dies, Moses and Aaron rebel against God by striking a rock when Yahweh had told them to speak to it and bring forth water, and the nation of Edom refuses to let Israel pass through on their way to Canaan. The sacrilege of Moses and Aaron seals them to share in Israel's fate; they must perish in the wild and cannot enter the land.

AT THE EDGE OF THE
PROMISED LAND

The travel narrative picks up at Kadesh (Num 20:22), where it was broken off forty years previously (Num 13:26). With a number of quick steps, Israel arrives on the plains of Moab, which is the eastern doorstep to the promised land. This expedited journey includes the death of Aaron as well as two battles that change Israel's history: victories over the kings Sihon and Og, which annex to Israel the lands of Gilead, Bashan, Jazer, and Dibon. In Numbers 32, the tribes of Gad, Reuben, and the half-tribe of Manasseh ask Moses for this territory east of the Jordan River to be their covenant inheritance. With a few conditions, Moses grants the request, and so two and a half tribes of Israel receive their inheritance in the Transjordan.

Yet before Israel can cross the Jordan into the land of promise, preparations need to be made. These are hindered by a series of events that begin with Balak the king of Moab peering from his mountaintop perch down on the hordes of Israel (22:1). Balak does not want Israel as his neighbor, so he hires Balaam, a famous diviner from a region far to the east, near the Euphrates River. Balak essentially makes a business contract with Balaam. In return for a large sum of money, Balaam has to curse Israel. Balaam is honest with Balak; he can only speak what God gives him. Then, on four occasions, Balaam stands next to Balak and attempts to curse. Each time, Yahweh puts a blessing in Balaam's mouth instead. These blessings grow in prophetic grandeur. Balaam does not complete the contract, and it appears that his pockets remain empty.

In the blink of an eye, though, this blessing is in jeopardy. The women of Moab and Midian paid a visit to the young men of Israel. The gorgeous foreigners invited the Israelites to their sacrificial feasts, not unlike new neighbors inviting you to a backyard barbecue. What could be wrong with a little hospitality? What's wrong is that these feasts included idol worship of the local deity, Baal of Peor. Sexual attraction, feasts, and idolatry were the three steps of Israel's rebellion.

And where there was idolatry in the camp, wrath soon fell. An intense plague flared up and consumed 24,000 Israelites before Phinehas, Aaron's grandson, put a stop to it.

From the caves of Qumran, looking east to the Dead Sea and the Moabite highlands

How did this happen? After the blessings, how did the Moabite women lead them astray? The readers are not told for a while, but then, after Israel defeats Midian in battle, Moses reveals why: "Have you let all the women live? Behold, these, on Balaam's advice, caused the people of Israel to act treacherously against the LORD in the incident of Peor" (Num 31:15–16). It turns out that Balaam was behind the temptresses of Midian. When he could not curse Israel, he hatched a plan for them to curse themselves.

With the dust settled after Peor, the final preparations for invasion needed to be made. A census was taken for the second generation who survived the wilderness. Moses appointed Joshua to be his successor. Next came various laws and regulations about vows, the holy calendar, murder and cities of refuge, and the promised land's boundaries. And finally, a covenant renewal ceremony, recorded in the book of Deuteronomy, transferred power from Moses to Joshua. Moses delivered the entirety of Deuteronomy to Israel on the plains of Moab before he died, and Joshua ushered them across the Jordan. Deuteronomy confirms Israel's loyalty oath to Yahweh to obey all his commandments, statutes, and judgments so that they may live long in the land.

THE CONQUEST OF CANAAN

The progression established at the end of Numbers jumps to the opening of Joshua, as Joshua takes the reins. After spying out Jericho, which ensures that Yahweh "has given all the land into our hands" (Josh 2:24), it is time to cross the river. But this river crossing is planned out in accordance with the demands of holiness. All the people must become ritually pure in order to worship and to witness a manifestation of Yahweh (3:5). It is necessary because the ark crowned with the glory cloud goes before them to part the waters. The feet of the priests carrying the ark touch the cool river, and it divides to form dry soil. Just like at the Red Sea, the children of Israel hurry across the Jordan riverbed on solid ground (3:15). Twelve stones of remembrance are set up on the tenth day of the first month, the day of crossing. This twelve-tiered monument will be a memorial for Israel forever (4:19). Then we learn that the younger generation has not been circumcised. Circumcision is the sign of the covenant; it is a mark of consecration to be Yahweh's and an oath to live as Yahweh's, so with flint knives Israel is circumcised at Gilgal (5:2–9). The inaugural feast of Israel arrives in a matter of days. On the fourteenth of the first month, the calendar flips to Passover, which requires circumcision for participation (5:10–12). The newly circumcised people keep Passover in the promised land, which brings an end to the manna, and it is the first recorded Passover since Mount Sinai (Num 9:1).

One more scene puts the icing on this holy cake (5:13–15). Shortly after Passover, Joshua is taking a walk near Jericho when he spots a man with a drawn sword. He inquires, "Are you for us or for our adversary?" The man clarifies that he is not a man; "I am the commander of the army of the LORD." Joshua pitches himself over to worship. Since angels in the Bible refuse to accept worship from humans, this means this must be Yahweh himself. The Divine Warrior, with drawn sword, stands ready to fight for his people. Then he demands that Joshua remove his sandals, as he is standing on holy ground. Unlike the burning bush of Exodus 3, though, this holy ground does not seem to be geographically limited. There is an openness that seems to extend to the area of Jericho and even to the whole land.

The Golan Heights, with
Mount Hermon in the distance

The holy preparations performed by the people align with the sacredness of the land, which brings up the topic of holy war—the type of warfare used to conquer the promised land. The Hebrew word for this distinct warfare is *herem*, which translates to "devote to destruction," "doom to destruction," or "utterly destroy." *Herem* means to be consecrated through destruction; it devotes an object to God by means of destruction. In this way, its analogy is the whole burnt offering that transfers the entire bull to Yahweh as smoke through flames. A person would say, "I *herem* this object to Yahweh," which makes the thing unusable and irredeemable by laity and priests (Lev 27:28–29). So, in *herem* warfare, Yahweh *heremed* the people of the land (Canaanites, Perizzites, Hivites, etc.), so they must be completely wiped out: man, woman, and child. Only what is named is devoted to destruction, which in Joshua always covers the people and religious shrines, and sometimes includes homes, possessions, and animals. As with Jericho, sometimes everything is *heremed*. Yet with the cities that stood on mounds, Israel got to keep the plunder of homes and cattle (Josh 11:14). Finally, *herem* warfare could be implemented by Israel only within the boundaries of the promised land; outside the land, Israel did not employ *herem* (Deut 20:10–18).

What role did this *herem* warfare, which seems terribly cruel for us moderns, play? First, it has a purifying function. The land laid defiled under the abominations of the Canaanites, so they had to be vomited out by death (Lev 18:25–26). The status of the land as holy demanded that the wicked Canaanites and their idolatry be purged by devoting them to destruction. Secondly, this devastation foreshadowed the final judgment and what all sinners deserve before the holiness of Yahweh. We should not think that this *herem* was easy for Israel; in fact, they failed to complete this order from God. Rather, the horrors of *herem* displayed the true wages of sin for all sinners, and it exhibits the full justice of Yahweh against sin and evil. This is why *herem* warfare was only commanded of Israel, for a limited time, and only within the borders of the promised land. The presence of *herem* in the Old Testament does not give Christians the right to endorse the use of something like it today.

With Yahweh ready to fight for his people, the conquest begins. After seven days of marching, Jericho falls like a sand castle hit by a wave. Once Achan's rebellion is punished, Ai too crumbles to the ground. The land soon lays subdued before Yahweh and his commander, Joshua. The language of complete conquest that we find throughout the book of Joshua, however, can be misleading. The long list of victories and defeated kings in Joshua 10–12 can give the impression that the land was mostly conquered and Canaanite-free. In 11:23, it even says, "Joshua took the whole land. ... Joshua gave it for an inheritance to Israel ... the land had rest from war." If this was all that was recorded, one could not be faulted for thinking that the conquest was universal.

A chapter passes, however, and Yahweh declares to Joshua, who is nearing retirement: "There remains yet very much land to possess" (13:1). And before Joshua is gathered to his kin, he charges the elders of the people to finish the conquest he began. They must fight so that Yahweh will push back and drive away the remaining nations (23:5). With all diligence, Israel must not mix with these nations, either by intermarriage or by religion (23:7, 12). In a covenant renewal ceremony at Shechem, Israel swears fealty to Yahweh as their God and to do all his commandments (24:16–18). These exhortations paint a clear picture of Israel's responsibilities and dangers to avoid: (1) they shall *herem* all the people, (2) they shall not let them live and be their neighbors, and (3) they shall not mingle with them by marriage or worship. These three points transition us from the end of Joshua to the opening of Judges.

THE JUDGES CYCLE

A hinge effect links Joshua and Judges. A hinge repeats the same event at the conclusion of one book and the start of another to indicate that the two volumes are connected. This hinge is Joshua's death and his last charge to take over the land (see Josh 24:28–30 and Judg 2:6–9). This bond further raises the question of whether Israel will succeed at Joshua's three-point charge. Judges 1, though, hardly keeps us in suspense. As Israel marches into battle after the funeral of Joshua, there is a regression into disobedience. The tribe of Judah gets an A for conquering Hebron and putting all the people under the sword, but they failed to defeat the iron chariots of the plain. Similarly, Benjamin did well, but he permitted the Jebusites to survive in Jerusalem, and Joseph performed about the same at Bethel. After these, a refrain enters the text: Manasseh did not drive out the inhabitants but put them to forced labor. Ephraim did not drive out the inhabitants but lived among them. Zebulun did not drive out the inhabitants but lived among them and put them to forced labor. Asher did not drive out the inhabitants and lived among them. Dan was oppressed by the Amorites and driven back into the hill country. This slippery slope into disobedience sets the stage for the first judges cycle in 2:11.

The judges cycle is a pattern that consists of five steps: (1) Israel does evil by going after other gods. (2) Yahweh gives them over to their enemies. (3) Israel cries out for mercy. (4) God raises up a judge who delivers them. (5) The land has rest. This sequence is put on rinse and repeat throughout the book, yet it does not return exactly where it began. More specifically, it should not be visualized as a two-dimensional circle but a three-dimensional downward spiral. As it says in 2:19, "whenever the judge died, they turned back and were more corrupt than their fathers." Each successive rebellion was worse than the one before.

This cycle does some heavy theological lifting in the book of Judges, with several themes at play within the cycle's rhythm. First, there is the standard of Joshua's three-point charge. Will Israel destroy the nations? Or will they live among them, intermarry, and serve their gods? Israel's primary failure was to not do *herem*. Judges 3:5–6 state this quite frankly: Israel lived among the nations; they took their daughters as wives; they served their gods.

Second, Yahweh employed the judges cycle as a test to see if Israel would truly obey him (3:1–4). The cycle is an exam to determine if Israel would keep all the commandments of the law. The pattern explores the question of whether Israel can be righteous by obeying the law.

The final theme, and probably the most prominent, deals with leadership. In fact, the entire cycle begins with a crisis of leadership. Joshua and all the elders of his generation died (2:8–10), creating a vacuum of rule when Israel went astray. The vacancy after Joshua harkens back to Numbers 27, when Moses was about to die. Yahweh told Moses that his funeral was near, so Moses asked for a successor "who shall go out before them and come in before them ... that the congregation of the LORD may not be as sheep that have no shepherd" (Num 27:17). This shepherding aligns with the work of a king. Joshua is never called a king, but he functioned as a king for Israel. Joshua, though, did not appoint a successor; he did not show the foresight of Moses. Leaderless Israel becomes like sheep without a shepherd, slipping down the spiral of idolatry and wickedness. Additionally, as Yahweh raises up judges to shepherd his people in obedience, the character and behavior of the judge is critical. Each judge is measured by several criteria: (1) their devotion to Yahweh, (2) their marriage and treatment of women, (3) their military conduct, and (4) the religious reforms they enact to help the people obey. These themes will weave together into a unified quilt.

Othniel walks up to the plate first and smacks it over the fence. The righteous Caleb, one of the two faithful spies, is his older brother. The Spirit of Yahweh rests on his shoulders. After his great victory over Cushan-rishathaim, the land attains peace for a full forty years. Othniel checks all the boxes, but the brevity of his account leaves us looking for more.

Ehud then bravely takes up the call of God to fight the corpulent Eglon. With cunning, this Benjaminite buries his dagger in the king's blubber and escapes to rally the Israelites to fight for Yahweh. The staggering victory wins eighty years of peace for the land. Ehud judged Israel well, except for one little detail: in Judges 3:19 and 26, Ehud passes by some idols near Gilgal. The detail seems random, but it is a mark against Ehud. Why did he just stroll by the idols? Why did he not destroy them? Did the idols remain under the rule of Ehud? Ehud excelled as a military leader, but his piety seems to fall a bit short.

Another note should be registered at this point. The text says Othniel's peace was forty years and Ehud's was eighty, yet the leadership of these men is regional and tribal. This peace does not include the whole promised land, but only the territory of the judge's tribe. The years of peace cannot be added up for a chronological timeline; instead, there is contemporaneity between the judges. This makes it impossible to figure out the exact chronology of the period of the judges. Rather, the organization of the judges serves the themes of the judges cycle, as we shall see.

A duo is next: the prophetess Deborah, who takes the initiative in this victory, and a man named Barak. Oppressed by king Jabin and his cruel general Sisera, Deborah summons Barak and rebukes him for his cowardly aversion of Yahweh's command. "Has not the LORD, the God of Israel, commanded you, 'Go, gather your men at Mount Tabor?'" (4:6). Barak has ignored the call to fight, and so he puts a condition on his acceptance of Deborah's call: "If you go with me, I will go" (4:8). Deborah agrees to be Barak's chaplain, but she makes clear that the glory of victory will not be Barak's; it will crown the head of a woman. At first, we expect this heroine to be Deborah, yet the heroine will arise from an unexpected tent. To foreshadow this, right before the battle takes off we meet a new character: Heber, a Kenite, who moved near Kadesh (4:11).

The Kenites were the descendants of Moses' father-in-law, who aligned themselves with Judah (Judg 1:16). Joining with Judah made the Kenites loyal to Yahweh and his covenant people. Heber, however, moved away, which signals a break with Yahweh and Israel. "Heber was moving away from his kin—and soon enough from the loyalties his people had forged with Israel."[2] In fact, Kedesh lies close to King Jabin's territory. Heber's defection from Judah included his alliance with the foe Jabin. This is why, when Jabin's general Sisera flees the battle he is losing, he thinks he will be safe in Heber's tent. The husband had sworn allegiance to Jabin, but Heber's wife Jael knew that it is better to obey Yahweh than your husband.

Once inside the tent, Sisera asks for water; she brings him milk. Jael's lavish hospitality is feminine and gentle. She brings out her best china and choicest foods. Sisera feels honored and comforted. Once he has fallen asleep, however, her gentle tone quickly swings to a harsh one. The hostess's hand extends not for the salt or another dish, but for a tent peg. Her right hand seizes a workman's hammer. We have shifted from Martha Stewart to *This Old House*. The verbs of Deborah's victory poem intensify what she did next: she struck, crushed, shattered, and pierced (5:26–27). Bones crack; a skull splits. Sisera's head lays crushed at the feet of a woman.

The devoted piety of Jael sets the bar high for our next judge, Gideon. This time the semi-nomadic Midianites have infested the land. The angel of Yahweh pays a visit to Gideon, who is of the tribe of Manasseh, while he is hiding from the Midianites. The angel addresses Gideon as "a man of valor" and tells him to "go in this strength of yours" (Judg 6:12–14). Gideon appears to hail from a powerful family, but he protests in modesty: "How can I save? ... My clan is the weakest in Manasseh, and I am the least in my father's house" (6:15). His shyness echoes that of Moses in Exodus 3–4; we feel that he protests too much. Yahweh's first task for Gideon is telling; he must tear down an altar of Baal and the goddess Asherah's pole and replace them with an altar to him. The judge's central duty is to turn the people back to Yahweh.

The attack on the Midianites unfolds smoothly. Gideon follows Yahweh's direction, narrowing his force to three hundred men armed with trumpets and torches in pots. We begin to suspect his modesty when he proudly gives the battle cry, "For the LORD and for Gideon" (7:18). The Midianites are quickly routed and the chase is on. Gideon's three hundred pursue Midianite kings Zebah and Zalmunna across the Jordan River eastward. After catching them, Gideon returns to the towns Succoth and Penuel, who refused to give him aid in his pursuit. He cruelly kills all the men of Penuel, who are fellow Israelites (8:17); this punishment extends beyond what he had threatened earlier (8:9). It seems harsh to do this to your own people, but the point is that it was a privilege for royalty in the ancient Near East. Gideon is increasingly acting like a king.

His interaction with Zebah and Zalmunna also betrays the royal pretensions of Gideon. The two kings sarcastically say his brothers look like sons of a king. They mock him as a pretend king, so Gideon proves his royalty by executing them and seizing the royal jewelry from their camels. Following Gideon's execution of the Midianite kings, then, the Israelites' offer to him to rule over them matches his behavior (8:22). Gideon's refusal has the tone of a coy refusal to accept, since he follows it with the universally understood prerogatives of kings: he takes part of the plunder (8:24), makes a religious device called an ephod for access to God (8:27), and amasses a harem that provides him with seventy sons (8:30). Finally, his ephod becomes an idolatrous snare for all the people. Gideon replaces the Baal altar he had torn down with an idol of his own making. The land gets its rest, but people are not more obedient.

In addition to all this, Gideon's legacy is the anti-judge Abimelech, born from one of Gideon's concubines. Abimelech, whose name means "my father is king," slaughters all seventy of his half-brothers, save one named Jotham. He makes himself king in Shechem, and after three years his oppressive rule leads to rebellion. Like any tyrant, Abimelech responds with violence: he burns up a thousand of his own people in a tower. He would have done the same in the city of Thebez if a woman had not dropped a millstone on his head. No peace comes on the land, but there is a great sigh of relief with the end of Abimelech (9:56–57). The enemy oppressor in this cycle did not come from outside of Israel, but creeped up from within it.

The sad pattern of Abimelech does not die with him. The next major judge is Jephthah, who lives east of the Jordan River in the land of Gilead. Two qualities are clear about Jephthah. First, he is the son of a prostitute. He was brought forth in the breakdown of covenant marriage. And second, he is a mighty warrior. His skills in violence propel him to become a successful bandit in the land of Tob, and his reputation is so unparalleled that the elders of Gilead beg him to be their ruler when the Ammonites invade. But Jephthah is all muscle and no brain; his diplomatic correspondence with the king of the Ammonites is dotted with error, what K. A. Kitchen calls "an ignorant man's bold bluster."[3]

This second trait leads him to make the foolish vow to sacrifice the first thing to exit his house upon returning victorious from battle. What did he expect to come out of his house other than a human? Does this mean he vowed a human sacrifice? His grief and shock on seeing his daughter imply that this was not his intention. Yet in his ignorant zeal he feels bound to keep his vow, even though the law provided ways to deal with a foolish vow (Lev 27 and Num 30). The end is the horrific death of his virgin daughter.

And his killing does not stop there. The men of Ephraim complain against Jephthah for not asking for help and threaten violence. Jephthah meets the charge with a civil war, and you do not mess with Jephthah in battle. He and the men of Gilead kill 42,000 of their brothers from Ephraim. Jephthah has the shortest reign of any judge (six years), and his burial brings no peace to the land. Israel sinks further down the spiral of wickedness.

The final major judge in the book comes on the scene with much fanfare. An angel appears to Manoah and his wife and announces that a special son will be born to them. This son, Samson, will be a Nazirite, one devoted to serve Yahweh marked by never cutting his hair and abstaining from alcohol, and he will "begin to save Israel from the hand of the Philistines" (Judg 13:5). Why just *begin*? Samson grows up with Yahweh's blessing and the Spirit's stirring, yet he still has a weakness for women, and especially foreign women.

Samson's parents attempt to turn his eyes toward a nice Israelite girl, but to no avail. After he weds a Philistine, Samson's aggressive acts all flow from jealousy and personal vendetta. He slays thirty men, incinerates grain, and strikes down a thousand with a donkey's jawbone. He claims he is seeking justice, yet he is driven not by God's law but his own desire for vengeance. Samson's love for a woman named Delilah eventually brings him down. He keeps coming back to her, even though he knows she is in cahoots with the Philistines. Delilah's nagging requests to know the source of his strength bring Samson to her knees, not unlike how Jael nailed Sisera to the ground. Eventually his long hair, the last vestige of his Nazirite vow, is razored from his scalp so that he becomes weak like any other man (16:17), and he is captured.

If it was not for a final mercy from Yahweh, this would have been the last we hear of Samson. But with his hair grown back, he asks Yahweh for one last moment of strength to crush the Philistines who have imprisoned him. Samson brings the house down, but his motive is still vengeance: "to avenge for my two eyes" (16:28). He kills more in his death than in his life, but no peace comes on the land.

It seems like Israel has landed at the bottom of this downward spiral, but the last episode in the book goes lower (Judg 19–21). It begins with an unnamed Levite who has a concubine but no mention of a wife—a unique case in Scripture. This makes the relationship dubious, as if the Levite considers his concubine merely a sex object or slave. The concubine is unfaithful, and the Levite goes to retrieve her from her father's house. After reveling for days with his father-in-law, the man and his concubine get on the road late in the afternoon. A foreboding darkness hangs over the journey, since it is not safe to travel at night. The Levite proudly will not stop in a foreign town, so he pushes on to the Benjaminite town of Gibeah. In the gray of dusk, though, he does not notice that he has entered a place as wicked as Sodom (Gen 19). A terrible reenactment unfolds in the city. A rabble of scoundrels lust after the Levite, so to save his own skin he tosses out his concubine to them. They gang rape and abuse her all night. Reaching out for justice, she dies with hands on the threshold. In the morning, the Levite steps over her like a sleeping cat, tosses her on his donkey, and goes home. No tears are shed; no funeral is held. Rather, he cuts her up into a dozen pieces and mails them to every tribe in order to goad them to action. In doing so, this hedonistic and narcissistic good-for-nothing sparks a forest fire that consumes the whole nation.

Outraged, 400,000 warriors immediately assemble. They demand only the worthless men of Gibeah, but the Benjaminites refuse. Eleven tribes marshal against one in a civil war. When the dust settles, the eleven tribes have massacred man, woman, and beast in every town of Benjamin, which they then burn. At the beginning of Judges, Israel had failed to *herem* the pagan Canaanites, but here they *herem* their own flesh and blood. Every last soul of Benjamin is dead, save for six hundred men hiding in a cave. When the men of Israel realize what they have done, they scramble to save the tribe from dying out. Yet before the battle, they had taken a rash oath not to marry their daughters to the men of Benjamin.

Then they remember that one Israelite town failed to show up for battle: Jabesh-gilead. The Israelites *herem* this town and save four hundred virgins for the men of Benjamin. That leaves them two hundred short, so they attend a festival near Shiloh and steal the remaining number. By massacre and kidnapping, six hundred wives were taken to keep Benjamin alive. The book ends with the statement that there was no king in Israel, so everyone did what was right in his own eyes (21:25). Without a righteous leader, the sheep were scattered.

Here we are given an indication that the events of Judges show Israel's need for a king. Further, in Judges 20:28, when the people inquired of Yahweh, we are told that Phinehas the son of Eleazar was ministering in those days. Eleazar was Joshua's contemporary! Phinehas belonged to the generation who saw God's deeds in the wilderness (Judg 2:10). This means that the events narrated at the end of Judges happened shortly after Joshua's death. This episode came not last in the period of the judges, but first. The bitter weeping of Judges 21:2 is connected to the weeping in Judges 2:4. Israel did not slowly slide into vile degeneracy, but jumped off the cliff at the very beginning.

The question Israel faced during the judges cycle was whether they could obey. Could they be righteous enough to live in the land? By the end of the book, at every point they had failed. Israel could not obey. They needed a leader to guide them. And this leader could not be some sword-swinging general; his first expertise must be righteousness and devotion to Yahweh above all else. The waiting for a righteous king has begun. This wait will last all the way to Jesus Christ, when Yahweh will remember his oath to Abraham for the forgiveness of sin.

STUDY QUESTIONS

1. How do the plagues reveal the superiority of Yahweh over Egypt and its gods?

2. How did Israel persist in their disobedience and disbelief?

3. What caused the incident at Peor, and how was it resolved?

4. What is *herem* warfare, and what does it reveal about Yahweh?

5. What was Yahweh's purpose with the judges cycle?

6. In what ways do the judges get progressively worse?

7. How does the end of Judges surprise you?

4

THE MOSAIC ECONOMY

Bible Reading: Leviticus, Numbers, Deuteronomy

When you travel to a foreign country, you are well aware that there will be culture shock. The language means nothing to your ears. The culinary arts are exotic and strange. Thus begins the wonderful trek of learning. You become a student of their manners and etiquette, dress and diet, habits and holidays. Full acquaintance with a culture and people, however, requires becoming competent in their laws, politics, and government. Culture and government go hand in hand.

If this is the case in present-day travel, how much more with time travel, with visiting the ancient societies of the world. A common hindrance to our Bible knowledge is that we know the stories and characters, but we are ignorant of their laws and traditions. We recognize the players on the field but not the game they are playing. Paul S. Minear poignantly states the issue:

> In ancient literature we encounter people who are marching to the sound of a different drummer; the tempo of their life is vastly different from ours. Their language is shaped by a different mentality, their mentality shaped by different experience. Their world has a different ceiling and different horizons; their

maps give expression to different beginnings and endings. As long as a student shies away from that alien world, so long does Bible study remain bland, superficial, and tepid. But each step of penetration will increase his excitement, though also bewilderment, for at each step he encounters a collision between two languages, two mentalities, two modes of existing in the world, in fact, two worlds.[1]

The world of the Bible ebbs and flows with strange practices and people. We are aliens to their ancient society. "This is why an effective study of the Bible produces culture shock; the more intense the study, the greater the shock."[2] Yet many Bible resources and translations attempt to minimize our feelings of being alien. Paraphrasing Minear: like Americans traveling in Asia who stay in Western-style hotels and go on guided tours, such resources give the illusion of

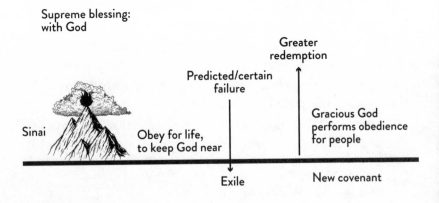

Chart 4: Sinai Map

travel, but without any of its risks and benefits. And if the Bible is alien in general for the modern human, then the ritual texts about sacrifice, impurities, and tabernacle worship might as well be from Jupiter.

It is safe to say that the Mosaic economy is the least understood part of the Bible for Christians. This misunderstanding cascades from being unpopular; Howard Eilberg-Schwartz has tracked how scholarly prejudice against the priestly literature in the nineteenth century trickled down to every Sunday School in the twentieth century.[3] If we, then, desire to profit from our travel through the ancient texts of Israel, we ought to embrace the culture shock. On our journey, we must leave the McDonald's and order the offal dish in the local mercado. God in his eternal wisdom revealed the law not to modern man, but to a group of wandering Arameans who sojourned as slaves in Egypt. To understand what Old Testament law means, then, we must first understand the characteristics of an ancient Near Eastern covenant.

ANCIENT TREATIES

As with any house, the house of Israel stands upon a foundation, and this foundation is a covenant. The covenant God made with the Hebrews of the exodus generation springs from the covenant God made with Abraham. They are intricately related, but also distinctly different. As we saw in chapter 2, ancient covenants were employed for a host of varying relationships, from adoption to business to international diplomacy. The nature of the relationship was embodied in the form and type of covenant. To understand the relationship, you must analyze the terms of the covenant. We see from Genesis 12 and 15 that the Abrahamic covenant was unconditional and unilateral. The character of the Mosaic covenant, likewise, can be seen from its form and terms. And there are two ancient text types that God used in the Mosaic covenant: law codes and treaties.

Law codes are lists or collections of laws whose form are often casuistic or case law. In them, a list of laws are encased in a preamble and prologue up front and an epilogue with blessings and curses in the rear. The early Mesopotamian codes we have date to about 2100–1700 BC. The practical legal use of these codes is debated, since their primary purpose is to demonstrate how the king maintained justice and righteousness. Many similarities between the codes can be observed, including a common form. The most famous law code belongs to Hammurabi, who was "King of Sumer and Akkad" in Babylon from around 1792–1750. Originally inscribed on black stone slabs, Hammurabi's law code was studied and copied in schools for nearly twelve centuries after his death. In the prologue, Hammurabi acclaims how the gods installed him for the good of all the people:

> At that time, the gods Anu and Enlil, for the enhancement of the well-being of the people, name me by my name: Hammurabi, the pious prince, who venerates the gods, to make justice prevail in the land, to abolish the wicked and the evil, to prevent the strong from oppressing the weak, to rise like the sun-god Shamash [the god of justice] over all mankind, to illuminate the land.[4]

Hammurabi goes on to list how he is the shepherd, the discerning king, the warrior, the one steeped in wisdom, and the judicious one who proclaims truth and quells rebellion. The closing blessings and curses obligate the people to follow the king and preserve his law. The laws number between 275–300, and several of them have considerable similarity with the laws of Scripture, especially the covenant code of Exodus 21–23.

The second text type that lies behind the Mosaic law is that of treaty, which was a type of covenant. Treaties administered international diplomacy between the nations and were solemnly sealed and witnessed by the gods. Moreover, "the ancient treaty was a *public* document. Copies of treaties were distributed, preserved, and published."[5] About sixty treaties still exist, most of which are Hittite, with a few handfuls from Syria and Neo-Assyria. The Hittite treaties date to the

mid-second millennium BC, the environment of Moses and the exodus.

There were two types of treaties in the ancient Near East: parity
and suzerain-vassal. Parity treaties
were enacted between nations of relatively the same size and power for their
mutual benefit, so the language used is
that of brothers (think of the agreement
between Solomon and Hiram in 1 Kgs

LAW CODE FORM

1. Title/Preamble
2. Prologue
3. Laws
4. Epilogue
5. Blessings/Curses

5:12). The suzerain-vassal treaty bonded a greater king with a lesser
king, a mighty nation with a puny one. This kind of treaty, then, was
often not a mutual agreement, but imposed by the suzerain on the
threat of annihilation (think of the agreement between Sennacherib
and Hezekiah in 2 Kgs 18).

There is a substantial difference, then, between modern treaties
and ancient ones. Modern treaties tend to be impersonal and sterile;
third-person language reigns. Ancient treaties are personal and emo-
tive, using second-person language to instill allegiance and fealty in the
vassal toward the suzerain. Jon Levenson summarizes this difference:

> The ancient Near East covenant was not an impersonal code,
> but an instrument of diplomacy founded upon the personal
> relationship of the heads of state. The essence of the covenant
> lies in the fact that the latter pledge to be faithful to one another.
> It is important to remember that even within one state, gov-
> ernment was conceived as personal, as it emphatically is not in
> modern states. Modern man wants a government of laws, not
> of men, one in which all legal relationships are described in
> abstract terms without reference to personalities—thus phrased
> in the third personal only. By contrast, in the ancient Near East,
> the king was thought to look after his subjects solicitously. In
> a ubiquitous metaphor, he was their shepherd and they were
> his flock. They loved and feared him. In parity treaties, the two

kings are "brothers"; in some suzerainty treaties, the greater king is the "father" of the lesser king, not in a biological sense, of course, but in a powerful metaphorical way.[6]

There is no false dichotomy between the personal and the legal. The legality of the covenant is rooted in the personal, and the personal is solemnized with the legal. The language of love found in Deuteronomy 6:4–6 rings with the covenantal tone.[7] So do many of David's psalms (such as Psalm 23). Yahweh, then, powerfully used this covenant form to relate to his people after coming out of Egypt.

A few quotes from these ancient treaties will help us familiarize ourselves with the world of Israel. A Hittite treaty between Šuppiluliuma and Aziru from the 1300s BC begins, "Thus says My Majesty, Šuppiluliuma, Great King, king of Hatti, hero, beloved of the Storm-god."[8] After a list of stipulations that cover military and extradition matters, the curses scare Aziru to fealty. "All the words of the treaty and of the oath which are inscribed on this tablet, if Aziru does not keep these words of the treaty and of the oath and he breaks the oath, let these oath gods destroy Aziru together with his head, his wives, his sons, his grandsons, his house, his town, his land, and all his possessions!"[9] In another Šuppiluliuma treaty, the warning curses directed at Kurtiwaza say, "May the oaths sworn in the presence of these gods break you like reeds. ... May they exterminate from the earth your name."[10]

These samplings of law codes and treaties help orient us to the climate and altitude of the ancient Near East and the world of Israel. Yahweh's accommodation to the time and place of his people gains focus and concreteness. But while the Mosaic covenant recruits features from both the codes and the treaties, it does not simply cut and paste. The covenant with Israel unites her not to a human king, but to the one King and God, Yahweh. The oaths in this covenant are not solemnized by the invocation of a herd of deities but Yahweh alone. Likewise, the Mosaic covenant is not only meant for political use; rather, it organically incorporates the very soul of Israelite religion and piety with the loving and holy God. Father/son, Lord/servant, God/people, Husband/wife, and King/citizen are all metaphors that illuminate the covenant relationship.

One clarification is needed here. When it comes to Scripture, we do not possess the original documents. We hold a historical record

HITTITE TREATY FORM

1. Title/Preamble
2. Historical Prologue
3. Stipulations (basic or detailed)
4. Depositing/Reading Treaty
5. Witnesses
6. Curses/Blessings

of the covenant making and the contents of the covenant, but not the documents themselves. The original documents were the dual copies carved by God's finger and later re-cut by Moses (Exod 31:18). For this reason, to expect Scripture to fit precisely the format of other treaties or codes is unreasonable. Nevertheless, the contents of the Mosaic covenant and its renewals show remarkable similarities. Table 1 lays the biblical texts over the flexible forms of a covenant.

THE MOSAIC COVENANT

With the analogues laid before us, we can now drill down into the details of the Mosaic or Sinai covenant to get acquainted with its character. The initial statement of the covenant is published upon arrival at Sinai, when Yahweh delivers to Moses a word for the people: "You yourselves have seen what I did to the Egyptians, and how I bore you on eagles' wings and brought you to myself" (Exod 19:4). This prologue lays out God's grand and gracious work for Israel as the basis of the covenant, which obligates Israel to Yahweh with fear and fealty. Yahweh purchased his people from Egypt; they belong to him.

The condition, then, stands firmly on the deeds of God: "If you will indeed obey my voice and keep my covenant" (19:5). Israel must do all God tells them, and they must keep his covenant. This includes guarding and upholding all his stipulations—in heart, word, and deed.

Conditions, though, are welded to sanctions, to rewards and/or punishments. "You shall be my treasured possession among all peoples ... you shall be to me a kingdom of priests and a holy nation" (19:5–6). This is the target placed in Israel's sights, the beautiful goal to attain. At the moment, Israel does not wear the ephod of a priest; she is not fully holy. Fulfilling the law is the condition for maintaining holiness and reaching greater holiness.

Exodus–Leviticus	Deuteronomy	Joshua 24
1. *Title/Preamble.* Exod 20:1 Now God spoke all these words	1. *Title/Preamble.* Deut 1:1–5 These are the words Moses spoke	1. *Title/Preamble.* Josh 24:2 Thus said YHWH, the God of Israel
2. *Historical Prologue.* 20:2 I am YHWH ... who brought you out of Egypt	2. *Historical Prologue.* 1:6–3:29 YHWH spoke to us (history, Sinai to Moab)	2. *Historical Prologue.* 24:2b–13 Forefather from Terah to new land
3. *Stipulations.* Basic: 10 Words, 20:3–17; Detailed: 20:22–26; 21–23, 25–31; Lev	3. *Stipulations.* Intro: 4. Basic: 5. Detailed: 6–11, 12–26	3. *Stipulations.* 24:14–15 (essence only)
4a. *Depositing Text.* 25:6 book by ark	4a. *Depositing Text.* 31:9, 24–26 book by ark	4a. *Depositing Text.* 24:26 in book
4b. *Reading out.* 24:7	4b. *Reading out.* 31:9–13 Read every 7 years.	4b. *Reading out*—
5. *Witness.* 24:4 (12 stelae)	5. *Witness.* 31:26 book; 31:19–22, song in 32	5. *Witness.* 24:22 people, 27 stela
6a. *Blessings.* Obedience Lev 26:3–13 If you follow my word, I send ... peace	6a. *Blessings.* Obedience 28:1–14 If you obey, you will be blessed ...	6a. *Blessings.* Obedience 24:20c After he has done you good (implied)
6b. *Curses.* Disobedience Lev 26:14–43	6b. *Curses.* Disobedience 28:15–68	6b. *Curses.* Disobedience 24:19–20

Table 1: The Sinai Covenant and Its Renewals[11]

This summarizes the covenant as a whole; the real thing comes in chapters 20–24. In chapters 20–23, Yahweh publishes the commands of his covenant, beginning with the foundation (The Ten Commandments) and moving to the detail (covenant code). Once the people learn the terms of the covenant, ratification can happen (Exod 24:1–11). The ceremony unfolds on three tiers. The people must stay at the foot of the mountain. Aaron, his sons, and seventy elders, representing the people, are allowed to climb the mountain, but they must bow down at a distance. Moses alone is permitted to approach Yahweh in his glory at the summit. With everyone in their place, Moses reads all the commandments to the people, who promise to do all Yahweh ordered (24:3).

Next, Moses commences with the covenant ratification ceremony. He first writes down all the commands of Yahweh. At the foot of Sinai, he erects an altar along with twelve pillars for the twelve tribes. Once the sacrifices are offered, the collected blood is split into containers. Moses dashes the first half of the blood on the altar that represents Yahweh. For a second time, Moses reads the covenant scroll to the people, who swear loyal obedience. Their oath is sealed with another blood rite. Moses dashes the second half of the blood on the people. The same blood act is performed on the altar and on the people, which means the blood is tossed on the twelve pillars (24:6, 8).

The blood has a twofold purpose. First, it consecrates the oaths as binding, both from God's perspective and the people's. Second, the blood evokes the death penalty for failure. Hence, Moses announces, "The blood of the covenant that the LORD has made with you" (24:8). This ceremony diverges crisply from the covenant ratification ceremony between God and Abraham in Genesis 15. In Genesis 15, God alone passed through the split animals. Here, though, the blood comes on the people as well to make the covenant conditional and breakable.

The final part of the ceremony takes place on the mountain, moving from the stipulations to the promised reward. A banquet table is set, and Moses, Aaron, his sons, and the seventy elders take their seats. Gazing upward, they behold the feet of God resting on a sapphire pavement. A pure blue glass ceiling is over their heads. Delicacies appear on the dining table for the men to eat and drink (24:11). As they behold Yahweh and feast, he does not raise his hand against them. Normally, for human beings to be this near to God spelled death and judgment, but an exception is granted here as a foretaste of the goal of the covenant. If Israel obeys and becomes holy, they will come to sit permanently where these men now eat.

The covenant ratification ceremony clarifies the conditional nature of the Mosaic covenant and forms the background for all the following legal material. At the covenant renewal ceremony forty years later on the plains of Moab, Moses declares to Israel, "The LORD our God made a covenant with us in Horeb. Not with our fathers did the LORD make this covenant" (Deut 5:2–3). "Our fathers" in Deuteronomy refers to Abraham, Isaac, and Jacob. There is an awareness in Israel that the Mosaic covenant differs from the Abrahamic covenant. As Moshe Weinfeld states, "The covenant with the Patriarchs is a covenant of grace, a divine promise to give them the land ... while the Sinaitic covenant is an obligation imposed on Israel to observe the law."[12] In Deuteronomy 6:25, parents shall answer their children who inquire about the commandments, "It will be our righteousness if we carefully do this whole commandment" (my translation). The people's obedience stands as their righteous credit in order to live long in the land.

The conditionality is front and center in Deuteronomy 11: "See, I am setting before you today a blessing and a curse: the blessing, if you obey ... and the curse, if you do not obey" (11:26–27). This is repeated in 30:19: "I have put before you life and death, blessing and curse. Choose life—if you and your offspring would live." In fact, the rhetoric of Deuteronomy repeats the language of "keep/observe/do carefully today so that you may live." Brent Strawn writes, "The content of Deuteronomy's repetition, therefore, is not only explicitly concerned with life, prosperity, and blessing, but the very repetitive rhetorical strategy of the book motivates one to enact these laws, statutes, and ordinances by means of valid and persuasive reasoning."[13]

From beginning to end, Deuteronomy beats the drum that Israel must read and live carefully the covenant stipulations.

Shechem as seen from Mount Gerizim

The reiteration of Deuteronomy, though, is hardly alone within the Torah. In Leviticus 18, the past ways of Egypt and the ways of the Canaanites to come are banned and replaced with the statutes and rules of Yahweh. The pagan practices scurry down the path to death, but the commandments of God climb the ladder of life. "You shall therefore keep my statutes and my rules; if a person does them, he shall live by them" (Lev 18:5). The single path of obeying the law will allow Israel to remain alive in the land. If Israel forsakes this path, then the land will spew Israel out as it vomited out the pagans before them (18:25–30). Being different from the nations is not the primary message, but conformity to Yahweh's holiness. The negative command matures into the positive: "You shall be holy, for I the LORD your God am holy" (Lev 19:2). Growing into this holiness consists in obeying the litany of laws, which include loving your neighbor and the sojourner, keeping Sabbath, eating the peace offering before day three, obeying reaping regulations, keeping just scales, and avoiding forbidden mourning rites. The law ends not only in the land of life, but also in the character of holiness.

Holiness by law displays what Yahweh demands to live in his presence, the best place ever. In love, Yahweh chose to redeem Israel from the yoke of Egypt. In patience and longsuffering, God puts up with his wayward son to forgive and to give second chances. But, at the end of the day, the demands of holiness cannot be compromised. As the blessings and curses make transparent, keeping the law is required to live in the land with God's presence, while disobedience can only end with exile and God-forsakenness (Lev 26; Deut 28).

Yet while Israel is commanded to choose life by doing all that Yahweh has commanded, she also gets the notification that she will fail. In addition to her own past adulteries, Yahweh tells Israel she will fail in the end. In Deuteronomy 4, Yahweh predicts that Israel will act corruptly, making idols for herself (4:25). He even calls heaven and earth as witnesses to the fact that Israel will soon perish from the land. She will not endure long, but Yahweh will scatter her like chaff to the four winds of the nations (4:26–27). Israel's effort to be holy is doomed to fail. In Deuteronomy 30:1–2, Moses declares that the blessing and curse will come on Israel; she will be driven to the nations. This collapse also gets written into the grand Song of Moses, the national anthem of Israel (Deut 32). Israel shall grow fat, lazy, and forgetful. Her vine is the vine of Sodom. Yahweh's vengeance will rain from heaven, and their day of calamity is near (32:35). And if Moses was not clear enough, Joshua frankly forecasts, "You are not able to serve the LORD, for he is a holy God. He is a jealous God; he will not forgive your transgressions or your sins" (24:19). His jealous holiness will consume them.

What is the point to such a destined failure? If holiness by the law is impossible for the hard-hearted Israelites, why does Yahweh demand it? Here a contrast arises between Moses' predictions and

Joshua's prophecy. Moses predicts that if, while in exile, Israel seeks Yahweh and returns to him, then he will not fail them or destroy them completely. In compassion he will remember the Abrahamic covenant that he swore to them (Deut 4:31). In Deuteronomy 10:16, Yahweh commands, "Circumcise therefore the foreskin of your heart." After they fail to do this, God promises that in exile he will do it for them: "The LORD your God will circumcise your heart and the heart of your offspring" (Deut 30:6). The heavenly doctor will transplant the hearts of his people. Similarly, Moses says that after the day of calamity Yahweh will vindicate his people. Yahweh is he who deals death and gives life. He wounds and he heals. He will purify his people's land (32:36–43). The sinners he slayed, he will make alive again. The sin-polluted land Yahweh will purify and make atonement for. And Leviticus adds its voice to Deuteronomy, saying that when Israel lays desolate among the nations and confesses her sins, then Yahweh will remember his covenant with Abraham, Isaac, and Jacob (Lev 26:42). He will not utterly spurn his people, but he will keep his covenant.

It is these postexilic promises that the prophets will later pick up on. Jeremiah preached a new covenant, one not like the one made coming out of Egypt that they broke (Jer 31:32). In this new, everlasting covenant, Yahweh will give his people a new heart, so that they can obey (Jer 32:39–40). He will forgive their iniquities and remember their sins no more (Jer 31:34). Ezekiel says that in the new covenant, Yahweh's kindness will purify them, purge their sins and idols, and grant a new spirit and heart (Ezek 36:25–27). Yahweh will plant his sanctuary in their midst forever, and he will be their God and they will be his people forever (Ezek 37:27–28). After the night of failure and judgment, mercy will dawn.

SACRIFICE, PURITY, AND HOLINESS

So far I have surveyed the Mosaic covenant with its conditionality, its demands to be holy by the law, and how, in the end, undergirded by the grace of the Abrahamic covenant, it leads to the new covenant. But I have not yet talked about its systems of holiness and purity, which are covered mainly in the later part of Exodus, Leviticus, and in the book of Numbers. Three main elements make up these systems: tabernacle, sacrifice, and purity. What connects these three is the priesthood. It's impossible in this chapter to analyze the holiness and purity systems in detail, but here I want to chart out some main features under four headings: tabernacle, priesthood, sacrifice, and ritual purity.

The tabernacle: "keeping heaven on earth"[14]

As moderns, when we trudge through the exacting details and precise demands of the tabernacle's furnishings or the sacrificial gore, our feet feel sunk in mud. What is the point? God gave the tabernacle as his dwelling place among his people. It was Yahweh's house on earth. The blueprint of its construction descended from heaven. Atop Sinai Yahweh told Moses, "Let them make me a sanctuary, that I may dwell in their midst. Exactly as I show you concerning the pattern of the tabernacle ... so you shall make" (Exod 25:8–9, 40). The glory cloud shifts from the summit of Sinai to fill the tabernacle, where Yahweh is enthroned, to meet and speak with Moses (Exod 25:22; Num 7:89).

In fact, Sinai, the mountain of God, forms the model to which the tabernacle conforms. Sinai was divided into three realms. The foot of the mount was where the people worshiped in ritual purity around the altar (Exod 19:10–13; 24:4–8). Not a finger of the people or a hoof of their livestock could touch the mountain, lest they die. The lower part of Sinai was holy, so Moses and the priestly family alone could tread there (Exod 24:1). Finally, the pinnacle was draped in the cloud of Yahweh; it was most holy, and only Moses could draw so near (24:15–18). Pure, holy, and most holy were the three steps up Sinai. Likewise, the courtyard of the tabernacle with its bronze altar for sacrifices could be entered by the people in a pure state. The holy place inside the tabernacle was forbidden to all save the priests. And the adytum, or holy of holies, barred all except the high priest once per year on the Day of Purgation. In this way, the tabernacle was a portable Sinai. Furthermore, as the holy decoration and furniture echoed garden imagery, the tabernacle moved as a portable Eden.

Model of the tabernacle

Later on with the temple, these realities become the joy of Israel's song. The sons of Korah harmonize, "My soul longs, yes, faints for the courts of the LORD ... for a day in your courts is better than a thousand elsewhere" (Ps 84:2, 10). The call to enter his courts with praise and thanksgiving reverberated in Israel's life (Ps 100:4). David's hope and confidence cheers to dwell in the house of Yahweh forever with his overflowing cup (Ps 23:6). The goodness of God's house and the holiness of his temple satisfy the people's longing soul. And the righteous are planted in the house of God like palm trees bearing fruit and cedars ever green (Ps 92:13). Levenson puts it this way:

> The temple serves, among many other things, as a survival of the primal paradise lost to the "profane" world, the world

outside the sanctuary (Latin, *fanum*) and as a prototype of the redeemed world envisioned by some to lie ahead. It connects the protological and the eschatological, the primal and the final, preserving Eden and providing a taste of the World-to-Come.[15]

The holy paradise persevered in the tabernacle, and later the temple. It was a foretaste of the Israelites' ultimate destiny in a world where death reigned outside. Victor Hurowitz concludes about God's presence in the temple, "Its design, decoration, and rituals made the Temple a virtual Heaven on earth."[16]

Yahweh's dwelling with his covenant people is their highest good and most blessed hope. The question is, How do they keep God near? And how do they enter his courts to live forever? As wonderful as it was for God to be near his people, such closeness created a lethal problem, because Israel were sinners. Sinners cannot live with the Holy God. Timmer puts it this way, "Yahweh's presence, in fact, is something of a dilemma, in that he freely chooses to manifest his special presence among Israel even though she is not qualified to experience this directly. This basic incompatibility is the *raison d'être* for the myriad provisions for accommodating Yahweh's presence."[17] Every last law, ritual, and feast is intended to preserve the presence of God with his people and separate the people from their sin and impurities. As Yahweh's glory on earth is a foretaste of heaven, an intrusion of paradise into history, then the holy sacrifices and rituals protect and maintain heaven on earth.

The entrance liturgies of the Psalms add their own voice to this truth (Psalms 15, 24). Not only must the holiness of the sanctuary be sustained, but the entering worshiper shall be upright. "Who shall sojourn in your tent? Who shall dwell on your holy hill? He who walks blamelessly and does what is right" (Ps 15:1–2). The people's lives have to measure up ethically before they can be admitted into God's house. But "those whom the 'entrance liturgy' qualifies for admittance become like the eternal and impregnable sanctuary into which they then come."[18] God's presence within the sanctuary is vouchsafed by the upholding of the cultic laws, and worshippers enter by being conformed to the law. The first element of keep God near in the tabernacle lies in the priesthood.

Priesthood: the necessity of mediation

Once Yahweh began announcing his commandments to Israel as Sinai rumbled, the people had a desperate problem. The theophany was too glorious; the law was too demanding; the people needed help. They ran to Moses, saying, "Let us not die, then, for this fearsome fire will consume us; if we hear the voice of the LORD our God any longer, we shall die. … You go closer and hear all that the LORD our God says, and then you tell us everything that the LORD our God tells you, and we will willingly do it" (Deut 5:22–24, NJPS). Like a burning in their bones, they knew they needed a mediator. And Yahweh responded that "they are right in all that they have spoken" (5:28). Moses became the first and archetypal mediator, and his mediation was passed on in two ways: first through the office of prophet (Deut 18:15–20), and second through the office of priest. Moses set up the tabernacle and oversaw the ordination of Aaron, but after Aaron's installation, Moses resigned from the priestly service.

The necessity of the priesthood also aligns with the overall goal of the Mosaic covenant to make the people a royal priesthood (Exod 19:6). The people are not presently priests, so Aaron and his descendants do the work until the finish line is crossed. There are two ingredients in the priesthood that make it effective: status and work.

The status of the priests involves their God-given rank and their maintenance of it. The baseline of the priestly status consists in Yahweh's election and word. Yahweh chose Aaron and his sons to serve as priests (Exod 19:24; 24:1; 28:1). The divine appointment, though, had to be ratified by a most elaborate ordination service (Exod 28–29; Lev 8). The ordination included a seven-step ritual of purification and sanctification, wherein by anointing oil and holy blood Aaron and his sons were elevated to the rank of holy. This sevenfold ritual was repeated in the same way for seven days during which Aaron could not exit the tabernacle. Finally, in a climactic eighth-day ceremony, Aaron performed the priestly duties to inaugurate both the public sacrificial system and his priesthood, which is capped by fire coming out from Yahweh's glory cloud to consume the sacrifices. By blood and smoke on the altar, and by blood and oil on their bodies, Aaron and his sons are sanctified as Yahweh's special property and servants. By these rituals, the Spirit of God invests the priests with authority and purity to carry the names of Israel before Yahweh and to bear away the sins of the people (Exod 28:29, 38).

The priests' status comes further into focus in the requirements of Leviticus 21–22. To begin with, a list of bodily blemishes bans a priest from sanctuary service (Lev 21:16–23). What these blemishes have in common is that they are caused by the effects of the curse of Genesis 3. They clearly depict that sin and death are in the world, that the corruption of sin affects us body and soul. To be free from these physical blemishes symbolizes being untouched by the curse. Moreover, the number of the prohibited priestly blemishes matches the imperfections that disqualify an animal from being sacrificed, twelve each (Lev 22:20–25). At the altar, priest and sacrifice copy each other in symbolically being untouched by the curse. In their bodies you can see the beauty of holiness, as they are whole, clean, and free from handicaps, deformities, and injuries. Similarly, the priests were barred from going to funerals to be defiled by corpse contamination (with a few exceptions, Lev 21:2, 11). The high priest had to marry a virgin from his own people. Additionally, the fabrics of the priestly garments are of the same type as those of the tabernacle, though in inverse order.[19] The chaos-free paradise represented by the garden imagery of the sanctuary also glistens in the appearance of the priests. As the tabernacle echoes Eden, so Aaron echoes Adam.

The work of the priesthood falls into two general categories. The first is intercession, bearing Israel's names before Yahweh in remembrance and bearing their sin away (Exod 28:29, 38). This includes performing all the rituals inside the holy place, offering all the sacrifices (daily, public and private), and conducting the annual feasts. The second duty is teaching and discernment. The root of this duty sprouts from Leviticus 10:10–11, "to distinguish between the holy and the common, and between the impure and pure and to teach the Israelites all the laws" (my translation). As Jacob Milgrom states, "the making of distinctions ... is the essence of the priestly function."[20] Judging, declaring, and treating appropriately what was holy and what was common or impure was the priest's task. A holy item (food, space, or time) belonged to Yahweh as his special property, and so could only be used as laid out by him. A common object was owned by the people, who were free to use it however they saw fit within the law. Holy and common, then, are statuses defined by God with very concrete realities. The priest was holy while the layperson was common. Sabbath and feast were holy time, but workdays were common. These well-defined statuses could not be mingled or confused.

Purity and impurity, though, are better understood as states than statuses. Two general rules aid in making this clear. First, the common must be pure in order to enter a holy space. For example, a common person could become impure by touching a corpse, but after purification, he could go to the tabernacle. Purity was the necessary prerequisite for the holy. Second, the holy may not meet the impure. An impure layperson who entered the holy space of the tabernacle had to be struck down. Holy time could not be defiled by common work. The exact way these four categories relate varies some depending on the topic (objects, people, time, and space). Nevertheless, the two main jobs of the priest lead us into the final two ways that God's presence was preserved in the tabernacle.

Sacrifice: sustaining and remedy

As moderns who are accustomed to shrink-wrapped meat from the supermarket, our minds struggle to process the necessity of animal sacrifice. Yet animal sacrifice was ubiquitous in the ancient world and a regular chore of life. Much could be said on the complex topic of sacrifice, but two factors help orient us to how Israel thought of and practiced it.

First, ritual in general—and sacrifice in particular—were ways to connect the visible realm of human life and the invisible realm of God. Edmund Leach states that "the purpose of religious performance is to provide a bridge, or channel of communication, through which the power of the gods may be made available to otherwise impotent men."[21] A sacrifice was believed to effect change in the unseen abode of God. Guilt before God and the need to remedy it is abstract and inaccessible to the material world, yet dabbing blood on the altar brought it into the realm of the tactile, sensual, and fleshly. The concrete ritual acts are used to express abstract ideas and to remove intangible forms of evil.[22] Yahweh ordained animal sacrifice so that communication and effected change could travel from the human plane to the divine.

Second, this transmission from earth to heaven, from the human to the divine, was understood in terms of gift, tribute, and legal payment. Some sacrifices were free gifts offered from the people in love and gratitude. When you love someone, you joyfully lavish him or her with presents and favors. No reason is necessary; love suffices. Yahweh's blessings and provision naturally invoke in the pious heart a longing to return the love. The gift offerings are particularly evidenced in the free will and peace offerings (Lev 7). Other sacrifices took the form of tribute. The analogy of lord and servant comes in to play here. When your lord summons you, you did not come empty handed. Your master and king deserves a portion of your income for his protection and oversight of you. The whole burnt offering could serve as an offering of approach, while the daily offerings and tithe fell under the idea of tribute. Finally, other sacrifices were legal payments as sin created defilements and debts demanding redress. Certain sins defiled the holy house of God, so the purification offering was brought to purge his house and effect forgiveness (Lev 4). Other sacrileges profaned Yahweh's name and desecrated a holy item, so the reparation offering paid restitution to Yahweh's honor (Lev 5:14–6:7). These sacrifices appeased Yahweh's wrath (propitiation) and paid the debt or removed the stain of sin (expiation).

These ideas of tribute and remedy undergird how Israel kept heaven on earth and preserved God's presence among them. In terms of tribute, Israel had to provide an unceasing stream of sacrifices. The fire on the bronze altar could never go out (Lev 6:9–13), and the fuel for this everlasting flame was the daily burnt offerings along with all the Sabbath, new moon, and holy festival sacrifices. Yahweh explicitly commanded Israel to provide these offerings (Num 28:2). Likewise, Israel had to perpetually provide the oil and bread for the menorah and shewbread (Lev 24:1–9). If the altar's flame was extinguished, if the river of offerings ran dry, Yahweh would judge his people and depart from them.

With respect to remedy, there was no presumption that Israel would not sin. Sin was expected; remedy was built in. As sin infested Israel, individually and corporately, the people could bring whole burnt, purification, and reparation offerings to pay the debt of sin, purify the sanctuary, and appease Yahweh's wrath so that the covenant relationship could be reconciled. The people paid the sacrifices, the priests offered them correctly, and Yahweh's presence was maintained among his covenant people.

Ritual purity: separation from impurities

The final element in the holiness system is ritual purity. The impure things listed as part of the Mosaic covenant were those things that separated you from God's presence in the tabernacle but were not themselves sin. This is why they were called ritual impurities, because they were not sins but barred the Israelites from the holy ceremonies that demanded purity. These impurities are covered in Leviticus 11–15 and Numbers 19. They include eating forbidden food, touching of animal carcasses, giving birth, having a scale disease, having sex, male and female genital flows, and touching human corpses. From this list, it is clear that these ritual impurities did not indicate sinfulness; in fact, some were necessary. Having babies was near and dear to the heart of the covenant. Israel had to raise up godly offspring, but the sexual act defiled a person for a day, and giving birth defiled the mother for either forty or eighty days. Menstruation and semen emission are natural, biological operations. The Israelites expressed their family duty by burying their dead. These everyday chores and functions defiled them and prevented them from going to the tabernacle.

While it was not a sin to contract such ritual impurities, it was a sin to fail to purify yourself. Yahweh minces no words: "You shall separate the Israelites from their impurities, lest they die through their impurities when they defile my sanctuary that is in your midst" (Lev 15:31, my translation). To defile the holy tent with their impurities spelled death for the people and the threat of Yahweh's departure.

The purification process came in two basic methods depending on whether the ritual impurity was major or minor. Major impurities included scale disease, childbirth, human corpse contamination, and abnormal, chronic genital discharges. What these had in common is that the defiled person was contagious to others and a purification sacrifice had to be brought for final purity, though all four had unique variations with regard to infection and purification. The rest of the impurities were minor ones. For these, the defiled person was not contagious to others (with the exception of the menstruating woman), and the remedy consisted of washing, laundering clothes (sometimes), and waiting until sunset. If an Israelite touched a dead mouse, they washed and then waited until evening. If they carried a dead animal in their clothes, they washed, laundered, and waited. It is evident from this that purity concerns would have been part of the everyday realities of the Israelites. If you were far from the sanctuary, your impure status was no danger to you, but as you walked near to the tabernacle gates, you had to be confident of your pure state. Your life depended on it.

What was the reason for these ritual impurities? Why did God set these as defilements, but other things like spitting and urinating were not? The reason is that these impurities orbit around two hubs:

death and sex. As we saw above with the blemishes for Aaron and the sacrifices, death and sex are flashpoints for the cursed world. These two recall the original curse in Genesis 3: the difficulty of childbirth and returning to the dust. The impurities were not sins, but through the laws surrounding them God was teaching Israel that the chief sources of impurity that keep them separate from him are not outside of them but within them, part of their bodies. Full and free access to Yahweh, then, did not just require the extinction of actual sin, but also the cure of these bodily impurities.

In this way we can see that these legal regulations were intended to teach the Israelites, not remain in effect for all time. Later, in Ezekiel's ode to the new covenant, Yahweh promises to sprinkle away even our ritual impurities (Ezek 36:25). And when Jesus came on the scene, he touched the bleeding woman and the leper and declared them pure, so that ritual purity ended as his blood purified our conscience from dead works to serve the living God (Heb 9:14).[23] Indeed, just as Jesus became our righteousness by fulfilling the law, so he was our holy and unblemished priest to perfect for all time those who are sanctified by his single offering (Heb 10:14). The alien customs of ancient Israel have carried us to the sweetest place of life everlasting, the very side of Jesus Christ in heaven.

We can also see that the law was meant to point to Christ. At Sinai, Israel's obedience would have allowed them to live righteously before God (Deut 6:25). But when they were found wanting, Yahweh became their righteousness for them through the branch of David's line (Jer 23:6). Within this noble prophetic heritage, Jesus Christ received the title the Righteous One (Acts 7:52; 1 John 2:1; Luke 23:47). The righteousness of God the law testified to became known apart from the law in the person of Jesus Christ unto justification and eternal life (Rom 3:21–22).

STUDY QUESTIONS

1. What similarities can you name between ancient treaties and the Mosaic covenant?

2. What was the condition of the Mosaic covenant?

3. How did the strictness of the law drive Israel to Christ?

4. What was the overall purpose of the holiness system?

5. How did the tabernacle resemble Mount Sinai?

6. What were the two main categories of the priests' work?

7. What is ritual purity?

5

THE KING WHO BRINGS PEACE

Bible Reading: 1–2 Samuel

With a heave and a ho and a grunt, the house came down and the dust scattered. Such was the finale for Samson, whose strong arms were no match for his foolish lust. By his death, he slaughtered more Philistines than in his life, but he ushered in no peace for Israel. The Philistine taxes still whipped the backs of God's people. No king reigned in Israel, so everyone did what they felt like. A moral and cultic chaos blanketed the land.

Into the midst of this chaos steps Elkanah and his two wives, Peninnah and Hannah. The book of 1 Samuel opens where the book of Judges closed. Something rotten is in the state of Israel, and it can be smelled within Elkanah's own family.

Elkanah pilgrimages faithfully every year to the tabernacle at Shiloh. He shares portions of the sacrifices with his wives and children. And even though Peninnah gets many portions, he shares a special portion with Hannah, who held a special place in his heart. Yet Hannah cannot have children, and her infertility comes from Yahweh himself: "The LORD had closed her womb." The text says this twice so we do not miss it (1 Sam 1:5, 6). Barrenness was a curse of

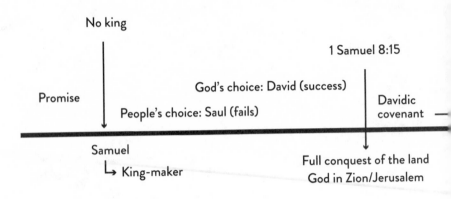

the covenant; it was a symptom of sin and Yahweh's disfavor (Deut 7:14; 28:18). Yet the cause does not seem to be in the family. Sure, Peninnah dishes out cruel taunts and Elkanah displays insensitivity toward Hannah's plight, but there are no gross idolatries in this household. Hannah's barrenness signals not so much a personal scandal but a national one. Hannah herself recognizes this as she links her trouble and deliverance to the coming salvation over all the foes of Yahweh (1 Sam 2:1–10). In fact, she first displays this faith in her vow to Yahweh (1:11). If Yahweh will grant her a male child, then she will dedicate him to Yahweh all his days as a Nazirite. The life-long Nazirite Samson failed to save Israel, so if Yahweh will remove her shame, then this Nazirite will finish what the first one started. Hannah weaves her predicament with the national one.

After her prayer is answered, a second prayer at her son's dedication sketches out the role he will play. In the second line she says, "My horn is exalted in the LORD" (1 Sam 2:1, my translation). A horn can represent power and royalty, but here it means Yahweh honored Hannah by raising up for her a son. The image of a horn closes

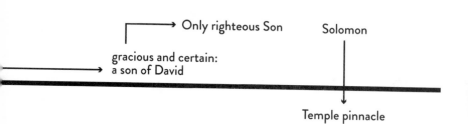

Chart 5: David

her prayer as well: "He will give strength to his king and exalt the horn of his anointed [messiah]" (2:10, my translation). Hannah's horn merges with the horn of the anointed king. Her vision is not perfect, yet Hannah believes that her son Samuel will play a part in Yahweh raising up a king to deliver his people. She prays for the precise problem made clear in the book of Judges—the lack of a king and the right type of king. Hannah is the heroine not just over chapters 1 and 2 but over both books of Samuel. The rest of these books depict Yahweh's answer to her prayer.

SAMUEL: JUDGE, PROPHET, PRIEST, KING-MAKER

The first major theme of Samuel is the need for a king to perform the salvation of God. A second key theme also appears early on. The chaos of Judges poured forth both from a failure in royal leadership and from priestly apostasy. The scattered sheep of Israel chased after other gods, and the pure worship of Yahweh fell into shambles, which describes what was happening at the tabernacle at Shiloh. With Samuel dropped off, we meet Hophni and Phinehas, sons of the corpulent priest Eli. These two forced sex with women who served in the tabernacle, and also lifted their hand against Yahweh by robbing him of the choicest portion of the sacrifices. Unruly, perverse, and lacking the fear of Yahweh, they corrupted the priesthood to feed their urges. And Eli sat and watched; he did nothing to discipline his boys. Yahweh, though, is not like Eli; he will not tolerate such sacrilege and abuse in his sanctuary, so he sends a man of God, a prophet.

This man of God joins a second prediction to Hannah's: judgment will come on the house of Eli. His two sons will perish in one day. The priesthood will transfer to another. The key promise, though, is in 1 Samuel 2:35: "And I will raise up for myself a faithful priest, who shall do according to what is in my heart and in my mind. And I will build him a sure house, and he shall go in and out before my anointed forever." Note that God combines four things: (1) a faithful priest who is (2) after God's heart and will (3) have an enduring house and (4) go in and out before his anointed. We do not know who this priest will be, but this promise keeps us on the lookout. Hannah alerts us to watch for a king, and this man of God puts on our radar a priest. Our anticipation grows. And so the story begins.

Raised by Eli, sleeping in the sanctuary, the young Samuel soon matures under the hand of Yahweh into a priest and a prophet. He ministers in the house of God to learn the arts of the priests and the word of Yahweh comes to Samuel so that from Dan to Beersheba he is recognized as a prophet. God's word was strong with Samuel. The ascendancy of Samuel, however, is countered by the fall of Eli and his sons.

The Philistines were a people originally from the Aegean Sea who settled along the coastal plain of Canaan in the fourteenth or thirteenth century BC. The government structure of the Philistines consisted of a confederation of five cities: Ashdod, Ashkelon, Ekron, Gaza, and Gath. Israel desperately needs a win at this time, so they summon the ark of the covenant from the tabernacle to be their

Shiloh

magic talisman. The people do not trust in Yahweh, but they treat the ark like a lucky rabbit's foot, and so the time of Yahweh's judgment is upon Israel. Both Hophni and Phinehas die, as the man of God predicted. The ark is taken prisoner and Israelite blood stains the ground. When news reaches Eli, it is not the fate of his sons that is troubling; rather, the news about the ark seizes him with despair. He topples from his seat and crushes his neck. The calamitous report then reaches Phinehas' pregnant wife and moves her into pre-term labor. With her son's name, she labels the next chapter of the story: Ichabod, "Where is the glory?" The glory has departed from Israel. The glory of Israel is Yahweh, and his portable throne is the ark. The whole goal of the law was to keep God with his people. But with this defeat, Israel is forsaken; the ark has gone into exile. The appalling crisis cuts the people to the quick. How will there be resolution?

As we have seen, in the ancient Near East, warring armies on earth paralleled gods at battle in heaven, so that the Philistines' victory over

Israel was seen as their god Dagon's defeat of Yahweh. This is what the Philistines think, so the ark is set at the feet of Dagon's statue (1 Sam 5:2).

But not so fast. The next morning, Dagon's statue is found lying face down before the ark of Yahweh. Surely this is just a fluke, so the Philistines set Dagon back up. But on morning two, Dagon has fallen before Yahweh with his head and hands broken off. Yahweh has slayed Dagon. Israel's loss is not Yahweh's downfall, but Yahweh's judgment on his people. Yahweh will vindicate his sovereignty over the Philistines. Tumors hatch on the people, a plague explodes within the city, and the ark must be banished. From Ashdod to Gath to Ekron, Yahweh lays waste to the Philistines for seven months. With echoes of the exodus, Yahweh marches victorious out of Philistia riding on a cart. The glory departed from Israel, but now it returns.

However, Yahweh's return does not mean all is well in Israel. The Israelites in the town of Beth-shemesh thought so, but after looking

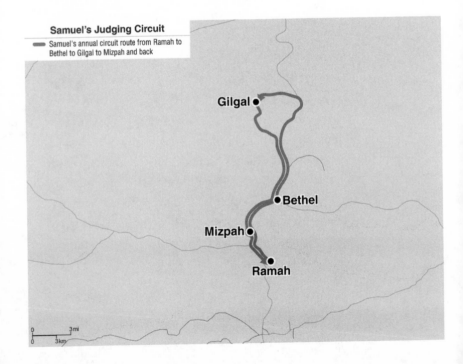

Samuel's Judging Circuit

Samuel's annual circuit route from Ramah to Bethel to Gilgal to Mizpah and back

in or at the ark, Yahweh struck them with a plague. He demands holiness from his people. Hence, the Beth-shemites ask a question that will hang over our story for a long time to come: "Who is able to stand before the LORD, this holy God?" (1 Sam 6:20). This was the question of the Mosaic covenant. The people need to be holy to remain in God's presence, but Israel has shown itself sorely lacking. Who is able to stand before Yahweh? Who will bring the holy ark all the way home? This matter gathers dust as the ark remains tucked away in the backwater town of Kiriath-jearim for many years.

With the ark back, though, the story returns to Samuel. His long, successful judgeship is summed up in a chapter (1 Sam 7). Summoning Israel to Mizpah, Samuel calls the people to repent and return to Yahweh; he leads them to victory in battle, and his annual circuit weaved through Bethel, Gilgal, and Mizpah, and back to home to Ramah.

Samuel, once young, has ripened into an old man, and the time has come to think about a replacement. Three offices rest on his shoulders and must be carried on: priest, prophet, and judge. Samuel's sons do not qualify, as they are corrupt and easily bribed. The elders of Israel have a problem before them, so they put a request to Samuel: "Appoint for us a king to judges us like all the nations" (1 Sam 8:5). They want a king to be Samuel's replacement.

This request is central to the narrative and shapes the rest of the story to the end of 2 Samuel, even casting its shadow over the rest of biblical history. Therefore, it is important to pause to grasp its nuances. First of all, the text makes evident that Samuel takes personal offense; he hoped to pass his mantle to his sons. Yahweh even has to tell him that "they have not rejected you, but they have rejected me" (1 Sam 8:7). Even when Yahweh tells him to give the people a king, Samuel rants on about all the evils of a king to dissuade them. The second time Yahweh orders Samuel to appoint a king, Samuel sends the people home and does nothing (1 Sam 8:22). Samuel resists the command of Yahweh.

Second, the request for a king itself is not problematic. Back in Deuteronomy 17, on the plains of Moab, Yahweh told Israel that if they wanted a king, then they could have one as long as he kept the law. In many ways, Moses performed the role of a king and passed this mantle on to Joshua in Numbers 27. And the crisis in Judges happened in the absence of leadership. The issue was not if they would have a leader, but the type of leader they truly needed. Hence, Yahweh tells Samuel to give the people a king, only Samuel must testify to them and inform them of "the justice of the king" (1 Sam 8:9, my translation). The justice (*mishpat*) of the king refers to what the Mosaic law requires (especially in Deut 17), and it is on this point that Samuel missteps again. In verse 11, he tells the people, "This is the justice of the king," but then he goes on to list nothing but the injustice of kings as they amass wealth and weapons to themselves (contra Deut 17). Hence, Yahweh permits them to have a king who is conformed to his law.

Third, even though a king is not problematic, the elders add a phrase that is: "like all the nations" (1 Sam 8:5, 20). The people want to be like all the other pagan nations. They lust for the glory of royalty as it is displayed in Egypt or Assyria. And this is why Yahweh says, "They have rejected me" (v. 7). There is an antitheocratic force to their demand. A king like the nations means a god like the nations. Hence, Yahweh rebukes them for their habit of idolatry since the exodus and orders Samuel to "testify to them about the justice of the king" (v. 9, my translation). That is, give them a king after God's law and not like the nations. As in Judges, the issue is what type of king. The people demand a king like the nations, and Yahweh counters with a just king according to the law. There is a tug-of-war between what the people want and what Yahweh has ordained. And this tension will play out in the unfolding story.

SAUL: THE PEOPLE'S CHOICE

As mentioned above, Samuel dismisses the people and sits on his hands. He makes no effort to find a king for the people, so Yahweh finds one. In walks Saul, who was born to a wealthy family of Benjamin and is tall, dark, and handsome. His appearance matches the royal type. Yet as we get to know Saul, the text continues to recall the stories of the judges. Similarities echo with the old stories to create comparisons. Will Saul take after the virtues of the judges or their vices? In their first meeting, Samuel honors Saul by telling him that he is desired by all of Israel; he is the king they have been longing for. Saul responds, though, with unconvincing self-deprecation: "Is not my clan the humblest of all the clans of the tribe of Benjamin?" (1 Sam 9:21). These are like the words of Gideon's false modesty (Judg 6:15), an unsettling resemblance.

Once Samuel anoints Saul, the prophet gives the new king three signs that will culminate at the garrison of the Philistines, and then Saul should "do what [his] hand finds to do" (1 Sam 10:7)—the clear implication being to attack the garrison. Saul, however, does nothing; he does not even tell his uncle about being anointed. Samuel soon gathers Israel to Mizpah and casts lots to select Saul as the new king, but Saul is hiding amid the luggage! Saul's reluctance to take the office reminds one of Barak in Judges 4. Finally, when the towering Saul stands up, the people ooh and aah at his royal stature and shout, "Long live the king!"

In contrast to his first day in office, which was not that impressive, Saul's second day on the job proves to be much more positive. The king of the Ammonites besieges the Israelite town of Jabesh-gilead with cruel terms of surrender, and news of it reaches Saul. Filled with the Spirit of God, Saul springs into action. He slices and dices a yoke of oxen and overnights the pieces to the twelve tribes of Israel, with the sworn curse that whoever does not help fight will be cut up like the oxen. Saul does to the cows what the Levite did to his concubine in

Judges 19:29. Doing this to cows is better than doing so with a human, yet the resemblance is uncomfortable. Nevertheless, Saul wins a great victory, and when the people want to kill those who rejected Saul's authority, Saul lets mercy triumph over judgment (1 Sam 11:13).

With Saul's kingship confirmed with a victory, Samuel assembles everyone to Gilgal, where the Israelites had previously crossed over into Canaan, to renew the kingdom/kingship. During this ceremony, Samuel officially retires as a judge and delivers to Israel his farewell speech. Two points stand out. First, he points to Saul and says, "Behold your king whom you have chosen, for whom you have asked" (1 Sam 12:13). Samuel makes clear that Saul is the people's choice. God gave them what they wanted. Second, he puts a charge before both the people and the king. If they obey the commandments of Yahweh, it will go well with them. If they do not, Yahweh will be against them and the king (1 Sam 8:14–15). This is the condition of the Mosaic covenant. The only way forward, the only path to blessing, is obedience, both for the people and the king. How will Saul perform?

The smooth road to victory that Saul had with the Ammonites does not get replicated with the Philistines. Even with his growing army, Saul is hard pressed by the Philistine thousands encamped at Michmash. The Israelite soldiers rally to Saul at Gilgal, and he has one order to follow: wait seven days until Samuel shows up to sacrifice. Samuel, though, is late; day seven came and went. The waiting lays waste to the people's courage; it pokes holes in Saul's army like a leaky bucket. The soldiers flow out to find safety, to hide in caves and holes. Saul must plug the leak, so he sacrifices the burnt and peace offerings. Of course, such is the irony of providence when you decide to do something wrong, the police show up in the rear-view mirror or your parents get home. So also, while the blood is still wet on his hands, Samuel shows up to catch Saul in the act. Saul attempts to make excuses, but Samuel does not mince words: "You have done foolishly. You have not kept the command of the LORD your God, with which he commanded you. For then the LORD would have established your kingdom over Israel forever. But now your kingdom shall not continue. The LORD has sought out a man after his own heart" (1 Sam 13:13–14). Note the details. One, for his disobedience, Saul's dynasty will not come to be. The kingship will end with Saul so that it will not get passed on to one of his sons. Two, had Saul obeyed, Yahweh would have rewarded him with an everlasting dynasty. The obedient king gets an enduring house. Three, Yahweh has turned his eyes to another whose heart images the heart of God. The character of the king must align with the holiness of Yahweh. Samuel's words map out the way ahead for the story.

After Samuel's rebuke, the two men seem to go their separate ways, which leaves Saul and his son Jonathan with a mere six hundred men at Gibeah of Benjamin. The Philistine horde swarms Michmash like ants, while the puny few of Israel cower without sword or spear, save the two in the hands of Saul and Jonathan. Jonathan, though, is immune to the cowardice that infects Saul and his men. With a hardy trust in Yahweh, Jonathan and his armor-bearer scale a cliff and start killing Philistines. Panic and confusion fall on them from Yahweh and they flee in terror, and the Israelites creep out of their caves to join the route for a marvelous victory. Yet as Israel is in pursuit, Saul utters an oath, "Cursed be the man who eats until it is evening" (1 Sam 14:24). Upon pain of death, Saul imposes a fast on his men as they run and fight. Yet Jonathan did not hear this oath, so he ate honey for energy. As the day ends, Saul casts lots to discover who violated his oath and the lot falls on Jonathan. This father sharpens his sword to slay his son, who won the victory. The foolish zeal of Jephthah dwells within Saul; deep problems lurk in the soul of Saul. Thankfully, the people know the law enough to redeem Jonathan from the rash oath so that he lives. They do what Jephthah was ignorant of.

Saul's performance does not improve at all, but continues to avalanche. A second major commandment comes to Saul from Yahweh through Samuel. Saul must march his army out to *herem* the Amalekites (1 Sam 15:3). Every human and animal must be destroyed to fulfill Yahweh's promise in Exodus 17:14. Saul gears up and devotes to destruction all the people and everything that is worthless; yet the best of the livestock he spares to sacrifice at Gilgal. Sacrifice does not measure up to the terms of *herem* warfare, especially since these sacrifices were the type that the men got to eat from (15:15). Saul is so proud of himself that he pats himself on the back when Samuel arrives. Like a giddy toddler, he boasts, "I have performed the commandment of the LORD." Wryly Samuel spits back, "Then what is all this mooing I hear?" (15:14, my paraphrase). Animal noise should not be heard after *herem*. The second major failure of Saul gets nailed next to the first one. Yahweh has rejected Saul as king, tearing the kingdom from him and handing it to a neighbor who is better (1 Sam 15:26–28). Saul has proven himself to be a king like the nations; this is what the people wanted, but it is not what they need. They need a king who will obey Yahweh.

THE RISE OF DAVID

And so, without much delay, Samuel ends up in the neighboring tribe of Judah, in the little town of Bethlehem. The seven strapping sons of Jesse parade before the old prophet, and he thinks them all to be perfect candidates. Strong, tall, and handsome, what could be wrong? Yahweh chastens, though, "Do not gawk at the outward appearance, for the LORD sees not as man as he looks on the heart" (1 Sam 16:7, my paraphrase). All seven are refused. Does Jesse have any other sons? Well, there is the runt, but he is out with the sheep and goats. The boy who was not important enough to be invited to the feast comes in from the field. Samuel arises and anoints him king, and the Spirit rushes upon him. We meet the man after God's heart, David. A pair of columns is set before us. In one there is Saul, the people's choice, with his deeds and failures listed. In the other is Yahweh's pick David, with his qualities ready to be filled in. How will the two measure up to each other?

The Valley of Elah, where David fought Goliath

The meet-and-greet with David begins with his appearance, ruddy and handsome. More than likely, to be ruddy was to be darker skinned than the average Israelite. It wasn't looked down upon, but it was not the norm. Next, we discover that David is a musician and a poet who can heal with his harmonies. Healing lays in the hands of this king, and his first patient is the now-tormented Saul. It is only after we listen to his musical therapy that we see David perform in battle. In the felling of Goliath, the bright spot shines not from David's self-confidence but from his confidence in Yahweh. Before he charges the giant with sling and stone, David cries out, "You come to me with a sword and with a spear and with a javelin, but I come to you in the name of the LORD of hosts, the God of the armies of Israel, whom you have defied" (1 Sam 17:45). Yahweh is his strength. David trusts not in horses or the legs of men but in the name of Yahweh.

Therefore, after the stunning victory, one by one, the people fall in love with David. Jonathan loves him first, and as the crown prince, he even makes a covenant with David with the gifts of his sword and armor (1 Sam 18:4). Once David's successes start piling up, all of Israel and Judah love him (1 Sam 18:16). Even Saul's daughter, Michal, loves him (1 Sam 18:20). Yet as the love for David grows so does Saul's hatred. The king's jealousy, hatred, and insecurity swirl into increasingly bold assassination attempts. The covert ventures soon become a royal warrant for the arrest and execution of David. As David goes on the run, the contrast between David and Saul develops along the lines of obedience. For David, the test plays out on the stage of being an upright servant. Will David rebel with violence against his lord Saul? Will he slay Yahweh's anointed one to secure his throne? For Saul, the trial unfolds on the field of defending his throne with violence. Will he devour David and all who protect him? Will he corrupt his power for self-preservation or use it for the will of God?

The deciding ordeal ignites for David in chapter 25 with Nabal and Abigail. Out in the wilderness of Paran, David and his men have been performing unsolicited protection and aid to the flocks of the wealthy Nabal. During the festive season of shearing, a small taste of Nabal's massive yield is all David asks for. Nabal both refuses and shames David by calling him a runaway servant, the very thing David is not (1 Sam 25:10). Infuriated, David takes his four hundred men and marches for vengeance. An open road lays before David to stain his innocence, but in steps Abigail. Armed with gifts, Abigail lays down in front of David and wins the award for the best speech since Hannah (1 Sam 25:24–31). With the courage of fifty men, she takes the guilt of her foolish husband on herself. She states that Yahweh will restrain David from bloodguilt. She asks for forgiveness and predicts in faith that Yahweh will grant David an enduring house (the same house spoken of in 1 Sam 2:35), and that evil will not be found in David. The eloquence and bravery of Abigail blows the anger of David away and leaves him in awe. David blesses Abigail and admits that she saved him from bloodguilt and avenging himself (25:32–33). Abigail was the servant of Yahweh to save David. Abigail is the heroine behind the blamelessness of David. Hence, David passes the test by not raising his hand against Yahweh's anointed and by not committing bloodguilt.

En Gedi, where David hid from Saul

Saul, on the other hand, flunks one test after another. Out of anger and jealousy, he keeps trying to murder David. Saul chases David all around the wilderness of Judah like a hungry lion. Saul has an addiction to his jealousy that he cannot shake, despite moments of clarity. He hits rock bottom, though, with the priests of Nob (1 Sam 22:6–19). The priest Ahimelech had aided David with the shewbread and the sword of Goliath before he even knew that Saul had it out for David. After learning of this help, Saul's jealousy is convinced of Ahimelech's sedition. The logical and reasoned defense of Ahimelech bounces off Saul's stubbornness like a flea off armor. The suspicious king cannot tolerate the slightest whiff of mutiny. His instability reads Ahimelech's integrity as betrayal and issues the decree of death. The priests must die. His Israelite servants, however, fear God and dare not lift a hand against a priest. The testimony of this piety will not hinder Saul's blood lust, so he turns to his mercenary Doeg the Edomite. By the blade of this foreigner, Saul cuts down in Nob every man, woman, child, ox, donkey, and lamb. Saul would not *herem* the Amalekites, but he does *herem* the priestly town of Nob. This Benjaminite king embodies all the vices and crimes found within the book of Judges. The people's choice monarch brings only sin and judgment.

And so, without much further ado, Yahweh renders his verdict. On the slopes of Gilboa, Saul prepares for battle with the Philistines by consulting a necromancer (1 Sam 28:7). His money to the witch only buys him one last oracle from the dead Samuel, who reminds him of Yahweh's promise to give the kingdom to Saul's neighbor for his failure with Amalek. And Samuel signs off with the doom of Saul and his sons the next day in battle (1 Sam 28:17–19). Like Eli and his boys, in a single day Saul and his sons perish on Mount Gilboa (1 Sam 31:8). Meanwhile, at the very same time, what business occupied David? He is destroying the Amalekites for plundering Ziklag, and he freely offers part of the spoils to the people of Judah (1 Sam 30:6–30). As Saul died for his failure with the Amalekites, David succeeds, innocent of bloodguilt, upright as a servant, and fighting Yahweh's battles.

In fact, David's blamelessness continues to shine after the death of Saul and the opening of 2 Samuel. He does not celebrate the end of Saul as an enemy, but he laments the beauty of Saul and Jonathan as loved ones (2 Sam 1:17–27). When an Amalekite takes credit for Saul's death, hoping for a reward, David executes him on his own testimony. It is only after he inquired of Yahweh for divine permission that David returns to Judah to be crowned king (2 Sam 2:1–4). When Saul's son, Ish-bosheth, and his general Abner attempt to hold the kingdom of Saul together, David labors to minimize bloodshed. He happily accepts Abner's terms of peace to unite Israel. And when Joab kills Abner, David weeps bitterly and forces Joab to mourn as well. Finally, when the two scoundrels assassinate Ish-bosheth and bring his head to David, David executes them for murder. The virtue of David cleanly marches one step at a time to become king over all

Israel, sealed with a covenant (2 Sam 5:3–5). The righteous king after Yahweh's heart is the one Yahweh carries to the throne to be the one shepherd of Israel.

Bethlehem, David's hometown

And David's first acts in office further polish his shine. He marches on Jerusalem, puts the Jebusites to the sword, and makes the stronghold of Zion his capital. "And David became greater and greater, for the LORD, the God of hosts, was with him" (2 Sam 5:10). According to the word of Yahweh, David deals a fatal blow to the Philistines (2 Sam 5:25). And with them out of the way, David can turn his devotion to Yahweh and the ark. He travels to Kiriath-jearim, which is where the ark was dropped off back in 1 Samuel 7:2. After Uzzah is struck down, though, David feels the same unworthiness of the Beth-shemites, who cried out, "Who is able to stand before the LORD, this holy God?" (1 Sam 6:20). Likewise, David asks, "How can the ark of the LORD come to me?" (2 Sam 6:9). Yet with renewed effort, David brought the ark from Kiriath-jearim to Zion with a sacrifice every six steps and passionate dancing. By righteousness and sacrifice, David installs the ark, upon which Yahweh of Hosts is enthroned, in his capital, at the center of Israel. David restored God's presence among his people. After hundreds of years of failure, David fulfills the law and finishes the conquest of Joshua.

For his fidelity, Yahweh rewards his royal servant with a covenant. David desired to construct a house for Yahweh, but Yahweh will build a house for David (2 Sam 7:11). As we have seen, to understand the nature of a covenant one must look at its form, its terms. What stands out in 2 Samuel 7 is the string of Yahweh's unilateral promises. "I will make for you a great name. ... I will give you rest from all your enemies. ... I will raise up your offspring ... I will establish his kingdom. ... I will establish the throne of his kingdom forever. ... I will be to him a father. ... My steadfast love will not depart from him. ... Your house and your kingdom shall be made sure. ... Your throne shall be established forever" (1 Sam 7:9–16). These are unconditional, gracious promises, which matches the Abrahamic covenant. Even when a Davidic son misbehaves, Yahweh will discipline, but he will not take his favor away (7:14–15). The disobedience of the heirs cannot prevent God from keeping his promise. This is the foundational layer, or first prong, of the covenant—Yahweh's eternal and gracious promise. Moreover, this promise is fulfilled not in David but in his son. David will die, but his son will ascend the throne and be the temple-builder (7:12–13).

Nevertheless, there is a second layer or prong to this covenant, which is barely hinted at here but shows up later. This second prong peaks out in 7:14 about fatherly discipline. Yahweh will graciously fulfill his promises apart from human works, but the behavior of the king matters. Hence, after David's son Solomon builds the temple and Yahweh reaffirms this covenant with him, Solomon's behavior takes center stage. In 1 Kings 9, Yahweh appears to Solomon, "As for you, if you will walk before me, as David your father walked, with integrity of heart and uprightness, doing according to all that I have commanded you, and keeping my statutes and my rules, then

I will establish your royal throne over Israel forever, as I promised David your father, saying, 'You shall not lack a man on the throne of Israel'" (9:4–5). Righteousness according to the Mosaic law is required for Solomon for him to receive the promise of David. Likewise, if Solomon or his sons break the law and turn to idols, then the full exile curse of the Mosaic law will be poured out (9:6–9). The conditional obedience of the Mosaic law is demanded from the heir of David to receive the eternal throne. Only the righteous son will become the everlasting king.

The first layer, which aligns with the Abrahamic covenant, establishes God's sure grace to perform the promises for David's house. The second layer, which picks up the conditionality of the Mosaic covenant, demands that the son be righteous by the law. These are the two layers of the Davidic covenant, and they will govern the hopes and history of Israel until Jesus, the holy Son of David. But for now, Yahweh is not finished with David. After bestowing this wonderful covenant on David, the pinnacle of his career is reached in 2 Samuel 8.

This chapter lists the military victories of David to show how his enemies were subdued all around the borders of Israel, Yahweh giving him victory at every point. But verse 15 names his crowning achievement: "David reigned over all Israel. And David administered justice and equity to all his people." This pair of justice and righteousness epitomizes the ideal king, who obeys all the commandments of the law in service to the people. This justice and righteousness fulfill the law to keep God near to his people and to bring the people into the fullness of covenant beatitude.

DAVID FOUND WANTING

Nevertheless, the righteous glow of David's crown does not last long. After this high point, David takes a few more good steps and then tumbles. The first slip-up is when David breaks a habit, a custom. It's the season for kings to go out and do battle, but David remains in

Jerusalem (2 Sam 11:1). And idle hands will play. Evening is approaching, and David arises from his bed to stretch his legs on his rooftop patio. His eyes are scanning the cityscape of Zion when he spots the beautiful physique of a naked woman bathing. Lust is conceived in his heart and gives birth to sin. He fetches her, she comes to him, he lies with her, and she returns (2 Sam 11:4). David commits adultery with Bathsheba, the wife of Uriah the Hittite, who is one of David's mighty men (2 Sam 23:39). However, this is likely more than adultery. The text doesn't reveal her intentions, but you do not say no to a king; David imposed himself on her. Pregnancy outs the sexual indiscretion, so David has to devise a cover up. He invites Uriah back from the battlefield in hopes he'll lie with Bathsheba so the child will appear to be his. But Uriah, full of integrity, will not sleep with his wife while his fellow soldiers abstain in the field. Uriah's empathy with the military only shames David's lack thereof (2 Sam 11:11). In desperation, David puts Uriah in the front line so he'll die in battle. And in order to take out Uriah, many more die by an incompetent battle strategy. David seems unaffected, as he gets another wife and son.

Yahweh, however, is not going to let David get away with his crime. This sin must be punished, and so Nathan the prophet confronts the king. He tells a parable about a rich man who, though owning much livestock, steals a poor man's only lamb—one so close to his family she was "like a daughter" (2 Sam 12:3). David erupts in anger, saying the man deserves to die and must pay back four times the price of the lamb, to which Nathan responds, "You are the man!" (12:7). The brilliance of Nathan's little parable is that he provokes David to condemn himself.

To David's credit, he repents. Yahweh forgives and spares his life, but the debt of David's rebellion demands full repayment. The recompense is twofold. First, in return for David stealing a wife in secret, God will give David's wives to other men to lay with them—in broad daylight (12:11–12). Second, since David sent Uriah wrongly into battle, warfare will haunt David's family (12:10). And as we will see, death takes four of David's sons, just as he demanded a fourfold restitution of the rich man.

The first son of David to perish is the son of adultery; Bathsheba's firstborn dies on the seventh day. Yet God has mercy, and Bathsheba conceives another son—Solomon, whom Yahweh favored (1 Sam 12:24). Once Solomon is born, however, the lethal drama within David's house is underway. The king's firstborn son, Amnon, is flooded with passion for his half-sister Tamar. He eventually gets Tamar alone and rapes her, only to cast her out. The tears of Tamar cry out for justice, for an advocate, but her brother Absalom silences her and David does nothing. The king is supposed to perform justice and righteousness but does not, not even for his own daughter (2 Sam 13:21). David likely would not punish Amnon because he was his firstborn.[1] David failed to get justice for his daughter because he showed favoritism to his son.

The inaction of David opens the window for vigilantism and bloodshed outside the law. Absalom was not about to let Amnon off the hook. After carrying out a plot to kill Amnon, Absalom flees to Geshur for three years, during which time David longs to bring him back but again does nothing. Finally, by the cunning of his chief general Joab, David comes to understand that the right thing to do with Absalom is to show mercy and equity instead of demanding strict justice. A summons goes forth and the banished son comes home, yet David puts him under house arrest and refuses to see him. Absalom returned but was not restored. And where forgiveness and mercy are not extended, the demands of the law remain. David is still punishing Absalom; he is letting the debt of bloodguilt remain. And this miscarriage of justice catapults Absalom into another plot.

The handsome Absalom, with his gorgeous mane of hair, will show Israel what true justice tastes like. He sets up a rival court that steals the heart of the people, and before long he has baked up a full-blown conspiracy to slay his father and seize the throne. As David flees Jerusalem with some of his supporters, he is despondent and humbled as he seems to realize this is part of the punishment for his sins. He says, "If I find favor in the eyes of the LORD, he will bring me back. ... But if he says, 'I have no pleasure in you,' behold, here I am, let him do to me what seems good to him" (2 Sam 15:25–26). With David safe for the time being on the east side of the Jordan, Absalom marches into the capital, puts a tent on the palace roof, and in the eyes of all he goes into David's concubines. Yahweh's punishment has come to pass. Absalom's though, must have the head of his father. Only this will secure his reign. The armies of Israel line up for a civil war.

Yet before the battle begins, David issues one final command: "Deal gently for my sake with the young man Absalom" (2 Sam 18:5). David actually orders his army not to kill Absalom, the arch-rebel behind this. What we see in David are the complex and mysterious emotions of a dad, where we can sympathize with and be critical of him at the same time. The royal order of gentleness, however, contrasts with Yahweh's will, which we were told of in 2 Samuel 17:14, "so that the LORD might bring harm upon Absalom." David's command for mercy swims against the current of God's justice. And when David falls short, Joab has a way of making up the difference. Joab pin-cushions Absalom with three javelins to the chest. Son number three is dead. And when David freezes with grief and depression, Joab again kicks him into gear of being king.

Once Absalom's conspiracy has been quelled and David is back in Jerusalem, the book of 2 Samuel closes with a few chapters that cover assorted matters. The majestic poems of David's song of deliverance and his last words are the jewels that adorn chapters 22:1–23:7. The heroics of David's mighty men deck the halls in the rest of chapter 23. And in the final chapter, the pride of David's heart tempts him into counting the myriads of Israel. He takes a census for his own glory. Once Yahweh convicts David and he repents, David has the choice of his punishment: three years of famine, three months of defeat, or three days of plague (2 Sam 24:13). He selects the three days in the hope of the mercy in God's hands. The plague is unleashed, and 70,000 perish in a tsunami of holy wrath. The plague storms lethally towards Jerusalem and pauses at the threshing floor of Araunah. The prophet urges David to build an altar, so after buying Araunah's property, David raises an altar and offers sacrifice to appease Yahweh's wrath and to avert the plague.

The final act of David in the books of Samuel places him humbly before an altar lifting up sacrificial smoke to Yahweh. Yet as we know from 2 Samuel 24:1, the people did not just die for David's sin, but God's anger was against Israel for some other undisclosed sin. David's sin was just the trigger for the punishment, which means David became the way for the people to find forgiveness. David's sin sparked the plague, but his sacrifice also quenched the fire of the storm for the people. Throughout the first part of David's life, his bright eyes sparkled with blamelessness; with every step, he plateaued on the mesa of righteousness and justice. Righteousness sketched David as the ideal king. But his plateau soon cascaded into a ravine infested with the thorns of murder, sexual perversity, passivity, and pride. The faults of David are entangled in the scrub-brush of sin. And yet the mercy of God did not forsake him to the briers; instead, David overcame by humility and sacrifice. The humble David returned to Jerusalem; the sacrificing David averted the plague. And these humiliations profited both David and the people of Israel. In David, then, the two necessities demanded by the law are provided by the king. The law required righteousness and sacrifice; both were fundamental to keep God near and the people close. And where Israel flunked under the judges, Yahweh did for his people in David what they could not do. By David's righteousness, Israel came into their inheritance. And in the face of sin, David provided atonement at an altar. In this way, Yahweh molded David into the exemplary king by which all his sons shall be measured, even leading God's people to David's greatest Son, Jesus Christ.

Nevertheless, the story of David has one more chapter. Only three of his sons have perished (2 Sam 12:5–6). David is in the winter of his life, and Adonijah, David's third son, sees his dad's old age as his moment. He was next in line for the throne, so he prepares his own enthronement party. Why wait for another to exalt you when you can do it yourself? Nathan the prophet and Bathsheba, however, are of a different mind, stepping in and advocating for Solomon instead. David agrees that Solomon shall be king instead of Adonijah. After his inauguration, Solomon agrees to spare Adonijah, yet once David is laid to rest and Adonijah betrays his royal pretentions, Solomon swiftly executes him. The fourth son has died.

David's final charge to Solomon is the closing note to his life. On his deathbed, David exhorts his son: "Be strong and show yourself a man, and keep the charge of the LORD your God, walking in his ways and keeping his statutes, his commandments, his rules, and his testimonies, as it is written in the Law of Moses" (1 Kings 2:2–3). Obedience to the law is the burden of his office, and the reward of success is Yahweh's fulfilled promise to David: "You shall not lack a man on the throne of Israel" (1 Kings 2:4). Yahweh's unconditional promise will never fail for David; yet only the righteous son will taste the everlasting fruit. As the stone is rolled over David's tomb, will Solomon be this son?

STUDY QUESTIONS

1. What roles did Samuel fulfill?

2. What was wrong with the people's request for a king?

3. What were the two main failures of Saul for which Yahweh tore the kingdom from him?

4. What was so impressive about Jonathan's love for David?

5. Describe the heroism of Abigail.

6. What were the two prongs of the Davidic covenant?

7. How was David punished for his sin with Bathsheba?

6

THE DIVIDED KINGDOM

Bible Reading: 1–2 Kings

If you tour many of the beautiful cities of our globe, you will marvel at the marble buttresses, ancient structures, and cloud-scraping towers. The Piazza San Marco in Venice serenades you with its arches and clock spire. Times Square's forest of lights put a pirouette in your step. Shimmering against the night sky, Bangkok's Wat Arun glows like a star. Yet if you let your feet stray too far, soon you will step where it is unpleasant. Just off the swept street lies a dark alley, the red-light district, or the unfamiliar hustle and bustle of a local market. Behind the makeup of these beautiful cities are the wrinkles and blemishes of real life.

In a similar fashion, the tour of Solomon's Jerusalem in 1 Kings begins by keeping us largely within the manicured places. Solomon's wisdom has painted the streets with gold. The priceless craftsmanship of Tyrian cypress and cedar mark every door, window, and frame. Costly stone cut from the earth cements the foundations. It took seven years to build the temple, but Solomon's palace cost thirteen years of labor. Ivory plated in gold is his throne. Spices, gold, horses, and treasure from across the Near East flowed into Israel. Silver is as common as stone and cedar as plentiful as sycamore.

Hence, King Solomon excels in wealth and wisdom over all the kings on earth (1 Kgs 10:23). And Israel flourishes! From Dan to

Beersheba, the people are as many as the sand by the sea, as each human sits safely under her vine and fig tree. They eat and drink and are happy (1 Kgs 4:20, 25). In Israel, there is no adversary and no misfortune (1 Kgs 5:4). The promises of Abraham are in full bloom. The glitz and glamour deluge every sense: the perfume of the incense, the golden glow, the soft fabrics, and the fine wine.

But if you pay attention to the details, you start to notice that not everything that glimmers is gold. The hygiene of Jerusalem is not up to code. On this building over here, the plaque says, "The Temple of Chemosh." The monument on that corner is dedicated to Ashtoreth. The bell on the Mount of Olives rings for Milcom, and there is a shrine to Molech, who demands child sacrifice. There are idols in this Jerusalem, and the patronesses of the shrines are the wives of Solomon. Seven hundred wives and three hundred concubines—a ludicrous rejection of God's command (Deut 17:17). And Solomon pays homage to the deities of his brides; he bends the knee and kisses the bull. The temple-builder king, whose devotion eloquently prayed after the glory cloud filled the temple, added gods and goddesses to his pantheon. The cedar forest of the holy Jerusalem is infested with idols. Solomon may have judged cases with wisdom. His publications on wildlife and proverbs may be filled with astute scholarship. But, when it comes to the ground level of righteousness, to worship Yahweh alone, he fails. This son did not surpass his father. And yet for the father's sake, Yahweh did not rip the kingdom from Solomon's hands (1 Kgs 11:12).

This passage from 1 Kings 11 is actually a good example of how the Davidic covenant works. Solomon flunks the righteousness exam, but Yahweh graciously preserves the kingdom for the sake of his promise to David. Mercifully, Yahweh puts another son on the throne, but only the righteous son will sit there forever. In Solomon's case, his judgment did not even fall in his lifetime but on his son. Therefore, after Yahweh condemns Solomon, he raises up three foes who will strike once the king is dead: Hadad the Edomite, Rezon in Damascus, and in Israel Jeroboam the son of Nebat. And it does not take long before Jeroboam walks out on center stage.

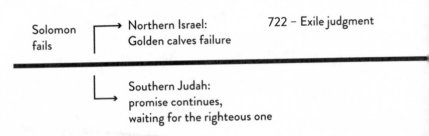

With the funeral of Solomon completed, the time comes for the new king to be installed. The scepter is being passed to Rehoboam, and all of Israel travels to Shechem for the inauguration ceremony. Yet before he is crowned, the people have a request; "Lighten the hard service of your father and his heavy yoke on us, and we will serve you." (1 Kgs 12:4). Another rust spot corrupts the armor of Solomon; he overtaxed and overworked his people to build his empire. The magnificent buildings rubbed their backs raw. Rehoboam has an opening to be better than his father. He, though, needs three days to think and take counsel. First, the elders of Solomon's administration share their insight: "If you will be a servant to those people today and serve them, and if you respond to them with kind words, they will be your servants always" (12:7, NJPS). Their counsel promotes a justice administered by service and kindness. A heavy hand does not make a good king. Yet the inexperienced Rehoboam is suspicious of these gray heads, so he turns next to the men of his age, those spoiled rich kids he grew up with in prep school. The immature counselors take a much more severe tack. They instruct him to tell those whiners, "My little finger is thicker than my father's loins. ... My father flogged you

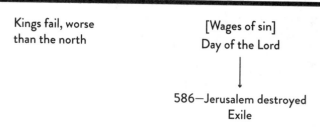

Chart 6: Divided Kingdom

with whips, but I will flog you with scorpions" (12:10–11, my translation). "It is better to be feared as a king than loved" is the motto of these men.[1] And Rehoboam is hooked; he plagiarizes the words of his buddies, but it provokes opposition: "To your tents, O Israel! Look now to your own house, O David" (12:16). The kingdom is split; ten tribes secede while the tribe of Judah remains loyal to Rehoboam and the house of David: the kingdom of Judah in the south, and the kingdom of Israel in the north.

Without delay, the northern kingdom forms a government and appoints Jeroboam, son of Nebat, king. Once Jeroboam makes his capital in Shechem, he must deal with a major political challenge. The temple resides in the south, and people travel there three times a year to worship and give offerings. If the people take their worship and hard-earned sacrifices to the south, their loyalty to Judah will soon follow.

Jeroboam then devises an ingenious solution. He builds two shrines to house a golden calf each. One will sit up north in Dan, and the other near the border with Judah at Bethel. He cuts the ribbon on these shrines by saying, "Behold your god, O Israel, who brought you up out of the land of Egypt" (1 Kgs 12:28), which is nearly

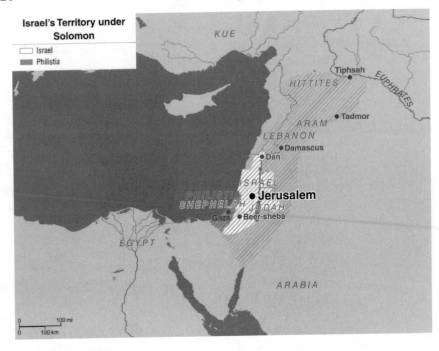

Israel's Territory under Solomon

□ Israel
■ Philistia

word for word what Aaron said about the golden calf in Exodus 32:4. Additionally, Jeroboam commissions cult places throughout his kingdom and bans the Levites from serving in them. Instead of one place of worship, there are many. Finally, he devises a new feast (1 Kgs 12:32–33). The Feast of Booths was celebrated in Jerusalem on the fifteenth day of the seventh month, and it was the biggest feast of the year. Hence, Jeroboam creates a new holiday on the fifteenth of the eighth month for his northern people to keep. For political survival, Jeroboam created false worship in Israel.

To clarify, though, Jeroboam may not have intended a violation of the first commandment (no other gods)—rather, he broke the second commandment (not make a carved image). The golden calves were likely intended as pedestals for Yahweh. Yahweh is jealous, however, for the second commandment just as much as the first. Moreover, the author of Kings presents Jeroboam's act as one of grand apostasy. As Gary Knoppers writes, "Jeroboam's cultus revives and perpetuates Aaron's apostasy. ... The cult of Jeroboam is counterfeit and secondary. The author goes beyond condemning the northern cultus as non-Judahite. He claims that Jeroboam's cult is fundamentally un-Israelite."[2] Therefore, this sin of Jeroboam son of Nebat becomes the cancer in the north that eats at Israel its whole life. Baal worship will come and go in the north, but the calves remain. Now we will survey the history of the northern kingdom, and then the history of the south.

NORTHERN ISRAEL: NEVER TURNING FROM EVIL

Once the kingdom splits into north and south, a new theme develops: the reliability and certainty of the prophetic word of God. Yahweh speaks through his prophet and his word will come to pass, even if it seems farfetched and unlikely.

The first scene with Jeroboam lodges this theme in our memories. We see Jeroboam standing by the altar in Bethel in the shrine of the golden calf. An unnamed man of God arrives from Judah and announces to the counterfeit altar, "O altar, altar! Thus said the LORD: A son shall be born to the house of David, Josiah by name; and he shall slaughter upon you the priests of the shrines" (1 Kgs 13:2). Josiah is one of the last kings of Judah, who reigns from 640–609 BC, and he fulfills this word in 2 Kings 23:15–16. Spoiler alert, Yahweh declares the end from the beginning. After he converses with Jeroboam briefly, we learn that Yahweh insisted that this Judean prophet cannot stop to eat or drink and must go home a different way (13:9). The Lord's word must be followed. Once the Judean heads for home, an old Bethel prophet catches up and lies, "The Lord told me to bring you back home for a meal" (13:18, my paraphrase). The Judean prophet believes the contrary word, but during supper, Yahweh truly speaks through the Bethel man, "Because you have flouted the word of the LORD ... your corpse shall not come to the grave of your fathers" (13:21–22, NJPS). To defy the word is to die. On the way home, a lion slays the Judean man, and the elder of Bethel puts the man's corpse in his own tomb with the obituary, "what he announced by the word of the LORD ... shall surely come true" (13:32). This odd episode raises questions, but one thing is for sure: Yahweh's word will come to pass and it must be obeyed.

And the second scene with Jeroboam echoes the first one (1 Kgs 14). His son Abijah catches a lethal illness, so he sends his wife incognito to the prophet Ahijah to learn the destiny of his boy. The wife's disguise is transparent to the prophetic eye, and Ahijah preaches against the sin of Jeroboam and predicts the demise of the lad Abijah as soon as his mother arrives. Ahijah's sermon also includes a prophesy of doom against the house of Jeroboam and the northern kingdom itself (14:13–15). An end will come to the dynasty of Jeroboam, and exile will scatter Israel beyond the Euphrates, which happens two hundred years later. Soon Jeroboam dies, and his son Nadab reigns for only two years before Baasha assassinates him for the throne. Similarly, Baasha rules for twenty-four years, gets a prophetic doom sermon, and dies. His son Elah is on the throne for two years, and then Zimri wipes out his entire house.

This succession of reigns and insurrections begins to form a rough pattern: First, the king does not depart from the sins of Jeroboam (e.g., 1 Kgs 15:26, 34). Then, Yahweh proclaims judgment on the dynasty of the king (e.g., 1 Kgs 14:14; 16:3). Finally, a seditious coup overthrows the king to replace him with a new dynasty in fulfillment of the word (e.g., 1 Kgs 15:29; 16:12). One of the attributes of the north's history is this regular changing of the royal dynasty; nine different dynasties govern Israel from 930 to 722 BC. Though the kings may change, their ways in following the golden calves do not.

Judean Kings[3]	Israelite Kings
Rehoboam: 930–914	Jeroboam I, son of Nebat: 930–911
Abijam: 914–911	Nadab: 911–909
Asa: 911–871	Baasha: 909–887
	Elah: 886–885
	Zimri: 885 (7 days)
	Omri: 885–875
Jehoshaphat: 870–849	Ahab: 874–853
J(eh)oram II: 848–842	Ahaziah I: 853–852
Ahaziah II: 842–841	J(eh)oram I: 852–841
Queen Athaliah: 841–835	Jehu: 841–814
Joash I: 835–796	Jehoahaz I: 813–806
Amaziah: 795–776	Joash II: 805–790
Uzziah (Azariah): 776–736 (not active post 750)	Jeroboam II: 790–750
Jotham: 750–735	Zechariah: 750 (6 months)
	Shallum: 749 (1 month)
	Menahem: 749–738
	Pekahiah: 738–736
	Pekah: 736–732
Ahaz: 734–715	Hoshea: 731–722
Hezekiah: 715–686	**Fall of Samaria: 722**
Manasseh: 686–642	
Amon: 642–640	
Josiah: 640–609	
Jehoahaz II: 609 (3 months)	
Jehoiakim: 609–598	
Jehoiachin: 598–597 (3 months)	
Zedekiah: 597–586	
Fall of Jerusalem: 586	

Table 2: Kings of the Southern and Northern Kingdoms

Zimri's reign expires before anything can really happen. After a mere seven days in Tirzah, his general Omri wins the support of the army and the people. Zimri burns the citadel down on top of himself; yet the text can still put on his tombstone, "He followed in the ways of Jeroboam."

Even though Omri only gets eight verses in Scripture, he is permitted twelve years on the throne and several notable accomplishments. First, Omri moves the capital from Tirzah to Samaria, which remains the capital until its destruction. Second, Omri's foreign dealings appear to have gained some success. He is mentioned on the Moabite stone as having oppressed Moab for many years.[4] In the Neo-Assyrian inscriptions, the kingdom of Israel is known as "the house of Omri." And he forms an alliance with Tyre by the marriage of his son Ahab to Jezebel.[5] Third, this influence from Tyre is probably reflected in Scripture when it says that he not only followed the ways of Jeroboam son of Nebat, but "was worse than all who preceded him" (1 Kgs 16:25).

Even though few readers of the Bible may know the name Omri, nearly all are familiar with his son Ahab. When Ahab brings Jezebel home, she brings with her Baal[6] worship. Whatever presence Baal worship had previously, with Jezebel it becomes one of the official religions with full backing and funding from the royal purse. With the reign of Ahab getting a big shot in the arm of Baal worship, the narrative slows down to introduce us to a big-shot prophet, Elijah.

Very little background information is given on Elijah; instead, he catapults in with the curse of Yahweh on Ahab: "There will be no dew or rain except at my bidding" (1 Kgs 17:1). After being on the run for three years, Elijah is sent by Yahweh to Ahab for a confrontation, an ordeal to see who the people will serve. The showdown happens on the top of Mount Carmel, with 450 Baal prophets on one side with Ahab, and Elijah all alone on the other. In the audience sits all of Israel. The Lord's prophet sets the challenge before the people: "How long will you keep hopping between two opinions? If the LORD is God, follow Him; and if Baal, follow him!" (1 Kgs 18:21, NJPS).

A test to prove the divinity of the gods is arranged. A young bull is given to each side, and both parties can invoke their god to respond with fire (18:24). The horde of Baal prophets dance, chant, and slash themselves from morning until mid-afternoon—to no effect. Elijah taunts the prophets, "Shout louder! Maybe Baal is on a journey or napping and needs to be awakened" (18:27, my paraphrase). Then, it is Elijah's turn. With twelve stones for the tribes of Israel, Elijah builds an altar and doses it—wood and animal—with twelve buckets of water. The altar swims in a moat of water. At the time of the evening sacrifice, Elijah utters one little prayer, "Answer me, that this people may know that you, O LORD, are God" (18:37). The heavens crack and fire shoots down from Yahweh to lick up stone, wood, flesh, and water. The fire of Yahweh leaves nothing but a scorch mark upon the ground. The people testify, "Yahweh is the God; Yahweh is the God" (18:39, my translation). Their positive declaration, though, does not seem to reverse their lack of devotion to Yahweh. After the Baal prophets are slaughtered and the rains return, Elijah drags himself in despair to Horeb (that is, Sinai) and he complains to Yahweh, "I alone am left and they are out to take my life" (1 Kgs 19:10). Elijah's zeal has borne no fruit as all of Israel has forsaken the covenant of Yahweh. He is ready to throw in the towel, but Yahweh has more work for him. Three he must anoint: Hazael to be king in Damascus, Jehu to be king of Israel, and Elisha to be his prophetic successor (19:15–16). And the three are for judgment. The one who escapes Hazael's sword will be cut down by Jehu; the survivor of Jehu will be killed by Elisha. Moreover, Elijah's loneliness is unjustified as Yahweh has preserved in Israel seven thousand who have not bowed the knee or kissed the bull of Baal (19:18).

Elijah's weariness appears to have taken its toll, for he completes only a third of the job. He anoints Elisha to be his replacement and he retires into the background for a few chapters. Meanwhile, as Ahab is in Samaria, Ben-Hadad king of Syria marches out to attack him, and the end looks near for Israel. A prophet shows up and promises Yahweh's deliverance so that Ahab will know that Yahweh

Beit She'an looking west, near Jezreel

is God (1 Kgs 20:13). After the victory, however, Ahab makes a covenant with Ben-Hadad and sends him home, which releases another prophetic word that Ahab will die for setting Ben-Hadad free. Sullen and vexed, Ahab returns to Samaria and then takes some vacation at his summer palace in Jezreel. From his balcony, Ahab eyes the vineyard next door and wants it. He makes an offer to the owner Naboth, but Naboth is God-fearing and loyal to the covenant. There is no way Naboth will sell his God-given covenant inheritance. This rejection makes Ahab pout on his bed like a spoiled child. Jezebel has no patience for a sulking husband and knows how to get things done. Jezebel's conspiracy gets Naboth falsely convicted for reviling both God and king; Naboth is stoned, and the vineyard belongs to Ahab. This property acquisition is no small matter, however, as it summons Elijah back to work. Elijah meets Ahab in Naboth's vineyard with two words of doom. One, the dogs will lick up Ahab's blood where they lapped up Naboth's (1 Kgs 21:19), and two, the dogs shall devour Jezebel in the field of Jezreel (1 Kgs 21:23). The house of Ahab is coming to an end.

To our surprise, Ahab hears of his ruin and repents, which moves Yahweh to mercy. The extinction of Ahab's dynasty will not come in his day but in the days of his son (1 Kgs 21:29). Ahab's humiliation, though, is not long lived. In three years' time, the king of Judah, Jehoshaphat, has come up to visit his ally Ahab, and Ahab convinces Jehoshaphat to fight Syria to reclaim Ramoth-gilead. As Ahab's prophets promise success in battle, Jehoshaphat wants to hear from another of Yahweh's prophets. Ahab knows of one, Micaiah, but he hates him, as he always declares misfortune to Ahab and never anything good. In a brilliant scene, Micaiah stands in the royal court and publishes the decree of heaven: Yahweh has spoken disaster upon Ahab. And what Yahweh says comes to be. Despite Ahab's disguise in battle, a random arrow finds a narrow opening in the king's armor, and the dogs lick Ahab's blood from the chariot (1 Kgs 22:38).

After Ahab's death, two of his sons get time on the throne. First, Ahaziah reigns for two years and continues the evil of his father, but he dies from an injury and the word of Elijah (2 King 1:17). Since Ahaziah has no sons, his brother Joram takes the throne. Yet at this time Yahweh takes Elijah up to heaven in a fiery chariot, and a double portion of Elijah's spirit comes to rest on Elisha (2 Kgs 2:9–13). This double-the-spirit is proven by a series of wonders. Nevertheless, there were two tasks that Elijah had left undone, the anointing of Hazael and Jehu. Elisha, then, journeys north to Damascus to anoint Hazael, saying, "I know the evil that you will do to the people of Israel" (2 Kgs 8:12). The sword of Hazael is Yahweh's judgment on his rebellious people. Next on the anointing list is Jehu, a commander in Israel's army, so Elisha sends one of the sons of the prophets to pour oil on Jehu's head in Ramoth-gilead. At this point, though, it is necessary to have a clear idea of Ahab's family tree, since the names are a bit confusing. The table lays out the names and the variations of spellings.[7]

These names are important due to God's commission to Jehu: "You shall strike down the House of Ahab your master. ... The whole house of Ahab shall perish, and I will cut off every male belonging

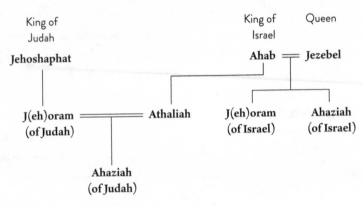

Table 3: Ahab's and Jezebel's Family

to Ahab, bond and free in Israel" (2 Kgs 9:7–8). The task of wiping out Ahab's line falls to Jehu, who does a good job of it. Without delay, Jehu's crazy chariot driving brings him to the palace at Jezreel, where King Joram of Israel is convalescing and King Ahaziah of Judah is visiting him. With an arrow to the heart, Jehu terminates Joram and has his body tossed on Naboth's vineyard in accordance with Yahweh's word. A fatal shot also expires Ahaziah of Judah, who was a grandson of Ahab. Upon entering the city, Jehu urges the eunuchs to launch Jezebel from the balcony, and she becomes dog food, fulfilling Elijah's word (2 Kgs 9:34–37). Over the next few days, Jehu gets the heads of Ahab's seventy sons and even forty-two of Ahaziah's relatives, which puts a final end to Ahab's dynasty (2 Kgs 10:17).

The demise of Ahab's house is not the only gold star Jehu earns; he also institutes religious reforms. Jehu boasts that he would worship Baal more than anyone else, and to celebrate his zealous piety he holds a rave for every Baal devotee in the massive temple of Baal in

Samaria. Once the worship party is in full swing, he locks the doors and releases the executioners. The blood of the idolaters paints the walls red, and the temple is deconstructed into a public latrine to eradicate Baal worship from Israel (2 Kgs 10:27–28). And for Jehu's religious zeal, Yahweh rewards him with four generations who will sit on the throne in the north. Yet despite Jehu's hatred of Baal, he does not turn from the golden calves of Jeroboam the son of Nebat. The evil of Jeroboam lives on in Jehu and all four of his generations.

The next four reigns pass with relatively little detail. Jehoahaz sits for seventeen years, his son Jehoash sixteen, and his son Jeroboam II forty-one (2 Kgs 14:23–29). Under Jehoahaz and Jehoash, Israel suffers dearly at the hand of Hazael and his son. Yet Yahweh's mercy grants his people a time of peace and prosperity under Jeroboam II. The loyalty to the golden calves, nevertheless, remains constant.

The death of Jeroboam II brings us to the year of the four kings, about 750 BC, which is the beginning of the end for the north. In that year, Jeroboam II dies; Zechariah, the last son of Jehu, perishes after six months, and Shallum only survives a month before Menahem seizes power. During Menahem's reign, a foe on the horizon arrives on the front step—Assyria. Menahem is forced to pay tribute to Assyria, and Assyria annexes the Transjordan and everything north of Galilee during the days of Pekah. Finally, Hoshea comes to power and first pays tribute as an Assyrian vassal. When Hoshea sends messengers to Egypt, he violates the terms of the covenant, so the king of Assyria besieges Samaria and destroys it in 722 BC. Hoshea receives the medal for the last king in the north. What the prophet Ahijah spoke several centuries previously has come to pass (1 Kgs 14:15). The Lord's word stands firm.

The violation of the Assyrian covenant, however, was just a symptom of another covenant desecration: that of the Mosaic covenant. Therefore, the narrator of 2 Kings interjects a covenantal sermon into the history as theological commentary. Why did God allow Israel to be demolished and exiled? "This occurred because the people of Israel had sinned against the LORD their God ... and had feared other gods and walked in the customs of the nations" (2 Kgs 17:7–8). They built shrines in every town and set up sacred pillars under every green tree instead of worshiping at the place where God made his name to dwell (Deut 12). The Israelites followed the defiling fetishes of the people who had profaned the land before them (Lev 18:24–30). Children were burned to Molech (Lev 20:2), and witchcraft and divination spread to every household (Deut 18:9–14). And even though Yahweh's long-suffering sent prophet after prophet to call them to repentance, the people's stiff necks and hard hearts refused to change. Long life in the land was conditioned on their obedience, so in the total absence of obedience, Yahweh's holy justice executed the full curse of the covenant, scattering them among the nations as God-forsaken. Holiness by the law was replaced with profane wickedness, so God "cast them out from his presence" (2 Kgs 17:20). Could sinful people earn a place before God's face with obedience? This was the question of the Mosaic covenant. The answer is in with a deafening NO. And the history of the north gets replayed in the south with only slight variations.

SOUTHERN JUDAH: WORSE THAN THE BROTHER

Let's rewind back to the reign of Rehoboam and see how Judah's wickedness compares to Israel's. Now, Jeroboam son of Nebat launched his kingdom off the cliff of apostasy right out of the gate. The idolatry of Jeroboam flows in the veins of Israel from conception to burial. Not much effort is required from Judah in the south to grade better on obedience. And in many ways, the south does score higher on righteousness, which results in Judah out-living Israel by just shy of 140 years. Many factors contribute to the righteousness found in the south that was lacking in the north, but two stand out in the history of Kings.

First, Judah retained Jerusalem and the temple. The holy place of God's name, where true worship was to be offered, continued to be the center for piety and restoration. As we will see, the temple will be sorely misused and abused, but the sacred vestiges of the temple prop up a place for repentance and renewal. Second, the promise to David handed down from king to king provided a sustaining grace for both king and people. Despite the failings of the king, Yahweh's fidelity placed another Davidic son on the throne, and with the promise came the demand to walk in the law. The south, then, was supported by the gifts of temple and royal promise. Yet the more one is given, the more is demanded. The higher you rise the harder you fall. Therefore, the high points of obedience in Judah are quickly chased by plummets into depravity.

Furthermore, in the north, there was a repeating measurement of royal performance, which was a negative standard: "he did what was evil ... he walked in the way of Jeroboam." Some kings were better, such as Jehu, and others were worse, such as Ahab, but they all kept the golden calves in Dan and Bethel. In Judah, however, the standard of measurement differs from the negative example of Jeroboam to the positive example of David. The refrain that echoes through the south first appears with King Asa: "And Asa did what was right in the eyes of the LORD, as David his father had done" (1 Kgs 15:11). A good king pleases Yahweh by following the manners of David. A wicked king, however, gets judged with language like, "he did what displeasing to the LORD" or "he walked in all the sins that his father did before him, and his heart was not wholly true to the LORD his God, as the heart of David his father." (1 Kgs 15:3). David is the yardstick by which the kings are measured.

Yet the fidelity of David focuses particularly upon the cultic. That is, did the king worship Yahweh in the temple alone or did he multiply shrines? And there are two levels in cultic failure. The first misstep relates to the "high places," as most English translations read, or better the "shrines." In Kings, "shrines" is a general term for a cultic place of worship that was Yahwistic. Yahweh was worshiped in these shrines, yet they were not the temple, but were scattered throughout the land and so were condemned as illegitimate.[8] These Yahwistic shrines were likely syncretistic, which means the worship of Yahweh was mixed with ideas and practices pulled from other religions. The second and more grievous error of the kings was active worship of foreign deities, like Baal, Ashtoreth, or Molech. This idolatry was the royal promotion of idolatrous worship. A good example how these two sins work in the kings of the south is found in the first three kings of Judah.

In 1 Kings 14, we are told that under Rehoboam the people built shrines (high places), and Asherim, pillars, and cult prostitutes were in the land (14:23–24). Like Solomon, Rehoboam had both shrines and idolatry. And in the steps of Rehoboam his son Abijam walked (1 Kgs 15:3). However, when the third king ascends the throne, he institutes religious reforms by banishing cult prostitutes, removing idols, cutting down the image of Asherah, and deposing his queen mother (1 Kgs 15:12–13). All this positive obedience, though, is chastened in the next verse, "But the high places were not taken away. Nevertheless, the heart of Asa was wholly true to the LORD all his days." (15:14). The final judgment of Asa is that he did what was pleasing to Yahweh, as his father David had done. Asa's wholehearted pleasing of Yahweh is expressed in his purging of the idols; yet his reputation is tarnished by leaving the shrines in business.

There is one more ingredient to this pattern found in Judah, which is God's faithfulness to David. Hence, after the wickedness of Abijam is summarized, the text asserts Yahweh's mercy: "Nevertheless, for David's sake the LORD his God gave him a lamp in Jerusalem, setting up his son after him, and establishing Jerusalem" (1 Kgs 15:4). Despite the king's wickedness, Yahweh puts another Davidic heir on the throne; God gives the son a chance to be the righteous one. The steadfast love of Yahweh sworn to David is what preserves the south, king and people, even in the face of their regular slides into idolatry.

Once Asa, though, is laid to rest with his fathers, his son Jehoshaphat grabs the royal wheel and steers ably like his father. He swerves clear of idolatry and further repairs the potholes of Asherah and cult prostitutes. Jehoshaphat's heart is also courageous in the ways of Yahweh by promoting Torah education in the cities and ensuring fidelity and anticorruption in the judges and priests. Jehoshaphat's tomb read, "He did what was right in the eyes of the LORD" with the caveat "yet the high places were not taken down."

Nevertheless, one action of Jehoshaphat tarnishes his legacy and proves to be hugely detrimental for Judah's history. This act could be mistaken as sensible foreign policy, but once in the grave, it explodes into a national calamity. This action was Jehoshaphat's alliance with Ahab by marriage (2 Chron 18:1). He took Athaliah, Jezebel's daughter, to be wed to his son Jehoram. Jehoshaphat takes as his daughter-in-law the princess of Baal. The prophet Jehu even rebukes Jehoshaphat for this alliance: "Should you help the wicked and love those who hate the LORD?" (2 Chron 19:2). The table of Ahab's family in the previous section shows how Ahab and Jehoshaphat gave their sons the same names, which betrays an unhealthy friendliness.

Hence, once inaugurated, Jehoram speedily rushes to imitate the ways of Ahab. For eight years, Jehoram spreads the poison of Baal and Asherah in Judah. He even slaughters all his brothers to keep power in his blood-stained hands (2 Chron 21:4). The evil of Ahab in the north had infected the south and spread like gangrene. For his wickedness, a letter from Elijah condemns Judah to a plague and Jehoram to a disease of the bowels. Jehoram's approval ratings were so low that it says, "He departed with no one's regret" (2 Chron 21:20). And Ahaziah's one-year reign after Jehoram does not change the status quo. Ahaziah continues to promote the evil ways of Ahab, and his mother, Athaliah, is his counselor in all things. The time of Yahweh's decreed judgment has come.

Ahaziah's uncle, King Joram in the north, is injured while fighting the Syrians, so he excuses himself to the palace in Jezreel to heal. Like any good nephew, Ahaziah goes to visit his laid-up uncle. Little does he know, though, that the horn of Elisha has recently anointed Jehu son of Nimshi to wipe out the house of Ahab, to which Ahaziah belongs. The therapy retreat in Jezreel soon turns into a blood bath. From his chariot Jehu shoots King Joram with an arrow, and after a bit of chase, Jehu also kills Ahaziah. In a single day, two thrones became vacant. Yet where Jehu filled the throne in the north, the house of Ahaziah could not produce a ruler in Judah. Queen Athaliah lost her husband, Jehoram, and now her son is dead, with no suitable males to rule. What is a queen to do? Seize the throne for yourself—who needs a man? This is exactly what Athaliah does; she claims sole authority in the south. Queen Athaliah becomes the only woman to rule as a king in the history of the south.

And once Athaliah grasps the scepter, she is feeling in the mood for a bit of revenge. For what just happened to her? At the command of Yahweh, Jehu wiped out the entire family of Ahab with one exception, Athaliah. She is the daughter of Ahab and Jezebel, sister of the kings Ahaziah and Joram in Israel, wife of the late Jehoram, and mother of king Ahaziah. Jehu had just killed her whole family, so she retaliates by massacring the entire royal family of David. From crib to chair, Athaliah slashes every male of David's house in order to outdo the zeal of Jehu. In Athaliah, the seed of the serpent sinks its fangs deep into the promise of God. The Lord swore to preserve the line of David, but if all the Davidic heirs are extinct, then the promise fails. By cutting off the line of David, Athaliah hopes to forestall the oath of Yahweh. The steadfast fidelity of Yahweh, though, never fails.

As the henchmen of Athaliah fill Jerusalem with murderous cries, Jehosheba steals away a son of Ahaziah named Joash. Jehosheba was the daughter of King Jehoram and sister to Ahaziah, and she had married the godly priest Jehoiada. This pious couple hides their nephew in the temple for the next six years while the terror of Athaliah's idolatry spoils the land. And on Joash's seventh birthday, the season for revolution becomes fully ripe. Jehoiada has everything planned out to unfold across the sacred geography of the temple. During the changing of the guards on the Sabbath, the armed guards usher in the young lad and declare, "Long live the king!" (2 Kgs 11:12). Athaliah shrieks treason, but to no avail, as Jehoiada has her seized and executed. Then Jehoiada makes a covenant between Yahweh and the king and people, so that they would be Yahweh's people alone. The people quickly demolish the cult of Baal that Athaliah had sponsored. Finally, "the city was quiet after Athaliah had been put to death with the sword" (2 Kgs 11:20).

The reign of Joash unfolds largely along the lines of the uprightness of his sponsor and protector, Jehoiada. He makes extensive repairs and reforms to the temple and is judged as doing what is right in the eyes of Yahweh, except for the shrines. Yet Chronicles adds an interesting footnote to the reign of Joash that is not mentioned in Kings. The Chronicler relays how when Jehoiada dies, Joash and the nobles turn away from Yahweh to the Asherah poles and idols (2 Chron 24:18). Joash even murders Jehoiada's son, the prophet Zechariah. For this, Yahweh's judgment comes in two waves: a defeat by the Syrians and the assassination of Joash.

After Joash is laid to rest in Jerusalem, but not in the tombs of the kings, his son Amaziah takes the throne for the next 29 years. The report card of Amaziah reads with a B for doing what is right in the eyes of Yahweh, but not taking down the shrines. This passing grade, though, is asterisked with two failures. First, after winning a victory over Edom, Amaziah brings home their gods and grants them shrines. Second, Amaziah's arrogance challenges big brother to the north, such that King Joash hands Judah a deep defeat, which ends up being Yahweh's punishment for Amaziah's turning to idols.

This pattern of starting well for Yahweh but then turning from him, seen in Joash and Amaziah, gets replayed over two more generations. The Lord blesses Amaziah's son, Uzziah or Azariah, with a long and prosperous reign of fifty-two years for doing what was right, save the shrines. Yet the fatness of the land puffs up the heart of Uzziah with pride. Uzziah appropriates for himself the right to enter the temple and offer incense like a priest. For this sacrilege, this king is struck with scale disease and is quarantined off into solitary confinement for the rest of his life. Similarly, King Jotham pleases Yahweh and becomes mighty because he orders his ways before Yahweh (2 Chron 27:6), yet he permits the people to continue in their corrupt ways.

This rough pattern that lasted four generations comes to a screeching halt in Jotham's son, Ahaz. Right out of the start gate, Ahaz ignites wickedness like a wildfire. He gives royal approval to Baal worship throughout the land and even sponsors child sacrifice in the Hinnom Valley. As punishment, Judah suffers a crushing defeat by Syria and Israel. But this only enflames Ahaz's rebellion (2 Chron 28:22). For relief from Syria and Israel, Ahaz hires the king of Assyria for deliverance at the cost of the temple treasures. Then, he replicates an altar he saw in Damascus and puts it in the temple to replace Yahweh's altar. Finally, Ahaz retools the shrines to offer sacrifices to other gods. Ahaz has met the wickedness of Ahab and surpasses it.

When Ahaz's sixteen years of evil finally come to an end, we find an apple that fell far from the tree. Ahaz wins the medal for worst king to date, but his son breaks the record for the most upright king since David. And King Hezekiah's righteousness stands tall on the legs of religious reform and trust in Yahweh. On the reform side, Hezekiah begins with a wholesale destruction of the defiling idols and their practices. He marshals the Levites and priests to purge the temple of detestable things. Once he restores purity to the temple and its worship, Hezekiah organizes a covenant renewal ceremony for all the people at Passover, to lead the people in national repentance and renewed devotion to Yahweh alone. The Chronicler even labels this as an unparalleled time of joy in Jerusalem since the days of Solomon (2 Chron 30:26). The people make good on their repentance by going forth to tear down idols scattered throughout the land. Even the shrines get put out of business. This was the first good leg of Hezekiah.

The second leg of his righteousness straightens out when Sennacherib the king of Assyria marches on Judah. When Hezekiah took the throne, Judah was still a vassal state of Assyria due to Ahaz's desire to be the "servant and son" of Tiglath-pileser (2 Kgs 16:7). The dates of Hezekiah are notoriously difficult and debated. Yet part of Hezekiah's reforms include fortifying Jerusalem's wall and water source in preparation to throw off the yoke of Assyria. Hence, in 705 BC when King Sargon dies, Hezekiah partners with Egypt in an alliance to rebel, and Hezekiah even attacks pro-Assyrian rulers in Philistia (2 Kgs 18:7–8).[9] By 701 BC, King Sennacherib has destroyed the fortified Judean town of Lachish and is on Jerusalem's doorstep. Assyria demands heavy tribute from Hezekiah, which he pays, but when he will not surrender, Assyria gives the final demand, "Surrender for peace or die!" In Sennacherib's ultimatum, though, he scorns Yahweh as being as weak as the other gods of the conquered nations. Hezekiah's faith causes him to tear his clothes, and he casts himself on the power and mercy of Yahweh to deliver his people from their enemies. Yahweh hears the king's prayer and answers with a mighty victory as the angel of Yahweh strikes down 185,000 Assyrians in a single night (2 Kgs 19:35). Hezekiah trusts in Yahweh to fight his battles, and his trust is not in vain. Besides a proud misstep with the Babylonian envoys, the biblical record judges Hezekiah as doing right in the eyes of Yahweh.

One would expect that such a godly king would father an upright heir. Yet with the coronation of his son Manasseh, we find ourselves on a spiritual teeter-totter. Ahaz's wickedness plummeted Judah down into idolatry; Hezekiah's righteousness rocketed Judah to the heights of purity. And Manasseh skydives from Hezekiah's peaks into a trench deeper than Ahaz's. The litany of his evil seems to have no end. Manasseh rebuilds the shrines, opens up altars for Baal and Asherah, puts idol altars in the temple, burns his son for Molech, employs wizards and mediums, and fills Jerusalem with innocent blood. In Manasseh, Judah not only matches the sin of Samaria, but proves to be worse. Therefore, due to the unparalleled degeneracy of Manasseh, Yahweh declares that Judah is going into exile (2 Kgs 21:11; Jer 15:4). For the sin of Manasseh, the ultimate curse of the covenant will befall Judah. Chronicles even informs us how Assyria took Manasseh captive in Babylon, which humbled Manasseh in repentance—but this did not stay Yahweh's judgment, only delayed it. Besides, Amon comes to power and continues the wickedness of his father. The cancer of iniquity had spread to the bones of Judah, and not even the skilled surgery of Josiah could remove it.

Josiah was only eight years old when the crown came to rest on his head, but he puts us back on the teeter-totter. Josiah restores Judah to a righteousness even greater than Hezekiah reached. His radical reforms begin in his eighteenth year after a scroll of the law is found in the temple by Hilkiah the priest. Then, Josiah begins a full-scale campaign to eradicate idolatry. From the profane images in the temple to the shrines in the countryside, Josiah demolishes the cultic statutes and defiles the shrines so that they cannot be used again. King Josiah even bulldozes Topheth, where babies were burned to Molech, as well as the abominations to Milcom and Chemosh on the Mount of Olives, which Solomon built. Finally, to fulfill the word of 1 Kings 13:2, Josiah strides up to Bethel to the altar that Jeroboam son of Nebat built, burns bones on it, and levels it (2 Kgs 23:15–16). Josiah's renovations also included purifying and repairing the temple, and like Hezekiah, he oversees a massive covenant renewal during Passover. The people's reconciliation to Yahweh is so grand that the Chronicler praises the celebration as "No Passover like it had been kept in Israel" (2 Chron 35:18). Therefore, Josiah receives a commendation unlike any king since David: "He did what was pleasing to the LORD and he followed all the ways of his ancestor David; he did not deviate to the right or to the left" (2 Kgs 22:2). For his devotion, Yahweh mercifully delays the final judgment decreed upon Manasseh until after Josiah's time.

Josiah's unexpected death at Megiddo in 609 BC, however, puts Judah on a fast-moving slide toward the end. Four more kings fill the next twenty-plus years of Judah's turbulent life, and all four do evil in the eyes of Yahweh. To begin with, Josiah's son Jehoahaz only reigns for three months before Pharaoh Neco carts him off to Egypt and puts Jehoiakim, another son of Josiah, on the throne, which makes Jehoiakim a vassal of Egypt. Three short years later, though, Babylon marches through Palestine after putting the final nails in Assyria's coffin. Nebuchadnezzar forces Jehoiakim to break his allegiance with Egypt and become a Babylonian vassal. The political forces in Judah that are still loyal to Egypt remained strong, so that in 598 Jehoiakim rebels from Babylon just before he dies, and his son Jehoiachin takes over. Nebuchadnezzar again marches on Jerusalem, where he deports Jehoiachin and exiles a large number of the most educated and skilled

Judeans. The Babylonian monarch also puts another son of Josiah on the throne, Zedekiah. For the next nine years, King Zedekiah is pulled back and forth by the pro-Egyptian and pro-Babylonian factions of his government. But in 589, Zedekiah puts his hope in Egypt and rebels against Babylon. A year later, Jerusalem is under siege, and by July 586 the wall is breached and the city and temple destroyed. The Lord's word of judgment is fulfilled.

The full curse of the Mosaic covenant steamrolled Judah for its disobedience. The Lord warned Solomon that if he and his sons did not do all the commandments, then he would forsake the temple of his name and make it a byword among the nations. One after another, the kings turned from Yahweh to fashion images and bow down to them. Even the bright shining stars of Hezekiah and Josiah failed to put righteous sons on the throne to carry on their heritage. In the Davidic covenant, Yahweh demanded a righteous son to inherit an eternal kingdom. Yet none of them measured up. The idolatrous cancer with which Solomon infected Jerusalem was never healed or removed. The only thing left to do is call hospice and turn up the morphine until death comes in 586. In an extended sermon of Jeremiah, he puts in the balances the last four kings of Judah (Jer 21:11–23:6). He weights them one after another for justice and righteousness, but none is found: Jehoahaz zero, Jehoiakim bankrupt, Jehoiachin nothing. And for the sins of the kings, the nation is going into exile. For the cancer of the kings, the people must die.

And yet after exile, when Judah appears dead as she is scattered to the winds, Yahweh will gather his people. He will bring his sheep back and will give them a new shepherd. Yahweh will raise up for David a righteous branch. And the name of this king will be "The LORD is our Righteousness" (Jer 23:6). The righteousness needed by the people, which neither they nor their kings could do themselves, Yahweh will give to them through a righteous king. The Lord will keep his oath to David; he will sprout a branch from David who embodies the righteousness of Yahweh. Though the prophets did not see this king in their day, Mary will. The angel will announce, "Unto you is born this day in the city of David a Savior, who is Christ the Lord" (Luke 2:11). On the horizon is Jesus Christ, the Righteous One in whom we become the righteousness of God by faith alone.

STUDY QUESTIONS

1. How does the fall of Solomon demonstrate how the Davidic covenant works?

2. What sin always crippled the northern kingdom of Israel?

3. Discuss how the prophetic word works in the history of Kings.

4. Who introduced Baal worship to Israel? Why does this matter?

5. How does the history of the south teach the lesson of the Mosaic covenant?

7

THE PROPHETS

Bible Reading:
Isaiah, Joel, Micah, Nahum,
Obadiah, Habakkuk, Zephaniah

When you meet someone, you form an impression first by what you see, then by what you hear. Our eyes scan hair, face, and clothing to gather information, and our ears listen to how they speak. We especially notice if they have an accent or what type of accent. The accent may be beautiful, funny, or even difficult, but after spending time with them, you come to understand their accent and even appreciate it. One's accent is part of what makes a person unique and dear.

Similarly, we have to recognize that the Old Testament genre of prophecy has its own accent, one much different from what we hear in the Gospels, the Law, or the historical narratives. Amid the varying voices of Scripture, the prophets have their own dialect, the prophetic idiom. If you have ever found your reading of the prophets to be clogged down with confusion, this may be why.

The prophetic idiom arises not merely in word choice or tone but also in organization of ideas and phrases. That is, the prophetic idiom consists of not just how they talk but what they say. The content of the prophetic message is at issue, and this is because the prophets served not only their generation but also those on the other side of Christ's coming.

The New Testament is quite frank about this. Jesus said, "Many prophets and righteous people longed to see what you see, and did not see it, and to hear what you hear, and did not hear it" (Matt 13:17). Paul told the Corinthians, "These things happened to them as an example, but they were written down for our instruction, on whom the end of the ages has come" (1 Cor 10:11). Peter talks about how the prophets searched diligently and inquired carefully about the sufferings of Christ and the subsequent glories, and how even the angels longed to understand such matters (1 Pet 1:11–12). Every Gospel labors to show how the prophets spoke about Christ. On the day of his resurrection, during the evening table time, the risen Lord also opened the minds of his disciples to understand how Moses, the Prophets, and the Psalms were fulfilled in him (Luke 24:44–45). Therefore, the prophets were preaching about the future realities of Christ, his work, the church, and heaven itself. The telescope through which they peered was not completely in focus. They saw the truth, but the details were blurry. This also contributes to why their dialect can be difficult for us to understand at times. This is also why, before we begin surveying the individual prophets, it is good to lay a foundation concerning the office of the prophet and the nature of prophetic imagery and typology.

THE OFFICE OF THE PROPHET

Nowadays, we dress the prophets in the garb of modern preachers. We color them as vibrant harbingers of spiritual and social reform, bold individuals who protested systemic injustice and idolatry. Yet even if they do possess some of these traits, casting them in our image isn't an accurate way to get to know the prophets. Instead, God's institution and definition of the prophetic office needs to be front and center, along with the prophet's own self-understanding of his office and work. As we saw with kingly office, David became the model and pattern for all subsequent kings. Likewise with prophetic office, there is an archetype, a blueprint after which all the other prophets are based, and this standard is Moses.

Moses is the paradigmatic prophet, which makes the office an integral part of the Mosaic covenant. The Old Testament prophets are officers of the Mosaic theocracy. The primary passage that pins Moses up as the paradigm comes from Deuteronomy 18. After a series of laws forbidding pagan methods of divination and soothsaying, the Lord publishes how Israel will know his will: "The LORD your God will raise up for you a prophet like me from among you" (Deut 18:15). From this one line, three attributes of the prophet emerge.

First, the Lord raises the prophet up; only God chooses and picks a prophet. You can't volunteer to be a prophet. One's individual choice does not get a nod. In fact, at a low point Jeremiah did not want to be a prophet any more. He tried to quit, but God would not let him (Jer 20:9). Furthermore, a person cannot inherit the office from his father. Prophethood is not dynastic like kingship or limited to the line of Aaron, like priesthood. Second, the prophet will come from Israel, one of Israel's brothers. The prophet will not be a foreigner, but he will live under the same law and promises as the people to whom he preaches. Third, the prophet will be like Moses. Moses was self-conscious of his paradigm status, and this rank originated from an event at Sinai. Moses mentions this in Deuteronomy 18:16, which refers back to Deuteronomy 5.

As the congregation stood at the foot of Sinai, the mountain of God was ablaze with the fire and dark cloud of the Lord's glory. The people saw no image of God, but they heard his voice roar from the flames. Cowering in terror, the people pled with Moses, "Let us not die, then, for this fearsome fire will consume us; if we hear the voice of the LORD our God any longer, we shall die" (Deut 5:22, NJPS). The perfection of the law and the majesty of the Lord's presence was too much for them. The people could not be so near to the holy God. They needed someone to mediate for them, so they asked Moses, "You go closer and hear all that the LORD our God says, and then you tell us everything that the LORD our God tells you, and we will willingly do it" (5:24, NJPS). Moses did so, and the Lord approved of and granted their petition. Thus Moses became the go-between for the people with the Lord. And this mediatorial role got passed on from Moses to the prophets in his image.

Moreover, the primary task of the prophet was to speak the Lord's words. "I will put my words in his mouth, and he shall speak to them all that I command him" (Deut 18:18). The prophet could not jabber on about his opinions or ideas; rather, he had to utter God's word and nothing but God's word. If the prophet presumed to speak for God, if he made up an oracle when God had not given him one, then the Lord would judge that prophet with death (18:20). Hence, the prophet's preaching bore the very authority and power of the Lord himself. As the Lord said next, "whoever will not listen to my words that he shall speak in my name, I myself will require it of him" (18:19). To disobey Moses or Isaiah or Amos was not to disregard some rambling human but to rebel against the Lord himself. This means that the prophet was a covenantal spokesman. The prophet was an emissary or ambassador for the Lord to deliver to the people God's word. And this nature of their office comes out in two ubiquitous formulas.

The first formula is the messenger form, which in English is translated as "Thus said the Lord," or in the old King James, "Thus saith the Lord." This messenger formula most often opens up an oracle or sermon and marks the direct speech of the Lord. The formula also imprints the oracle with the official authority and authenticity of the Lord. A good example of this comes from Ezekiel when the Lord tells him, "I send you to them, and you shall say to them, 'Thus says the Lord GOD ...'" (Ezek 2:4). What follows in verse 5 is not an oracle but the demand for Ezekiel to preach whether they listen or not. Hence, the messenger formula stands as the Lord's certified stamp of authenticity.

The second formula that dots the prophetic literature is the oracle formula, sometimes called the signatory formula. In English, this phrase is most often translated as "declares the Lord" or "says the Lord." Yet the Hebrew is not a verb, but a noun, "an oracle of Yahweh," which is a fixed technical expression to identify a prophetic oracle. Most often, the oracle formula concludes an oracle or a smaller section within a larger sermon. This is why it is called a signatory formula, a way for the Lord to sign his name to the word. Yet the oracle formula is also found up front or in the middle of an oracle to add stress, emphasis, or certitude to what is being said. Nonetheless, the oracle formula seals the prophetic message with the Lord's own name.

The prophet, then, delivers the word of God to the people as official correspondence of the covenant. Additionally, it matters how or where the prophet receives the oracle. Again, Moses' paradigm is normative. Moses was first handed the law and word of God on top of Sinai within the glory cloud. Later on, once the glory cloud filled the tabernacle, the Lord spoke to Moses above the cherubim within the adytum. In short, Moses was given the word in the divine assembly or heavenly council.

The heavenly council is a concept that permeates the Old Testament and is common among Israel's neighbors, but it is easily missed by modern readers. The heavenly council refers to the Lord's heavenly throne room, where he sits on the throne and angels and spirits attend him as servants. This image of heaven resembles the earthly throne rooms of monarchs. A clear image of this comes from Job 1:6, when the "sons of God" came to present themselves before Yahweh. The prophet, then, stood in the heavenly council like one of the angels to receive Yahweh's official communication and to go forth and herald it to the people.

This heavenly council continuity between Moses and the prophets also has a discontinuity. On Sinai or in the tabernacle, Moses is physically in the presence of the Lord's glory, but this does not happen for the prophets after Moses. As it says, "Never again did there arise in Israel a prophet like Moses—whom the LORD singled out, face to face" (Deut 34:10). Likewise in Numbers 12, the Lord clarifies the uniqueness of Moses: "When a prophet of the LORD arises among you, I make myself known to him in a vision, I speak with him in a dream. Not so with my servant Moses; he is trusted throughout my household. With him I speak mouth to mouth, plainly and not in riddles, and he beholds the likeness of the LORD" (12:6–8, NJPS). The face-to-face communication with Moses is contrasted with the visionary experience of all the other prophets. In addition, the clarity of Moses is differentiated from the riddle character of the prophets. If you have ever thought that reading the prophets is like solving a puzzle, you are not far off.

Now, the visionary experience of the heavenly council varies from prophet to prophet; there is no single vision. Yet one of the clearest dreams comes from 1 Kings 22 and the prophet Micaiah. Ahab begrudgingly summons Micaiah, and the prophet relays how he obtained his word from the Lord: "I saw the LORD sitting on his throne, and all the host of heaven standing beside him on his right hand and on his left" (1 Kings 22:19). Micaiah beheld the heavenly council of the Lord. This is the requirement for all true prophets of the Lord. Hence, when he is in the temple, Isaiah sees the Lord seated on a high and lofty throne and the seraphim are chanting, "Holy, Holy, Holy" (Isa 6:1–3). This probably is not Isaiah's initial call, but it is still a vision where he received an oracle. Ezekiel witnesses the cherubim chariot with the glory of the Lord enthroned above when he is called to service (Ezek 1–2). Many of the other prophets do not describe their visions, but they always use the messenger and oracle formulas as evidence of being in God's presence. Moreover, in Jeremiah 23, Jeremiah is fighting with numerous false prophets who are contradicting the Lord's word through him and leading the people astray. They plagiarize the messenger formula, covering their lies with the pious "says the LORD" signatory. But the Lord counters that he did not send them, he did not speak to them, and they did not stand in his council (23:22). A true prophet has stood in the council of the Lord and seen and heard his word (23:18). Therefore, even though the visionary experience differs and is not always mentioned, an essential qualification of a prophet is having stood in the council of the Lord.

The final attribute to the prophetic office deals with the function and role of their oracles. The prophet mediates between God and Israel; he delivers nothing but the Lord's word. But what is the overall purpose of their preaching? Simply put, the prophet prosecutes the terms of the covenant to uphold the holiness of the Lord. They administer the covenant relationship either toward mercy or judgment. They are like a district attorney who brings charges against the accused to uphold the law. There is even a distinct type of sermon they use to do this called the prophetic dispute or lawsuit. A clear example is found in Hosea 4.

Here, Hosea opens with, "Hear the word of the LORD ... for the LORD has a case against the inhabitants of the land" (4:1, my translation). Hosea then lists the broken laws pulled from the Decalogue: false swearing, lying, murder, theft, and adultery (4:2). Next, Hosea lists the punishments they are suffering for their sin, which are the curses of the covenant. Finally, he calls the people to repent or face further judgment. These prophetic disputes are a particular type of sermon, but the overall ministries of the prophets serve this purpose. The prophets are constantly condemning the idolatry and wickedness of the people. They point out the curses already suffered by the people as a testimony of their sin. They warn and forecast greater doom to come. They unceasingly urge the people to repent. Indeed, there are two goals of prophets: either mercy or judgment.

In terms of mercy, the prophets intercede on behalf of the people. They petition the Lord to forgive and beg the people to repent. Spiritual reconciliation and restoration is the business of the prophets. A regular image for this is standing in the gap or breach (see Ezek 13). The people are a city, and their sin has torn a hole in the wall. Yahweh's fury charges through the breach like an enemy, and so the prophet must stand in the breach to repair it. The prophet builds with the bricks of repentance and the mortar of God's kindness. Just as Moses interceded for mercy in the face of sin (Exod 32) and Samuel interceded for God's help against the Philistines (1 Sam 7), so the prophets seek to sustain the covenant relationship by the lifegiving steadfast love of the Lord.

Yet as is obvious, the people are not very fond of repentance. They refuse to be humbled; sin is more natural to them than obedience. Hence, judgment is necessary. The justice of the holy Lord has to be upheld. In fact, with both Jeremiah and Ezekiel, the Lord prohibits any further intercession. The Lord orders these two that they cannot pray for the people any more, but can only herald the devastation to come. As any reading of the prophets bears out, judgment takes up the most airtime. The prophets, then, vindicate the Lord's holiness and righteousness by laying out how he keeps his covenant in pouring out the curses for sin.

In summary, modeled on the paradigm of Moses, the prophets are the Lord's emissaries sent from his heavenly council to proclaim his word to the people. They intercede for the people to God. They prosecute the law of the covenant against sin and rebellion. The Lord chooses his prophet from among the Israelites. And their word is truly the Lord's word, which will surely come to pass.

PROPHETIC IMAGERY
AND TYPOLOGY

The second factor in growing accustomed to the prophetic dialect is growing familiar with their imagery and how they use it to forecast the great salvation to come in Christ. This is called *typology*. The prophets are famous, or maybe infamous, for their vivid images, earthy metaphors, and violent descriptions. The cup of wrath causes vomiting (Jer 25). Sheol, the land of the dead, is littered with heroes slain by the sword (Ezek 32). Locusts devour, the sun goes dark, lambs lie down with lions, and on and on. Westerners pair piety with PG ratings, but the prophets regularly delve into R-rated symbols and words. If given an honest, unvarnished reading, the prophets rattle us with a severe case of culture shock. Yet as was stated in a previous chapter, the greater the shock the more penetrating the benefits. In order to makes sense of the prophetic imagery, one must consider (1) the origin or source of the imagery and (2) the future fulfillment of their messages.

As to origin, the nature of the office is paramount. The prophet is a covenant spokesman. Therefore, the Mosaic covenant documents form the foundation of prophetic imagery. The prophets constantly quote, allude to, and echo the first five books of the Bible. It is fair to say that every prophetic sermon is a sermon on the law. This is why a thorough familiarity with Exodus, Leviticus, Numbers, and Deuteronomy is a prerequisite for understanding the prophets. The prophets were master students and teachers of the law. To get a grasp of how the prophets used the law, we will look at four parts of the covenant used by the prophets: stipulations, theophany, curses, and blessings.

But first, a quick note about the sociology of knowledge. The sociology of knowledge deals with the relationship between human thought and society. In terms of the prophets, it means their intellectual capacity is limited and shaped by the time and culture in which they lived and their period of redemptive history. Their language represents their world. The prophets do not speak like New Testament apostles, much less modern people. The truths they utter about future times and seasons are expressed in the imagery of their culture. Just as the Lord accommodated the law to the ancient Near Eastern context, so the prophets share much in common with their ancient neighbors. Therefore, we should not be bothered by the fact that the prophets use much of the language, ideas, and imagery of the surrounding nations. Just as modern preachers might use modern movies as illustrations, so these ancient preachers had no quibble borrowing from the myths and politics of their larger culture.

STIPULATIONS

The most obvious use of the Mosaic law by the prophets are the laws or stipulations themselves. Sin is defined as the lack of conformity or transgression of God's law. The law is the moral standard by which the people are weighed and measured. The entire relationship between God and Israel is fractured due to their wickedness. Examples of this hardly need listing, but a few are helpful. As mentioned above in Hosea's covenant dispute in Hosea 4, prophets regularly refer to the Decalogue (so also Jer 7:9), but two infractions stand out: idolatry and murder.

From Isaiah's taunts against the stupidity of idolatry (Isa 40) to Ezekiel labeling them as fecal deities,[1] nearly every prophet denounced Israel and Judah for idolatry. Not only do the prophets have the first and second commandments in mind, but also passages like Deuteronomy 4, which stresses not making carved images. Particularly in Leviticus 18, Molech worship is prohibited and linked to Israel being vomited out of the land if they practice such wickedness. Indeed, idolatry stands out as the primary trigger for the covenant curses. The Lord casts his people out of his presence and even leaves the holy temple, because the people had profaned the sanctuary with their idols.

Murder is the other main sin of the people, but here we see how the commandments function as principles or summaries for a category of sin. The prophets use murder to cover all sorts of violence and injustice. And the language is that of bloodshed or filling the city with innocent blood. In Isaiah 5:7, the Lord looks for justice, but behold, bloodshed. Ezekiel says, "The land is full of blood, and the city full of injustice" (9:9). Micah and Amos lash out against the corrupt judges and priests who are quick to shed blood. Hosea calls Gilead a city of evildoers, tracked up with blood (6:8). And Ezekiel labels Jerusalem "the city of blood" (24:6–9). The imagery that prevails in this language arises not from the sixth commandment but from Numbers 35 and Deuteronomy 19 and 21. These passages speak about how innocent blood pollutes the land, and only the murderer's death can atone for this sin. Yet if Israel defiles the land, in which the Lord abides with his people, then he will cast them out. Bloodshed and violence, then, is the second key trigger for the full curse of exile.

THEOPHANY AND THE DAY OF THE LORD

Since judgment and wrath cover the oracles of the prophets, the character and color of this judgment cannot be overlooked. The prophets forecast the coming wrath as the coming of the Lord himself. The Lord will appear in his glory to condemn and destroy. In this way, the prophets speak about the revealing of the Lord, which refers to theophany. Yet the revealing of the Lord is also the coming of the Lord, which is known as the day of Yahweh, or day of the Lord.

The day of the Lord includes a complex avalanche of astounding events and deeds, the order of which is not always entirely clear from the prophets' point of view. Yet three main acts of the Lord will unfold: judgment on God's people, judgment on the nations/enemies, and the salvation of God's people (the remnant). Moreover, even though the day of the Lord is somewhat of a technical term for this day, the prophets regularly speak of this day without using the full phrase.

The imagery of the day of the Lord is unmistakable and terrifying. "Howl, for the day of the LORD is near … with pitiless fury and wrath to make the earth a desolation" (Isa 13:6–9, NJPS). It is a day of darkness and gloom, of densest cloud (Joel 2:2). This day of wrath rushes hastily forth as a day of trouble and distress, of calamity and desolation (Zeph 1:15). On this day of wrath and fury, the Lord stands as an enemy against his people (Lam 2:5). He marches out like a warrior; he rides forth in his chariot shooting his arrows of lightning (Hab 3:11). As the Almighty treads on mountains, creation is undone. The earth returns to being without form and void, the hills quiver, and all living things are no more (Jer 4:23–26; Joel 3:4). Yet where does all this paralyzing ruination come from? The first source is Sinai itself and the manner of the Lord's glory as he descended upon it. In Exodus 19, the mountain shakes, trumpets blast, and deep darkness and gloom enshroud the summit. The people cowered in terror (Deut 5:24–25). The Sinai theophany did not merely reveal the Lord's glory, but it also pictured the shape of wrath for failure to obey.

The second source for the day of the Lord comes from the Song of the Sea in Exodus 15, the Song of Moses in Deuteronomy 32, and the Song of the Ark in Numbers 10 (plus other passages). The motif of these passages displays the Lord as a divine warrior who marches or rides across the desert, armed with lightning, wind, and earthquake. So, in Exod 15, the Lord is a man of war, whose nostril blast piles up the waters (15:3, 8). "The LORD came from Sinai; he shone upon them from Seir ... lightning flashing at them from his right" (Deut 33:2, NJPS). Likewise, "O LORD, when you came forth from Seir ... the earth trembled ... the mountains quaked before the LORD, him of Sinai" (Judg 5:4–5, NJPS). As expected, artistic variation echoes between these poems, but the overall impression is the same: the Almighty marching as the divine warrior to judge and/or to save. Similarly, with their own unique style and manner of expression, the prophets pull from these images to paint the day of the Lord in terrifying colors. For example, where Deuteronomy 33 and Judges 5 speak of the Lord striding out of the south (Seir), Jeremiah reverses the direction to become the "foe of the north" (Jer 4), which he does to forecast the coming direction of the Lord's agent of destruction, Babylon.

CURSES

The third library of texts that the prophets use as source material for their preaching comes from the list of curses in Leviticus 26 and Deuteronomy 28. Drawing from these curses is not merely a matter of creativity but of justice. In the law, the Lord declared that he would curse his wicked people for disobedience. The curses laid out the just consequences for violating covenant stipulations. Hence, the execution of the curses vindicates the Lord as righteous and just, who is jealous for his holy name.

Moreover, within Leviticus 26 and Deuteronomy 28, a pattern of increasing intensity builds within the curses. If rebellion is found in Israel, the first wave of curses crashes with drought, disease, barrenness, and poverty. In this regard, a key dynamic of the covenant floats to the surface, which is the land as a spiritual barometer. The units of this barometric instrument are stated explicitly in Deuteronomy 11. If Israel obeys, the Lord will send rain, green fields, and many babes; but for disobedience, the Lord will lock the heavens tight, turn soil to rock, and dry up wombs (Deut 11:13–17). The Lord orders the natural processes of the weather according to Israel's performance. Drought and barrenness were calls of nature for Israel to repent. Therefore, a regular feature is the prophet as weatherman. They list how the land languishes, the vines droop, and the rains do not come.

If, however, Israel fails to repent, then a second wave of curses are let loose. Poverty and disease intensify and enemies invade. Cruel nations will enslave them, destroy their towns, and slaughter their young men. Like the enemies in the book of Judges, Israel will be oppressed and exploited by hard-faced nations. If unrepentance keeps growing, then national destruction will spring on Israel. The people will be besieged within the capital, where cannibalism and plague will spread like wildfire. After the city lies in ashes, the final wave of curses blows Israel like chaff in the wind, scattering them to the nations. Israel will be so miserable among the nations they will beg to be bought as slaves, but no one will purchase their sickly and frail bodies. The ultimate curse has landed. Israel is God-forsaken, without God and without hope in the world.

This crescendo of curses is what we have already seen in the book of Judges and in the history of 1–2 Kings. And this is a favorite topic of the prophets. A common motif of this curse is exhibited by de-civilization or the bustling town becoming a ghost town, a haunt for jackals. The normal sounds of life—wedding bells, the grinding mill, and kids in the street—will be muffled with pervasive death. Jeremiah regularly summarizes the curse with three terms: sword, famine, and plague (15:2; 21:9; 24:10), which Ezekiel also uses (6:11; 14:21), sometimes adding "wild beasts." Likewise, the prophets end at the same place as Leviticus 26 and Deuteronomy 28, with the burning of Jerusalem and the scattering of the people to the nations. Hosea closes nearly every one of his oracles with Israel being carried off to Assyria or Egypt (7:16; 8:13; 9:17; 10:15; 12:1). In Zephaniah, the Lord had prepared a sacrifice in Jerusalem, and it is the people (1:7–8). Ezekiel depicts the glory cloud departing from the profaned and blood-stained temple (Ezek 11). Habakkuk sees Babylon sweeping in to devour Judah upon horses as swift as eagles (1:8). Micah hears of Zion being plowed as a field, and Jerusalem becoming a heap of ruins (3:12). With one voice, all the prophets announce that the Lord is a God who keeps his word. The Lord will judge his people to show all nations that Yahweh is God and is holy.

BLESSINGS

The final source from which the prophets drink is the blessings that are primarily found also in Leviticus 26 and Deuteronomy 28. Yet the pattern that we saw back in chapter 4 that Israel was going to fail is important. The national anthem of Deuteronomy 32 sang of Israel's foregone exile. Israel's failure was certain. Judgment would come, but then after exile the Lord would gather his people to save them. The prophets, then, prosecuted the people for their rebellion; they forecasted the weather of curse; they beheld the day of the Lord judgment that would disperse his people like dust in a windstorm. But finally, they lifted the banner of hope in the Lord's gracious blessing of his people on the other side of exile.

The basic design of this future blessing is seen clearly in Isaiah 40. The Lord comes, gathers his scattered remnant, leads them back to the promised land in a second exodus march, judges the nations, and then plants his people in the land, where they will enjoy peace and security. A regular term for this salvation is "restore your fortunes." And an essential step in this trek home is dealing with sin. That is, the Lord will forgive his peoples' sins in a new and greater way. Out of fidelity to the promises of Abraham, the Lord will cast their sins into the depths of the sea (Micah 7:19). Yahweh will not merely forgive their sin, but even forget it (Isa 43:25). And the new heart created in the people by God will be able to please and obey him in love (Ezek 36:25–27).

Yet the numerous decorations of this basic design lift the blessings to new and higher places. Jeremiah sees a new and better covenant that will be unbreakable (Jer 31), where the king whose name is "Yahweh Is Our Righteousness" will reign (Jer 23). Micah sees this king coming from Bethlehem to shepherd the people in the very majesty of the name of the Lord (5:2–4). Likewise, Ezekiel predicts an everlasting covenant where a people with newly formed hearts will dwell with the Lord forevermore (Ezek 37:24–28). Yet what stands out about these future blessings is how idyllic and other-worldly they sound. Hosea likens Israel to an evergreen cedar of Lebanon that blossoms like the vine (14:5–7). The cedars of Lebanon are not fruit-producing, so for Israel to be a fruitful cedar is a new species. Micah speaks of Zion being the tallest mountain to which all nations shall flow (Mic 4). Ezekiel pictures a river of life flowing from the new temple and lined with every kind of tree (Ezek 47). Isaiah's images of peace and safety can only be described as a new heavens and new earth (Isa 66:22). The grandeur of the blessings take flight from the earthly plane and soar heavenward into glory.

TYPOLOGY

With the foundation laid concerning the office of prophet and source of their imagery, the vista of fulfillment comes into focus. This vista is monopolized with the day of the Lord and its three basic parts: judgment of Israel, judgment of nations, and salvation for Israel. In the exile, Israel was judged, so this box is checked—so they thought. Yet after exile, when Israel gets the land and temple back, the other two did not really occur. The nations were not judged. And Israel's salvation was lackluster compared to the glory that the prophets

NT Fulfillment: Christ's Work

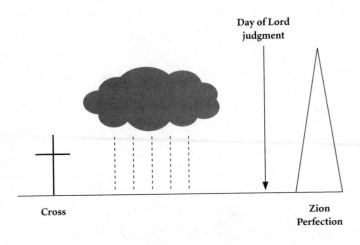

OT Prophets: Their Perspective

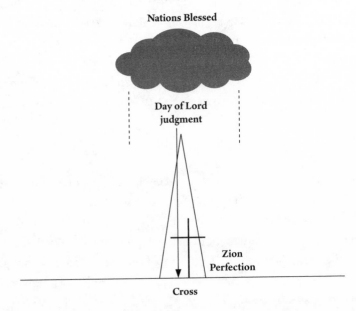

The time perspective of the prophets compared to the New Testament fulfillment

foretold—no new Davidic king. The prophets made it sound like all three parts of the day of the Lord happened together at about the same time, but as history unfolded, this was not so.

This brings us to the New Testament, where we see clearly the prophets fulfilled. As is shown opposite, the New Testament paints the promises of the prophets fulfilled in two major events. First, Jesus Christ comes as the true, righteous Davidic King, but he comes first to deal with sin on the cross. In his death and resurrection, Jesus won for us perfect forgiveness and justification. In his first coming, Christ inaugurated his kingdom in the salvation of sinners. After this, in the church age, the Spirit endows God's people to go forth to preach the gospel to the nations. Finally, in the Father's perfect timing, Christ will return in his second coming to judge the wicked nations and to raise his people to the heavenly Mount Zion of the new heavens and new earth. The Old Testament prophets gazed at the day of the Lord face on, so the events seemed simultaneous. The New Testament, however, gives us a profile perspective that reveals the distance in between them. As Peter remarked above, the prophets could not figure out the timing of the sufferings of Christ and the subsequent glory.

A SURVEY OF THE PREEXILIC PROPHETS

As we grow in familiarity and knowledge about the prophets, we cannot content ourselves with generalities. As necessary and helpful an overview is, the prophets love the particular, the idiosyncratic. The prophets are a creative bunch; they are the rhetorical artists of Scripture. Within the overall pattern laid out above, any particular oracle of a prophet will speak with its own voice and perspective. Not only does the accent of one prophet differ from another, but a prophet can change his tone, manner, and perspective from oracle to oracle. The pattern is simply a guide; it is elastic and stretchy. Therefore, we must be equally open and flexible in our reading. We need to respect the individual personality, time, and place of each prophet and get to know their books like the unique persons who wrote them. This summary, then, is intended as an introduction, helping you put faces to names so you can return later for more quality time. (Note: The prophets surveyed in this chapter will include only the preexilic prophets. The exilic prophets Jeremiah and Ezekiel and the postexilic prophets Haggai, Zechariah, and Malachi will be reserved for the following chapter.)

Prophets to Israel	Prophets to Judah
Jonah: during Jeroboam II's reign: 791–750	
Amos: during Jeroboam II's reign: 791–750	
Hosea: 750s—714?	Isaiah: 730s–701?
	Micah: 740s–714?
Destruction of North: 722	
	Nahum: 663–612 (window of ministry)
	Joel: no date; temple standing
	Jeremiah: 627–580s?
	Daniel: 605–539
	Habakkuk: 620s–600s
	Zephaniah: 620s–590s
	Ezekiel: 593–571
	Destruction of Jerusalem: 586
	Obadiah: 580s, post-destruction
	Decree of Cyrus: 538
	Zechariah and Haggai: 520–518
	Temple rebuilt: 515
	Malachi: postexilic, 500–450?

Table 4: Prophets to Israel and Judah
Dates with a "?" are uncertain, and "s" are rough.
Specific dates are used only when the oracle is dated by the prophet.

Jonah

One can safely posit that Jonah is the best-known minor prophet. Those raised in the church were wowed by his trip in the fish's belly. Even in pop culture, people catch references to Jonah. However, Jonah's modern popularity is somewhat ironic considering his relative obscurity in Scripture. Other than his book, we are given only one brief verse on Jonah in 2 Kings 14:25. Here we learn that Jonah had a ministry in the northern kingdom of Israel, prophesied about a border being restored to Israel, and was from Gath-hepher. Prophets are all about preaching, but Jonah is sermon-less. We know nothing about his words to Israel, and even though his preaching to Nineveh is reported, no transcript of his words is recorded. The most we find bubbles up in his prayer from inside the belly of the fish. Moreover, the story we do have concerning Jonah exposes him as having a bad attitude and resistant to the Lord. If any prophet of Israel could be buried in the sands of history, Jonah would be a prime candidate. Yet in the Lord's wise providence, he preserved Jonah as canonical, which means the book is profitable for our faith.

The time and place of our life molds us into who we are, and Jonah is no exception. Jonah lived and worked during the reign of Jeroboam II (791–750 BC), which was a season of relative peace and significant prosperity. The kindness of God allowed for Jeroboam II to restore the borders of the northern kingdom nearly to where they were under Solomon. Additionally, as we learn from Amos, the wealth of the north trampled the poor and outcasts. Hypocrisy aside, it was a good time to be an Israelite. This patriotism, however, was fueling a growing danger. The Assyrian Empire was winning battle after battle, solidifying its grip in the north and east, and it was starting to look south toward Palestine. It took no prophet to see that this foe would soon be on Israel's doorstep.

It is this setting that makes sense of Jonah's foul mood and outright prejudice. The Lord is extending mercy to the horrible Assyrians? No way! If the Lord told Jonah to preach judgment, he would have run to obey, but mercy sent him in the opposite direction. Hence, in Jonah we see our ugly tendencies to hoard God's grace for ourselves, our preference to see others judged rather than saved, and our resistance to the generosity of the Lord. In Jonah's pouting pride, he is exposed as no better than the violent Assyrians. Yet by a death and resurrection experience, the Lord's power to save extends even to the most undeserving.

Amos

The sheepherder of Tekoa never guessed that the Lord would pull him away from the flock and figs to be a prophet. But, when the Lord calls, you answer. Therefore, in the days of Jeroboam II (791–750 BC), Amos relocated from his little village in Judah to preach against the sins of Israel in the north. This places Amos as the contemporary of Jonah and within the prosperity that Israel enjoyed under Jeroboam II. Indeed, as Amos exposes, the wealth of Israel did not prosper it religiously but actually left it spiritually bankrupt.

Amos opens with the Lord roaring from Zion. The Lord's courtroom is in session to render justice. At first, the Lord roars against the evils of the surrounding nations: Damascus, Gaza, Tyre, Edom, Ammon, Moab, and even Judah. These rather brief woes, however, give way to an extended one, spanning 2:6 to 9:10. It begins, "For three transgressions of Israel, and for four, I will not revoke the punishment" (2:6a). The first mentioned is that "they sell for silver the righteous, and the needy for a pair of sandals" (2:6, my translation). This sin is repeated twice in Amos and in a sense it embodies what is rotten in Israel. If one could not repay a loan, the lender could foreclose and recoup his losses by selling the debtor into slavery. The law prohibited such a practice against fellow Israelites, but it was permitted with foreigners. Yet to sell the poor for a pair of sandals means the loan amount was the price of sandals. In modern terms, for a debt of $30, the rich sold the poor into slavery at likely a much higher price.

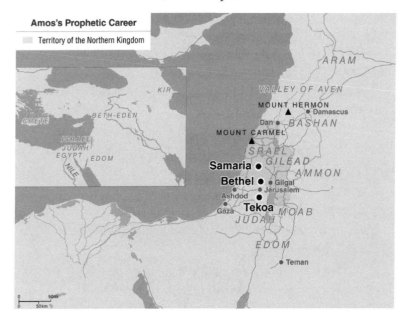

The widespread idolatry and recalcitrant wickedness of Israel, then, must be punished. The people refuse to repent, so the bitter day of wrath will not be turned away. The Lord has given a command to shake Israel among the nations. Israel will be joggled as one shakes a sieve, but not a pebble will fall to the ground. "All the sinners of my people shall die by the sword" (9:10). From beginning to end, Amos is an unrelenting message of sin and judgment. In fact, there is only one oracle of salvation that is tacked on as a conclusion. After the ruin of Israel, the Lord will restore the fortunes of his people, and he will do so by raising up the fallen booth of David. Salvation for the north will come through the royal house in the south.

Hosea

Hosea begins his work in the peaceful time of Jeroboam II, but the bulk of his ministry appears to play out in the turbulent decades before Samaria's destruction in 722. The opening verse even places Hosea at work during the reign of King Hezekiah in Judah, which means he may have ministered some after Israel's demise. This also makes sense of his several references to Judah as being no better than the north.

The prophet Hosea will always receive the award for having the marriage from hell. The Lord ordered him to take a wife of whoredom, which meant Gomer already had a bad reputation for sleeping around. Not surprisingly then, after their nuptials, the text makes clear that Hosea is the father of his firstborn son, Jezreel, but the text is ambiguous about the paternity of the daughter and second son. Hosea even names his daughter "Not-Loved" and his son "Not-My-People." Imagine if your dad named you not-loved or not-mine. Hosea seems convinced that he is not the father.

This rough family life, though, is a symbolic act. It pictures the covenant reality between God and Israel. Like Gomer, Israel has fornicated with other gods and she has given birth to children that are not God's. Israel's straying nature refuses to be corrected. Therefore, the names of the children are prophetic of judgment. Jezreel forecasts a swift end to the monarchy in Israel. Not-Loved portends of the Lord's judging without mercy, pardon, or compassion. And Not-My-People seals the Lord disowning and forsaking Israel for good. Yet the deaths of Gomer and the children set up a greater salvation on the other side of judgment. The Lord will raise his people up from the ground; he will remarry his people and reverse their names to "Loved" and "My-People." Judgment comes in death, but salvation in resurrection. And this motif of dying in exile and new life on the other side echoes throughout Hosea.

Isaiah

The New Testament authors draw on Isaiah more than any other prophet, likely for its abundance of references to Christ. Also, amid all the breathtaking poems in the Old Testament, the Pulitzer goes to Isaiah, whose poetic skill is unmatched. Scholars liken Isaiah to the Shakespeare of the Old Testament.

The ministry of Isaiah unfolded in the southern kingdom, mostly in Jerusalem. In chapter 8, we are informed that Isaiah was married to the prophetess and has at least two sons who are given prophetic names. His first son is Shear-jashub, meaning "a remnant will return"—a promise that a faithful minority will survive the destruction and exile. Isaiah's second boy is Maher-shalal-hash-baz, meaning "quick to booty, speedy to the spoil"—a portent of Assyria's quick destruction of northern Israel. Tradition held that Isaiah was related to the house of David. Though this cannot be confirmed, Isaiah does appear to hail from nobility with access to the royal court.

The first event dated in the book is the year that Uzziah died (736 BC), though Isaiah was likely ministering before this, and the final date comes with Sennacherib's siege of Jerusalem in 701. How long Isaiah ministered after the siege is unclear, but this establishes a rough window for his prophetic work. It also means that Isaiah was ministering during the fall of Samaria and the end of the northern kingdom.

There is no easy way to summarize the massive riches of Isaiah's book, but several themes stand out. Besides announcing the certain doom coming on Jerusalem for their violation of the Mosaic covenant, Isaiah paints the brightest eschatological picture on the other side. Four elements comprise this portrait. First, the Lord will usher his once forsaken people back to the promised land in a new exodus. The people will mount up with wings like eagles, and the Lord will make rivers spring up in the desert. Second, the servant of the Lord, who takes up the Davidic mantle, ushers in a new covenant for the people both through his suffering and his heralding good news. Third, the justice and righteousness of the servant of the Lord will be a light to the nations so that all nations will flow into Zion. Fourth, the blessings poured forth are nothing short of new creation, when death is swallowed up forever and the last tear is dried. The vision of Isaiah beheld Christ's greater exodus salvation, the church age, and the everlasting glory of heaven itself. The doomsday of wrath plummeted into the depths of Sheol, but the Lord's redemption of his peoples resurrects them to the undying fields of Zion.

Micah

The window for Micah's ministry spans the reigns of Jotham, Ahaz, and Hezekiah, which extends from 750 to 686 BC. Other than these kings, it is difficult to pinpoint any historical material in Micah, save the fall of Samaria. Micah's ministry served primarily the southern kingdom of Judah, but his opening oracle describes Samaria being plowed into farmland for vineyards. Once the dust settles on Samaria, Micah focuses his preaching on Judah, with the painful conclusion that the wound of Samaria will come to Jerusalem. The south will not escape the same cursed fate. In addition to idolatry, the prophet sets his sights especially upon the rulers, judges, and priests. Those in authority devour the flesh of the Lord's people. Just as Samaria was plowed, so Zion will be tilled up into a heap of ruins.

The certainty of judgment, though, is not the end of the story. As we saw in the law, curse was inevitable, but greater salvation would dawn. Hence, in the latter days, Zion will arise as the highest of mountains, nations will stream toward the Mount of the Lord, and God's people will never know war again. A shepherd king will hail from the little town of Bethlehem, and a remnant will be preserved through woe to be forgiven and brought back in love, just as the Lord promised to Abraham.

Joel

Locating Joel on the timeline of Judah is a problem that has yet to be solved. In fact, Joel has a reputation for being "notoriously undatable."[2] Safely, we can say that Joel's ministry serves Judah and most likely is located in Jerusalem. The temple is standing as Joel calls for a national assembly of repentance in the house of the Lord. Two images are pronounced within Joel's preaching.

First, as he broadcasts the coming day of the Lord, he colors the devastation as an overwhelming locust plague: "What the cutting locust left, the swarming locust has eaten. What the swarming locust left, the hopping locust has eaten" (1:4). Before the horde, the land is like the garden of Eden, but behind them, a desolate waste—nothing escapes (2:3). Sun and moon will be darkened before the great and terrible day of the Lord comes.

Second, the terror of the curse is balanced by the glory of the blessing afterwards. The Lord will restore what the locusts gobbled up. He will pour out his Spirit on all flesh, and God's people will never again be put to shame. As we have seen with the other prophets, the grandeur of God's salvation far exceeds earthly realities and rises to heavenly ones.

Nahum

Our knowledge concerning Nahum is confined to the opening line of his book, Nahum the Elkoshite, which is a town of uncertain location. Moreover, his oracle deals with Nineveh the capital of Assyria. As far as we know, this does not mean Nahum traveled to Nineveh, as did Jonah; rather, his word was preached to Judah, but its topic was the fall of Nineveh. Indeed, with grim detail, Nahum condemns Nineveh as the blood city, full of violence, where the killing never stops and the bodies pile up without number. For its love of murder, the Lord will repay Nineveh in kind. Fire will devour, the sword will finish her off, and her wound will be incurable. In 3:8, Nahum compares Nineveh's coming ruin to the demolished Thebes, which gives us a window for Nahum. Thebes fell to Assyria in 663 BC, and Nineveh was laid waste by Babylon in 612; hence, Nahum prophesied between these events.

This timeline helps clarify Nahum's pastoral effect on the Judeans. During the reigns of Manasseh and Amon, Judah suffered much at the hands of Assyria. In fact, the boy king Josiah was put on the throne to turn Judah away both from idols and their hated enemy of Assyria.

As the Assyrian wounds fester and leak puss in Judah, Nahum's forecast of destruction soothes like a balm for God's people. As he says, "The LORD is good, a stronghold in the day of trouble; he knows those who take refuge in him" (1:7). The Lord will work vengeance for his people. The destruction of your enemy amounts to a salvation for you, a restoration of the pride of Jacob (2:3).

Habakkuk

The personal information that we possess on Habakkuk is quite slim. The opening verse relays nothing about his father's name, his city of origin, or what king was on the throne. All that is preserved for us is his name and his book. Yet from his words, a rough historical setting emerges, as the Lord mentions how the Chaldeans are coming to destroy Judah. The book, then, dates before Jerusalem's fall in 586. In addition, Habakkuk seems well acquainted with the Babylonian war machine, which was put into production in the 620s BC with the rise of Nabopolassar, king of Babylon and Nebuchadnezzar's father. Less clear is if Habakkuk received this oracle before or after the fall of Nineveh in 612. Either way, this safely puts Habakkuk's ministry between 620 to somewhere in the 590s.

The oracle that Habakkuk saw consists of two complaints against the Lord. In the first complaint, the prophet protests that the law in Judah is numb and that justice does not go forth. How long can the Lord allow injustice to run wild? The Lord must do something. And he does, responding with a decisive judgment. The Lord is releasing the war steeds of the Chaldeans to swoop in and devour the wicked rebels of Judah. The dreaded Babylonian sword will be the Lord's agent of justice.

This reply, however, does not satisfy Habakkuk, so he retorts with a second complaint. "O Lord, we should not die!" (Hab 1:12, my translation). The Lord is too holy and pure to allow a violent man to swallow up a man more righteous than he. Babylon offers sacrifices to its war net by which it fishes the nations (Hab 1:16). Judah is bad, but Babylon is worse. The worse cannot punish the bad. Habakkuk must get an answer from the Lord. Yet in the Lord's second response, Habakkuk is told to wait. The Lord's word will come to pass; if it seems slow, wait for it.

When it comes, the word of the Lord consists of five woes against Babylon. Babylon will destroy Jerusalem, but the Lord will punish Babylon afterwards. After this, the prophet closes with a prayer of submission and confidence, in which he describes the holy terror of the Lord marching forth as the divine warrior. Habakkuk trembles, and rottenness enters his bones at the sound of the Almighty. And yet even though the fig does not blossom and the flocks are cut off—curse hems him in all around—the prophet will rejoice in the Lord and take joy in the God who delivers him (3:17–18). The day of the Lord must come, but Habakkuk will wait in faith for the salvation on the other side.

Zephaniah

The reign of Josiah (640–609 BC) is concurrent with the ministry of Zephaniah, who himself was likely of royal blood, as his genealogy traces back four generations to Hezekiah. Despite the pious reforms of Josiah and God's extension of mercy, Zephaniah trumpets the day of the Lord. The Lord has consecrated a sacrificial feast in Jerusalem, and who is the animal for slaughter? The officials and the king's sons! The people are the burnt offering going up in smoke. The utter demolition of this day of wrath filled with darkness and calamity will consume the whole land. A terrible end has been decreed.

Yet concerning the day of the Lord, Zephaniah shares a theme with his fellow prophets, namely that after the wrath comes on Jerusalem it will spill over into the nations. As with Nahum and Habakkuk, there is comfort for God's people to witness their foes punished for their crimes against Judah. Nevertheless, the pitch darkness of the day of the Lord does not eclipse the rising of grace. After the night of wrath, the Lord will turn the grief of his people into dancing. The Lord will dwell in their midst so that they never fear again, and he will restore their fortunes to remove their shame forever.

Obadiah

The final prophet to be surveyed in this chapter is Obadiah, who is another prophet that we know next to nothing about. No father, king, or place modifies him. Two words in Hebrew identify this brief book: "the vision of Obadiah." Additionally, like Nahum, this oracle does not aim at Israel or Judah, but at Edom. The origins of Edom date back to Esau in Genesis, which is why it is considered a brother nation.

Obadiah condemns Edom's pride and violence and publicizes the day of the Lord coming upon the house of Esau. These crimes against Judah were perpetuated on the day of her ruin and calamity, when foreigners cast lots for Jerusalem. We know that foreign mercenaries aided Babylon in the siege and burning of Jerusalem in 586. Mostly likely, then, at this time Edom came up to kick Judah while she was down and pridefully gloat over her misfortune (vv. 10–14). This would locate Obadiah's ministry after the destruction of Jerusalem.

Yet even if the subject of this oracle belongs to Edom, the primary audience still resides with God's people. Not only will the exiles of Judah see the Lord avenge their enemies, but in the latter days the Lord's kingdom will possess Mount Esau, and the exiles will dwell both in their land and the land of Edom. After judgment, the boarders of the new promised land will encompass even the borders of Edom.

The Lord will restore the fortunes of his people and grant them even more than they could ever imagine.

STUDY QUESTIONS

1. What is the prophetic idiom?

2. What are the functions of the prophetic office?

3. Describe some of the scenes when prophets stood in the heavenly council and received their call.

4. What were the four parts of the covenant that the prophets chiefly used for typology?

5. Discuss how typology worked for the prophets.

6. How does the historical context make sense of Jonah fleeing the Lord?

7. How does Obadiah's oracle against Edom help God's people?

8

EXILE AND RETURN

**Bible Reading:
Jeremiah, Ezekiel, Daniel, Lamentations,
Ezra, Nehemiah, Esther, Haggai, Zechariah**

When it comes to the past, we must confess that our memories keep poor records. As the saying goes, the single greatest contributor to the good old days is a bad memory. When age sets in, we dream of the long, youthful days of summer, but our teenage journal would read of complaints, frustrations, and the desire to grow up. At funerals, we swear in our obituaries to never forget, yet dementia can erase our most indelible loved ones. Nevertheless, some events are so significant that they burn forever in our memory. If you are old enough, you likely remember exactly where you were when you first heard of the assassinations of John F. Kennedy or Martin Luther King, Jr., or when you saw the footage of 9/11. The vividness of commercial jets slamming into the Twin Towers does not dull with time.

For the Israelites of old, it was the exile that marked forever their national memory. Two dates bookend this cataclysm. The Lord issues the first date to Ezekiel, January 15, 588 BC (Ezek 24:1–2). The British may remember the fifth of November, but the Judeans were never to forget the day Babylon began its siege of Jerusalem. After about two and a half years of starvation and plague, Babylon breached the city walls in July 586, and the temple was burned on August 14, 586. Due to a discrepancy between biblical dates, the rabbis set the day of remembrance two days later, the ninth of Ab.[1] To this day, both are days of mourning and fasting for the Jews. But there is good reason why this catastrophe of wrath should also be part of the identity of the church: the theology enshrined in this historical event is near and dear to our faith in Christ Jesus.

What was Jerusalem's destruction and the exile? As we have seen, the exile belongs to the ultimate curse of the Mosaic covenant. In the curses, the Lord displays the wages of sin. In Romans, we read the wages of sin are death, but this is not death as end of existence. Rather, what Paul means by death is teased out by the curses of the Old Testament. Hence, the curses of Deuteronomy 28 do not conclude with the extinction of Israel, but with the exiles being lost among the nations, without God and without hope—a fate worse than physical death. There Moses speaks about Israel being scattered to the four winds, where they are forced to worship other gods. In their rebellion, Israel could not keep their fingers off the worthless idols, but in exile, wood and stone statutes are all they have left. Moreover, the exiles will seek peace to no avail. Their despondent spirit will shiver in fear day and night. At sunrise they will long for evening, and at sunset they will dream of morning. So desperate will the exiles become that they will offer themselves as male and female slaves. For the slightest bit of security, they will auction themselves off in the slave market, but there will be no buyer (Deut 28:64–68). Not a single person will drop a penny on the ugly, frail exiles. This is the just punishment for sin.

The book of Lamentations explores Zion's destruction with harrowing detail. The entire book is a communal lament consisting in five chapters of alphabetic acrostics.[2] Yet Lamentations analyzes exile through the lens of the day of the Lord, which is especially pronounced in chapter two. In the burning of the city, the Lord clouds Zion in his wrath. He remembers not mercy but lays waste without pity. The Lord ravages Jacob like a flaming fire; his bow bends to kill.

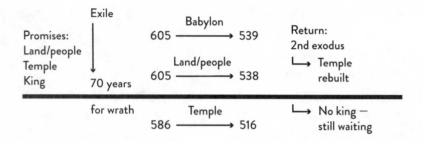

Chart 7: Exile & Return

He pours out ruin and destruction on every citadel and stronghold;
mourning spreads like a plague. The Lord forgets his appointed feasts;
he ends festival and Sabbath. King and priest are spurned. Altar and
temple are rejected and profaned. The law is no more, and no prophet
receives a vision (Lam 2:1–9). Every precious treasure of the covenant that marked Israel off as the Lord's has been burned up by the
fires of fury. On this day of the Lord, Israel suffers the punishment
of being God-forsaken.

Additionally, the agonies of destruction and exile are laid out as
the just payment for Israel's violations of the covenant stipulations.
This payment aspect surfaces in many different places and ways, so
just a few will be mentioned. First, in 2 Kings when Assyria laid waste
to Israel, the narrator tells us, this happened "because they did not
obey the voice of the LORD their God but transgressed his covenant,
even all that Moses the servant of the LORD commanded. They neither listened nor obeyed" (2 Kgs 18:12). In other words, Israel got
what they deserved. And as with the north, so with the south. Second,
one of the features of Ezekiel is his use of the recognition formula,
"then they/you will know that I am Yahweh." Yet the vast majority of
its occurrences results from the Lord's punishments. For example, "I
will punish you according to your ways … then you will know that I
am the LORD" (Ezek 7:9). The people's learning vindicates the Lord's
justice. Third, specific passages explicitly name the exile as satisfying
justice. In Ezekiel, the Lord speaks about "finishing his wrath" and

"I will get satisfaction" (Ezek 5:13; 7:8; 16:42; 21:17; 20:8, 21). Similarly, through Jeremiah the Lord says, "I will chastise you for justice; I will by no means leave you unpunished" (30:11, my translation). And this statement falls within a context of the Lord saving his people in the end. Likewise, Isaiah remarks about how the Lord will speak tenderly to Jerusalem "for her iniquity has been paid,[3] for she received the equiva-

KINGS OF THE NEO-BABYLONIAN EMPIRE

Nabopolassar 626–605

Nebuchadnezzar 605–562

Evil-Merodach 562–560

Neriglissar 560–556

Labasi-Marduk 556

Nabonidus 555–539

lent for all her sins" (Isa 40:2).[4] The point of this verse is that the punishment of Jerusalem must be paid in full before the tender mercy of the Lord can be spoken.

Finally, the satisfaction of justice of the exile comes out by the motif of the holiness of the land and the repaying of Sabbaths. In Leviticus 18, the Lord said if Israel defiles the land by practicing the abhorrent ways of its previous inhabitants, then the land will vomit Israel out just as it spewed out the Amorites. Infecting the land with sin makes it sick; sickness leads to puking—exile. Then, in Leviticus 26, once the people are dispersed, the Lord says, "I will make the land desolate … then the land shall be paid its sabbaths … the land shall rest and pay off its sabbath years"[5] (see Lev 26:33–34). The justice of God gets paid by the fallow land for the sins that stained it. As Jacob Milgrom states, "The justice of God decrees that Israel must repay the land for its lost sabbaticals."[6] And the Chronicler borrows this motif as a conclusion for his two-volume work: "to fulfill the word of the Lord by the mouth of Jeremiah, until the land had enjoyed its Sabbaths. All the days that it lay desolate it kept Sabbath, to fulfill seventy years" (2 Chron 36:21). As with the other passages, then, the necessity of exile arises from the demands of the Lord's holiness and justice. And with the quenching of the last drop of wrath, then the flood gates of mercy can be thrown open.

Fall of 605	First year of Nebuchadnezzar, fourth of Jehoiakim; first deportation (Daniel)
March 597	Nebuchadnezzar captures Jerusalem; second deportation (Ezekiel)
Oct 597	First regnal year of Zedekiah
Jan 588	Jerusalem siege begins
Oct 588	Jubilee proclaimed
Dec 588–Feb 587	Siege broken; slaves recaptured
July 586	Jerusalem breached
Aug 586	Temple and city burned; third deportation
581	Fourth deportation
Oct 539	Cyrus enters Babylon without a fight
Mar 538	First regnal year of Cyrus; decree of Cyrus for return
Fall 520	Second year of Darius; temple building restarts
March 516	Sixth year of Darius; temple finished
479	Seventh year of Xerxes; Esther becomes queen
458	Seventh year of Artaxerxes; Ezra arrives in Jerusalem
445	Twentieth year of Artaxerxes; Nehemiah arrives in Jerusalem

Table 5: Exilic and Postexilic Chronology

THE SEVENTY YEARS

There is one more important element of exile with regard to Sabbath repayment, which is its timespan of seventy years. We get this principally from Jeremiah 25. Jeremiah 25 dates to 605 BC, the first year of Nebuchadnezzar and the fourth year of Jehoiakim. Jeremiah announces that the Lord will use Nebuchadnezzar to exterminate the people and the whole land shall remain a desolate ruin. When seventy years are over, the Lord will punish the king of Babylon (Jer 25:11–12). The question, though, is when the seventy years begin.

Scripture points to several different answers, each with its value and point. To begin with, there is no necessity to understand the seventy years literally. The Hebrews regularly used numbers metaphorically, especially the number 7 and its factors. In Leviticus 26, the Lord declares four times that he will discipline or smite the exiles sevenfold (Lev 26:18, 21, 24, 28). This may even be Jeremiah's inspiration for the seventy years. Seventy, then, could be a stereotyped, approximate number, or it might signify complete justice. Yet the history and the prophets following Jeremiah point to three other options for understanding the seventy years: Babylon, the exiles, and the temple.

Babylon

In Jeremiah 25, the prophet links the seventy years to the life of Babylon. For seventy years the nations will serve the king of Babylon, and afterward, the Lord will make Babylon a desolation. Babylon fell to Persia in 539 BC. The dating of the rise of Babylon, however, does not come as easy. In 612, the capital of Nineveh fell to Nabopolassar. In 609, Babylon withstood the Egypt-Assyrian alliance at Haran. And in 605, Nebuchadnezzar drove the final nail into Assyria's coffin with a victory at Carchemish. Since Jeremiah 25 is dated to 605, this appears to be the most likely candidate, which would bring the lifespan of Nebuchadnezzar's Babylon to sixty-six years, a fitting approximation of seventy.

Exiles

When 2 Chronicles 36:22 and Ezra 1:1 refer to Jeremiah's seventy years, they pinpoint the fulfillment with Cyrus' proclamation for the exiles to return home. The decree of Cyrus was published in 538 BC during his first regnal year. Daniel also seems to locate this first year of Persia as the fulfillment of Jeremiah's seventy years (Dan 9:1–2).

This would mean the seventy years end when the Israelites return to the promised land, which makes their deportation its starting point. The exiles' exit and return also seem to be the natural reading of Leviticus 26:32–34. The departure of the people, however, unfolded over four deportations.

1. The first deportation occurred in 605 BC, when Nebuchadnezzar carted off a small group of the elites, including Daniel and his friends (2 Kings 24:1; Dan 1:2–4).

2. The second deportation registered as the largest in 597 BC, when Nebuchadnezzar squashed the rebellion in Jerusalem and exiled the educated officials and the highly skilled craftsmen in addition to King Jehoiachin. The numbers for this exile are given as ten thousand in 2 Kings 24:14 and as 3,023 in Jeremiah 52:28.[7] Ezekiel the prophet belonged to this group of exiles.

3. Once Jerusalem fell, Babylon carted off a third wave of exiles in 586 BC—much fewer due to fatalities of siege and war. Jeremiah records the tally of exiles as numbering a mere 832 people (Jer 52:29).

4. The final deportation happened in 582 BC, when another 745 Judeans were dragged off to Babylon by Nebuzaradan (Jer 52:30). Yet we have no further information about this deportation.

If the first wave of exiles started the march home in 538 with the decree of Cyrus, this locates the beginning of the seventy years with the first deportation in 605, coming in at sixty-seven years. The satisfying of justice counted the time that the people were away from the land exiled in Babylon.

Temple

The final measurement for the seventy years counts the decades of the temple lying in rubble. In Zechariah, the prophet receives a vision during which the angel of the Lord decries how long the curse on Israel has lasted (seventy years; Zech 1:12). This oracle is dated to the second year of King Darius of Persia in 520 BC. And the lifting of the seventy-year curse comes only with the rebuilding of Yahweh's house (Zech 1:16). The Judeans had been back in the land for nearly eighteen years, but the seventy years were not complete. Zechariah tying the seventy years to the temple also makes sense with the decree of Cyrus. In his decree, Cyrus both gave the exiles a passport home and a building permit for the temple. In fact, the temple rebuilding holds the place of higher importance: "The LORD, the God of heaven ... has charged me to build him a house at Jerusalem" (Ezra 1:2; 2 Chron 36:23). Therefore, under the leadership of Zerubbabel and Joshua the high priest, the temple was finished in 516 BC, which lines up with 586 BC right at seventy years.

The point of these different readings of the seventy years is to show how Scripture can find several layers of meaning. The same seventy years to satisfy justice can have multiple referents, and each referent makes its own point. For seventy years, the Lord judged the nations through Babylon, and then condemnation fell on Babylon. The land and the people belong at the heart of the covenant relationship with the Lord, so for seventy years God's people were banished from the land. The temple signified God's face shining upon his people; hence, the Lord hid his face in wrath for seventy years as dust and debris covered the temple mount. With each fulfillment of the seventy years, another aspect of justice was satisfied and sin paid for.

There is one more concept through which the exile is presented in Scripture. In Isaiah 61, the Spirit anoints the servant of the Lord in order to proclaim liberty to the captives. The phrase here for "proclaim liberty" is pulled directly from Leviticus 25:10, which is the unique announcement of Jubilee. And Jubilee both forgave all debts and returned the displaced Israelites back to their family plot of land. We know from Jeremiah 34 that in King Zedekiah's tenth year he made a covenant to proclaim Jubilee and to free all the Hebrew slaves. This proclamation, however, occurred during the Babylonian siege, the fall of 588 BC. Yet, when Babylon dropped the siege for three months to fight Egypt, Zedekiah and the other Judeans reneged on Jubilee to re-enslave their fellow Hebrews.[8] This confirms the year of 588 to 587 as a Jubilee year. And fifty years later, during another Jubilee year in 538, Cyrus published his decree to send the exiles back to the promised land, their covenantal inheritance. For fifty years, debts were paid in the land of exile, but when Jubilee dawned, the Lord sent his people home. Liberty from exile came to God's people.

The theology and history of exile, therefore, underscore that the wages of sin are indeed a God-forsaken death. The Lord was just and righteous in punishing his rebellious people. And once the debt of sin was paid, once wrath was satisfied, then the Lord would remember his promise to Abraham in order to show mercy and love that would bring his displaced people back to the land of promise and to himself. This design of exile further builds the stage for the ultimate fulfillment of these promises in Christ. In a real sense, Jubilee came to the Judean exiles in 538. Yet for Jesus, the decree of Cyrus did not satisfy the full realities of Jubilee. Hence, in that Nazarene synagogue, Jesus reads Isaiah 61 and closes the scroll to declare its fulfillment in him (Luke 4:17–21). Heavenly liberty will free those captives of sin, death, and the devil by the perfect sacrifice of Christ to satisfy justice once and for all and to offer the forgiveness of sin.

THE RETURN HOME

One might think that after exile, once the people got the land back, everything would be fine and dandy. The images of post-exilic salvation painted by the prophets were drenched in the idyllic colors of untold prosperity, peace, and righteousness. One cannot blame the returning exiles for having high expectations; in fact, faith in the promises demanded grand anticipations. The hard facts of history, though, spell out a lack-luster, disappointing story. As is expected, many of the details of the post-exilic chronology are murky and uncertain. Nevertheless, the overall flow of history is clear enough.

A few points are necessary to get us started. To begin with, the decree of Cyrus did not bring all the exiles home at once. There was not one march home but rather several larger waves of returning exiles mixed with a slow trickle of individuals. And many of the Judeans never relocated to the promise land but remained in Jewish communities scattered from Egypt to Asia Minor to modern day Iran, which became known as the Diaspora. Secondly, the arrangement of the book of Ezra is primarily thematic and not chronological, which is very typical of Hebrew narrative. For example, a letter from the

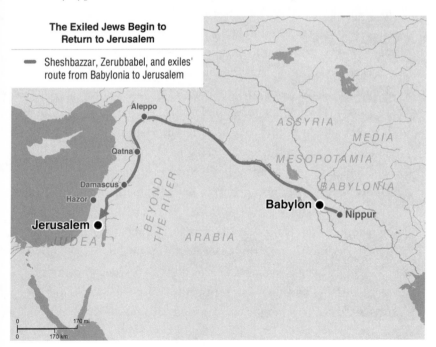

The Exiled Jews Begin to Return to Jerusalem

— Sheshbazzar, Zerubbabel, and exiles' route from Babylonia to Jerusalem time of Artaxerxes (465–424) is cut and pasted back into the days Cyrus (539–530) to show the kind of opposition that the Judeans faced (Ezra 4). Yet from several biblical books and Persian history, we can patch together a reliable history.

In 538, the decree of Cyrus put on the train the first group of return-ees, who were led by Sheshbazzar (Ezra 1:11), the first governor of Judea. Sheshbazzar's career remains obscure. In Ezra 5:16, he is cred-ited with laying the foundation for the new temple. Yet Ezra 3 gives credit to Joshua the high priest and Zerubbabel for the altar and foundation. The problem with this is that Joshua and Zerubbabel mainly operate in the days of Haggai and Zechariah in 520 and fol-lowing. It seems like Zerubbabel and Joshua are newer on the scene when the Lord sends Haggai and Zechariah. The following, then, is the probable scenario.

Sheshbazzar governed Judea and oversaw the altar and the foun-dation in the first years of return. Here, we already find disappoint-ment as the tears of the older generation mix with shouts of joy, as the new foundation paled in glory compared to those of Solomon (Ezra 3:12–13). Joshua and Zerubbabel are likely projected back into this scene.[9] Shortly after the foundation is finished, opponents push against the exiles and halt building efforts for the next 18 years (Ezra 4:4–5). Then, in the 520s, the Lord rouses the spirit of Joshua and Zerubbabel to restart the construction. Haggai says that "they came and worked on the house" (Hag 1:14). And Ezra 2:2 credits Zerubbabel as leading home a large number of Judeans. It is likely that Zerubbabel led a new group of exiles home and became the governor in the first two years of Darius' reign (522–520). With pro-phetic support from Haggai and Zechariah, Zerubbabel gets Tattenai to write a letter to King Darius to locate the original building permit for the temple issued by Cyrus. Darius finds Cyrus' decree and then gives permission and financial support to finish the temple. In 516, Darius' sixth year, the temple is completed and dedicated at Passover (Ezra 6:15, 19).

Once the temple has been rebuilt, Judea's history goes silent for the next fifty-eight years. This time is a possible window for the ministry of Malachi, as well as Esther's reign as queen of Persia (dating to Xerxes' time on the throne, 486–465). The affairs and welfare of Judea, though, are unknown. The chief question for this period lies with the wall. Was the wall of Jerusalem built and then torn down by Nehemiah's

KINGS OF PERSIA	
Cyrus II	539–530
Cambyses II	530–522
Darius I	522–486
Xerxes	486–465
Artaxerxes	465–424
Darius II	424–405

arrival in 445? Or was the wall never rebuilt? The account of Ezra's earlier work in Jerusalem that began in 458 does not mention the rebuilding of the wall. The simple truth is that we do not know. The letter to Artaxerxes in Ezra 4 does mention the finishing of the wall (Ezra 4:12), which the king stopped. Yet Artaxerxes must have changed his disposition about the wall, as he sent Nehemiah for this very purpose. Either way, the periods of Ezra and Nehemiah shed a bright light upon the mentality of the Judeans living within the tension of the prophetic promises.

THE MINISTRIES OF EZRA AND NEHEMIAH

The returning exiles arrived in the land of their fathers armed with the promises of Isaiah, Jeremiah, Ezekiel, and the other minor prophets. And the summary of their expectations can be added up as land, temple, kingship, and glory. The people would get the land back, the temple rebuilt, and a new Davidic king—and it would all be drenched in the riches of God's glory. In 538, the people were handed the land back, but it was a small slice of Solomon's domain. In 516, the temple returned to Jerusalem, yet it was tearfully small and unimpressive. These two grants were undeniable fulfillments by the Lord; however, where was the king? And where was the glory? A tension strained the people's faith. Yes, God kept his promises, but no, the fulfillments were not the entirety of the promises. Ezra and Nehemiah give us a view of this tension on the ground level.

In the seventh year of Artaxerxes (458), Ezra comes on the scene with impressive credentials. His genealogy traces a direct line back to Aaron himself, so he belongs to the priestly family. And Ezra bears the qualification of an expert scribe in the law of Moses (Ezra 7:6). He possessed everything he needed for the job before him. At the good pleasure of the king of Persia and the will of God, Ezra had been commissioned for a noble work in Jerusalem. After leading home a group of Judeans, which included priests, singers, temple servants, and a disappointing number of Levites, Ezra lands in Jerusalem with a letter from Artaxerxes. And this imperial order is very telling. By the edict of the king and his seven counselors, Ezra has two tasks. The first is to appoint magistrates and judges in the province Beyond the River and to put in order the law within Judea, which reflects the dual court system of Persia of imperial law and customary law. According to his wisdom, Ezra is to institute the law of the king of Persia and the law of his God (7:14). Ezra orders the people of Judea to heed the law of Artaxerxes and the law of God, which would have included the elaborate tax regulations.

This means Ezra the priest is also a Persian government official, something that would not have been permitted before the exile.[10] Pre-exile, for a priest to be in the employment of a foreign king would have amounted to treason. This rather anomalous situation reflects how Judea was no longer a sovereign nation, but a client state of the Persian empire. Additionally, the penalties to be meted out for crimes included death, corporal punishment, confiscation of possessions, or imprisonment (Ezra 7:26). These penal sanctions are Persian and not Israelite, since imprisonment and confiscation do not find a place in the Mosaic civil code.

Ezra's second task, however, entails the bringing of an offering to the temple on behalf of Artaxerxes and his advisors (7:15). A regular political policy of Persia consisted in royal gifts to local cults to secure the good will of the local population, which also could include tax-exempt status for the cult workers, as it is granted to the priests and Levites (7:24). For this reason, the king grants Ezra both monies and animals for an offering in Jerusalem and permits the Jews to take up whatever gold and silver they can find (7:16). Yet the poignant aspect of this rather common Persian policy surfaces in how Ezra understands it. Ezra adds an amen to Artaxerxes' letter by saying, "Blessed be the LORD, the God of our fathers, who put such a thing as this into the heart of the king, to beautify the house of the LORD" (7:27). By this phrase, "to beautify the house of the LORD," Ezra alludes to Isaiah 60, where it is found twice in reference to the wealth of the nations flowing in to adorn the temple (60:7, 13). Ezra believes that the Lord is fulfilling this wonderful promise from Isaiah in him. While acknowledging the Lord's fidelity to his word, at the same time Ezra thirsts for more glory, a greater fulfillment.

Once Ezra is on the ground in Jerusalem, he is confronted with the need for more. The bulletin comes in that the Israelites have not separated themselves from the foreign peoples, but have intermarried with them (Ezra 9:1–2). Ezra knows that intermarriage hatched the disaster of Baal-Peor in Numbers 25; it has been Israel's gateway drug into idolatry. Despondent and desolate, Ezra crumbles to his knees in confession. Amid his humble prayer, Ezra thanks the Lord for granting them a surviving remnant, a stake in his holy place, a brightening of their eyes, and a little reprieve in their bondage as slaves (Ezra 9:8–9). Describing their present state as slaves under Persia, in the very same breath Ezra admits the Lord's deliverance and their slavery, the need for more restoration. By this slavery, he does not mean that as individuals they were owned by a master; rather, as a nation, they were in servitude to Persia. Judea was not an independent nation with a king, but it paid taxes to the empire. In a real sense, Ezra beautified the temple along the lines of Isaiah 60. Yet Isaiah 60 painted Israel as master over other nations and not as being a slave to another nation. The true glory of Isaiah 60 was far from a reality for Ezra and his fellow Judeans. This was the tension in their faith and life after exile. They possess the land in part and enjoy a rebuilt temple, but the Davidic king is missing and there is no glory. When will the Lord rain down the full splendor of his prophetic promises?

Nehemiah, likewise, puts his own spin on this yearning for a greater fulfillment of God's promise. The curtain opens for Nehemiah in the twentieth year of Artaxerxes, which dates to 445, thirteen years after Ezra. Once his heart is torn by the news of Jerusalem's walls and gates, Nehemiah's prayer sets the table for the rest of the book. In his petition to God, he confesses both his sin and his fathers' before him, with an allusion to Solomon's prayer in 1 Kings 8. Next, his language borrows from both Deuteronomy 30:1–6 and Leviticus 26:40–46, where the Lord promised to bring his people home if they returned to him and kept his commandments. Finally, he adds a line from Deuteronomy 12, "bring them to the place that I have chosen, to make my name dwell there." (Neh 1:9). His hope is aimed at Israel dwelling in the place of the Lord's name. These three points pour the foundation for his request for success with regard to the wall.

In doing this, Nehemiah fashions two themes. First, he uses a term for the temple—the place of God's name—to refer to the entire city of Jerusalem and the shame of its rubble walls. Yet in times past, the limit of the sanctuary's sanctity was the temple wall, not the city wall. Nehemiah appears to expand the holiness of the temple to the whole of Jerusalem. Second, he stresses the conditional obedience of the people for the Lord to restore the full fortunes of his people. If the people repent and obey, then they will enjoy the place of his name. And Nehemiah takes this yoke upon himself to lead the people in obedience. Hence, he prays that Artaxerxes would grant permission to rebuild the wall (Neh 2:4–5). In short, Nehemiah believes that if he leads the people in obedience, then the full postexilic restoration will dawn, which is precisely what he labors to do in the rest of the book.

Nehemiah does not let the grass grow under his feet. Without delay, construction commences with a counterclockwise tour of the wall, starting in the north, down the west side, and back up the eastern border to end at the beginning. Yet the starting line sets the tone for the whole job. It is not Nehemiah who gets pride of place, but rather the high priest. Eliashib and his fellow priests build the Sheep Gate and consecrate it. To consecrate is to set apart as holy, and this consecration extends to the Towers of the Hundred and Hananel (Neh 3:1–2). This original consecration glues the whole wall together with the mortar of the holy. The wall is being raised as holy boundary, and the holy requires more than bricks. Therefore, Nehemiah's to-do list includes many other tasks.

In the middle of construction, the laborers and their wives cry out for food and debt relief. Their fellow Israelites have been practicing predatory lending, charging exorbitant interest rates and enslaving people when they cannot pay. Nehemiah fixes this with a functional Jubilee. He absolves the debts and returns the mortgaged property to their owners, and he prohibits the charging of interest, in line with the Mosaic law. Next, once the wall is completed after fifty-two days (Neh 6:6) and Nehemiah realizes how sparsely populated Jerusalem is, the Lord lays it on his heart to gather and enroll the people by genealogy, which begins a month of covenant renewal. All the people are gathered to celebrate the Day of Trumpets on the first day of the seventh month, when Ezra reads the scroll of the law of Moses to the people. On the fifteenth of the same month, the Feast of Booths is celebrated with great rejoicing. Finally, two days later, in a covenant assembly led by the Levites, the people confess their sin to the Lord (Neh 9) and renew the covenant to fully obey the Lord (Neh 10).[11] Raising the holy temple requires the covenant being in good working order.

The people living in Jerusalem, however, remain few in number, so lots are cast to bring one out of ten people into the capital (Neh

11). Leviticus identified the tithe as holy to the Lord (Lev 27:30). A tithe of the people, a sacred portion, moves into Jerusalem, which is explicitly labeled the holy city in Neh 11:1. And with the people nestled in their town-houses, now the final dedication of the wall can be celebrated. Nehemiah organizes this celebration into two choirs made up of Levites, priests, and other officials. The opening ceremony includes the purification of all the people as well as the gates and the wall (Neh 12:30). Starting on the west, these choirs parade on top of the wall, one heading south and the other north, singing and playing music as they go. They meet up on the eastern wall and finish this consecratory procession in the temple and with worship. This circumambulation consecrates as holy everything inside its perimeter and echoes David's bringing the ark to Jerusalem (1 Chron 15). Finally, Levitical officers are appointed over all the storerooms and contributions within the temple, according to the regulations of David.

Thus, the overall picture painted by Nehemiah is one in which the covenant, people, and Jerusalem are all set in holy order. The covenant has been renewed. A tithe of the people dwells in Jerusalem. The priests, the Levites, and the offerings are organized. The borders of holiness have been expanded from the temple to the whole city. Nehemiah has completed the repentance and obedience of the people, so the Lord's full restoration may rest on them as the morning dew. In fact, so many items have been checked off of Nehemiah's to-do list that one wonders what remains to be done.

Tucked away in all the names listed in Nehemiah, one that keeps popping up is David. The wall wrapped around the king's garden near to the tombs of David, but there was no king (Neh 3:15–16). The temple regulations all matched David's commandments, but there was no Davidic king. Sanballat accused Nehemiah of attempting to be a king (6:7), but Nehemiah rejected it fervently. Nehemiah forgave debts as kings do, but he refused tribute or tax from the people (5:18). Besides, there is no evidence to tie Nehemiah to the Davidic line. Nehemiah is not a priest, nor is he a king; he is a cupbearer to a Persian king. Yet he got everything ready for the king. Nehemiah is the steward who remembered the words of Zechariah, "Rejoice greatly, O daughter of Zion! ... Behold, your king is coming to you" (9:9). Hence, he closes his book by saying, "I cleansed them from every foreign element, ... O my God, remember it to my credit" (Neh 13:30–31, my translation). This book signs off with the steward waiting for the return of the king.

This is Nehemiah working out the tension between the fulfilled promises and those remaining to be fulfilled. His stance of faith embodies the life of the Judeans as they await the coming of Christ. Nehemiah is the last dated figure of the Old Testament.[12] He is the steward on the wall, watching the horizon for the procession of the king. They have the land, temple, and holy city, but without the glory of the king the pain of exile still throbs. As long as their taxes go to a foreign monarch (Neh 9:37), the glory of restoration remains unfulfilled. For the sins of the king, Judah was strewn among the nations; it will take the righteousness of a king to completely end its exile. Nehemiah served the people—and us—by preparing them to wait with the uplifted eyes of faith for the true Son of David to be born in Bethlehem.

THE EXILIC AND POSTEXILIC PROPHETS AND BOOKS

As was mentioned in the last chapter, a complete survey of the prophets was withheld for this chapter, since several of the prophets served during or after the exile. Furthermore, with the history of the exilic and postexilic period freshly set forth, theses prophets can be nestled more easily into their context.

Daniel

For many in the church, the book of Daniel has two faces. On the front side, the childhood stories of the fiery furnace and lion's den smile gently at you. On the back side, the obscure beasts and tyrants

of Daniel's visions growl you into a corner of confusion. The reconciliation of this split personality seems insurmountable, so we leave
face up the side we prefer. Yet the outline of Jeremiah's seventy years
given above constructs a frame upon which the whole book can be
stretched. To begin with, Daniel and his friends belong to the small
group of nobility that Nebuchadnezzar transferred to Babylon in his
first year (605). These were fine, young lads with the highest poten-
tial from the royal and noble families.

Once in Babylon, the best three-year education shapes these boys
for service to the crown. Over the next six chapters and seventy
years, Daniel remains loyal to the Lord alone, which nearly costs
him his life several times. He also faithfully serves Nebuchadnezzar
by interpreting his dreams, which all touch on the end of Babylon.
This is the first aspect to note about Daniel's first few interpreta-
tions and visions—they foretell the destruction of Babylon, which is
one purpose of the seventy years. Yet added to Babylon's demise are
the risings and fallings of other future empires. The future horizon
broadens to the great beyond. Then, in his prayer in the seventieth
year (Dan 9:1–2), the image of seventy years gets translated into the
seventy-weeks prophecy about the coming times.[13] In this way, the
seventy years becomes a type, a pattern for the events of the latter
days, both for Christ and his work, and even for the end of this age.
The theology of exile and restoration form the blueprint for understanding the salvation that will soon dawn.

Jeremiah

Considering how little we know about some of the other prophets,
the information we have for Jeremiah is considerable. He hails from
the town of Anathoth, which likely gave him a rearing and education
within a priestly family. When he was still a boy, in Josiah's thirteenth
year (627 BC), the word of the Lord first came to him, calling him to
be a prophet. Right from the start, the Lord warns Jeremiah that every
level of Judean society will oppose him, but he is making Jeremiah

into a bronze wall, an iron pillar so that he cannot be crushed. A long, turbulent ministry lies ahead.

Early on, the men of Anathoth sought to slit his throat if he kept preaching the Lord's word (11:21–23). With Jehoiakim on the throne, the political and religious climate became even more hostile against the prophet. The priest Pashhur beats Jeremiah and leaves him in stocks overnight. Jeremiah is prohibited from getting married as a sign of the coming judgment (Jer 16:1–4). After Jehoiakim burns Jeremiah's scroll, he and his scribe Baruch have to go into hiding (Jer 36), from 604 to 597. Another prophet, Hananiah, challenges him (Jer 28). Zedekiah keeps Jeremiah in prison during much of the siege (Jer 37) and even tosses him into an empty cistern, but Jeremiah is rescued by the Ethiopian Ebed-melech (Jer 38). After the fall of Jerusalem, Jeremiah remains in the land for about four years, when he is carted off to Egypt against his will. After a few oracles, he is never heard from again.

The preaching of Jeremiah weaves together an elaborate quilt of varied images, powerful metaphors, and profound religious faith. From the divorce court to rotting figs to the terrifying foe from the north, doom and devastation monopolize most of his sermons. Yet in his piety, Jeremiah earnestly grieves for his people. He writes that "my heart is sick within me. Behold, the cry of the daughter of my people" (Jer 8:18–19). Likewise, he bears the yoke of his suffering with a bold honesty to complain to the Lord that he enticed him into the ministry, so Jeremiah wishes that his mother's womb would have been his tomb (Jer 20:7–18).

Though grim and atrocious portraits of wrath and judgment may get more space in Jeremiah, they are eclipsed by the rising sun of redemption. Jeremiah's most famous prophecy comes in chapter 31, when he announces a coming new covenant, eternal and offering forgiveness and a new heart. After exile, the Lord promises to raise up a righteous branch for David. This future king will save Judah and Israel with justice and righteousness, and his name will be called, "Yahweh Is Our Righteousness" (Jer 23:5–6). This promise is particularly poignant because no king returned after exile, that is until Christ was born.

Ezekiel

Though Jeremiah's afflictions are severe, in some ways Ezekiel's are worse, as they come mostly from the Lord as opposed to being dished out by hostiles. Ezekiel was a priest carted off to the Chebar Canal in Babylon in 597, and his ministry commenced in 593 after seeing the glory of the Lord enthroned above the cherubim chariot. The dozen or so date formulas in the book give us a window of ministry for July 593 to April 573.

In the opening call of Ezekiel, which extends to the end of the third chapter, the burden of the divine call sits heavily upon the new prophet. After Ezekiel falls down before the Lord's glory, the Lord feeds him a scroll of lamentation, dirges, and woes. He is informed that the rebel people to whom he will be preaching will reject him with their brazen foreheads and hard hearts. The Spirit sweeps him back to plop him down among the exiles, where he sits stunned for seven days. Then, after being told that he must speak God's word, whether the people listen or not, the Lord puts Ezekiel under house arrest and strikes him mute, except when the Lord has an oracle for him. When he is not out preaching and doing symbolic acts, Ezekiel is housebound and mute. Unlike Isaiah and Jeremiah, who have salvation oracles peppered throughout their books, with just a few exceptions Ezekiel is dense with judgment all the way through chapter 33.

The nucleus of Ezekiel's theology and imagery appears in the vision of chapters 8–11. As a student of priestly educators, he was well at home with the motif that we teased out in chapter four, about how holiness kept God's presence within the sanctuary, but sin defiled his house and led to his departure. In this vision, Ezekiel is beamed to the north gate of the Jerusalem temple. As the Lord's glory leads him within the temple complex, the stench grows more nauseating with every step. A statue of the goddess Asherah greets him before the gate. The gate

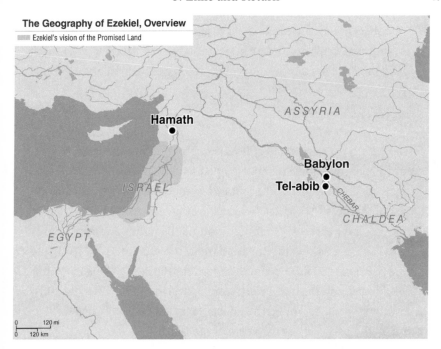

The Geography of Ezekiel, Overview
Ezekiel's vision of the Promised Land

room is riddled with murals of every detestable image venerated by the seventy elders. Within the gate, women weep for Tammuz. In the inner court, twenty-five priests bow to the sun-god Shemesh with their backs to the Lord. Their abominations pile up in God's holy home like roach-infested trash, crawling with maggots. The verdict has been rendered: their terrible abominations are driving Yahweh far from his sanctuary (Ezek 8:6). Just as Ezekiel travelled further into the temple, so God travels outward. The glory of the Lord moves from the adytum to the temple steps. He mounts his cherubim chariot just south of the temple. They take flight and soar to the eastern gate with glory above them. Then, the chariot ascends from the midst of the city, and the glory stands outside on the eastern hill. The Lord of glory has left the building. A fate worse than death struck the people.

Despite the long train of horrific visions, a word of hope and salvation comes at the end. The Lord will gather his scattered lambs and replace their rocky hearts with hearts of flesh filled with the Spirit. And this seed of hope sprouts into the grand oaks of salvation in chapters 36–37 and blossoms into a grand temple vision when the glory returns to his holy home never to leave again (Ezek 43:7). Once again, the road of exile and judgment leads us to Christ and heaven.

Haggai and Zechariah

The pairing of these two prophets is not to diminish their two books, but to recognize their teamwork, just as Ezra always groups them together. Tongue-in-cheek, scholars sometimes refer to Haggai as the only successful prophet. Where the other prophets were regularly ignored and persecuted, Haggai mounts his pulpit and gets immediate results. His several oracles date to the second year of Darius, king of Persia, 520 BC. He aims his word most directly at the governor, Zerubbabel, and the high priest, Joshua, declaring, "Go up to the hills and bring wood and build the house" (Hag 1:8). Zerubbabel, Joshua, and all the people obey the voice of the Lord.

Zechariah's ministry mirrored Haggai's, but he was more prolific. In the opening visions, several problems are dealt with, two being a defiled priest and a defiled place. Since the ordination of Aaron, a holy priest was required to anoint his successor. In the exile, however, all the priests had become defiled; the holy succession had been snipped. So, in 3:1–10, the Lord strips the filthy garments off of Joshua and adorns him with festal robes and a pure diadem. Secondly, the curse and iniquity upon the land had to be destroyed. So, with a disposal rite that echoes the removal of the scale disease in Leviticus 14, birds fly the curse away and dump it in Babylon. The iniquity of the land was carried away in a single day (Zech 3:9).

After the visions, the horizon of Zechariah expands further into the future, particularly toward the coming of the king to Zion and the Lord's own coming. The completion of the temple did not satisfy the full appetite of the people for restoration.

Malachi

The superscription of Malachi provides no information concerning its historical setting; neither does the prophet receive any biographical detail, either genealogical or geographical. Furthermore, Malachi means "my messenger" or "my angel," which opens the possibility of it being a title rather than a proper noun. The evidence favors a personal name for the prophet, but it remains disputed by scholars.

Concerning Malachi's dating, the reference to a governor (Mal 1:8) implies a Persian setting, which fits with the issues in the book about mixed marriages, tithing, cultic laxity, and social injustices. Since the temple is in use, Malachi must date after 516 BC, and since the problems he castigates anticipates the work of Ezra and Nehemiah, many scholars date the book between 480–450.

The book is made up of eight sections, including the superscription and conclusion. Malachi's form or genre is sometimes labeled as a disputation or dispute, as there are a series of questions and answers. The theme of covenant is central to the book, surfacing with Jacob versus Esau, the covenant with Levi, the marriage covenant, tithing, and the messenger of the covenant. Yet the prophet's overall purpose is the purification and moral renewal of the people. Malpractices in worship require cleansing. Their marriages need the garment of lawlessness removed. The covenant messenger will purge injustice and wickedness like a smelter's fire and a fuller's lye. Their tithing failure must be reformed for the blessings to rain. And the people must be obediently waiting for Elijah to come before the awesome and fearful day of the Lord. As with the other postexilic books, Malachi sets his crosshairs on a greater work of God to come, with the firm faith that the Lord is their God in the present and in the future to come. Judgment awaits the rebellious, but the faithful can set their hope on the Lord's ultimate deliverance.

Esther

Esther is no prophet in any usual sense of the term, but this book's religious and theological value earns it a rightful place in Holy Scripture. Sometimes criticized for not naming God, Esther's silence is its power to speak to the faith of God's people in exile. Whereas prophets shout, "Thus said the Lord," this book whispers of the Lord's faithfulness through story, characterization, and irony. Her story dates from Ahasuerus' (Hebrew name for Xerxes) third year, 482. Yet despite the existence of the temple back in Judah, the book assumes the ongoing state of the exile.

The four main characters provide an excellent way to hear God's silence.[14] First, there is King Ahasuerus and the Persian Empire. By the repetition of the 127 provinces and the lists of riches, Ahasuerus seems all-powerful and wealthy beyond belief. He always seems to be feasting, and even though he has many concubines, he is capable of loving Esther. Ahasuerus enjoys showing generosity and is ever concerned with law and protocol. And yet everyone else is always telling him what to do. Ahasuerus is lazy; he never fact-checks. He is not particularly cruel, but he is thoughtless and egotistical. At the end of the day, he is a pawn, capable of great good and horrendous evil.

Mordecai, though, is rather the opposite. He registers as the ideal character who is caring, stable, and loyal. Mordecai is solid; his character is unchanged and consistent; he is a brick. He is all action, but we can never really perceive his motives, which leaves him a bit inscrutable and unapproachable. You want him on your team, but it is hard to identify with him.

Where Mordecai is all action, Haman is all motive and emotion. We are always informed about his reasons and moods, whether he is mad, giddy, overconfident, or hopeless. The prime motive of Haman, however, is his lust for honor and power. Haman is not first a racist or a genocidal maniac. His whole plan began because his pride was bruised. This is what makes Haman a fool; he had eyes only for himself. He wanted to slaughter every last Jew so that he could feel more important. He tried to destroy their faith over a personal slight.

Finally, where Mordecai is stable, Esther dynamically develops and grows. We first meet her as a vulnerable and insignificant orphan. She gets swept up in the life of a queen, herded by eunuchs, and dosed in perfumes. She won the queenship by a night with the king. At first, she balks when Mordecai asks for help, but then she risks her life with no certainty of success and takes charge. Her speeches are a brilliant mixture of politeness, deference, and delay composed to maximize persuasiveness. In the male-dominated court of the king, Esther's wisdom topples the powerful Haman and steers Ahasuerus right where she wants him. The orphaned girl has become the authoritative queen of Persia. Some of what Esther did was very morally gray. There is no way to fully approve or disapprove of her actions. But there is also no doubt that she is the heroine of this story.

The drama of this book unfolds against the backdrop of the exodus motif. Haman is an Agagite, a descendant of the Amalekites that God swore to wipe out (Exod 17:16). Mordecai heralds from the tribe of Benjamin and reminds us of Saul. That ancient rivalry between the forever foes, Amalek and Israel, is playing out in Esther. Hence, Haman publishes his decree of extinction the day before Passover (3:12). Five days later, during the week of Unleavened Bread, Esther defeats Haman and delivers her people. God is not mentioned by name, but his salvation is clearly seen as he rescues his people in an exodus manner. God's people may live as sojourners in exile, but he is still faithful to them.

STUDY QUESTIONS

1. How does Lamentations picture Jerusalem's destruction?

2. How does the exile portray the satisfaction of the Lord's justice?

3. Discuss the various ways that Jeremiah's seventy years can be understood.

4. Discuss how the promises of God were fulfilled and unfulfilled after exile.

5. How do Ezra and Nehemiah show the tension in their faith after the exile?

6. Describe how Jeremiah and Ezekiel spoke of God's restoration after exile.

7. Who are the characters in Esther?

9

PSALMS AND WISDOM

Bible Reading:
Job, Ecclesiastes, Proverbs, Song of Songs, Psalms

As we walk through the Old Testament, the grand drama of the Lord's redemption sweeps us off our feet with its engaging stories and vivid prophetic preaching. Yet within this saga, we come to several intermissions. These books are not concerned in the same way with the Lord's historical plan for a particular people, but with how humanity lives within the created world. These books are Job, Ecclesiastes, Proverbs, Psalms, and Song of Songs, which are commonly referred to as the wisdom literature of the Old Testament.[1].

The presence of wisdom books in Scripture reflects another similarity that the Old Testament has with the ancient Near East. Wisdom literature is a wide phenomenon across the ancient Near East, present in Egypt, Syria, Palestine, and Mesopotamia over several millennia. Yet despite its wide representation, no definition of wisdom literature can clearly demarcate its boundaries. Wisdom literature is not a neat and tidy genre. Rather, as Michael Fox comments, "We should not think of Wisdom literature as a field that can be marked out and fenced in. Wisdom literature is a *family* of texts."[2] There are a wide variety of texts that belong to the family of wisdom literature, including a son's education and advice to rulers.

However, Fox divides the diverse collection of wisdom literature into two general types: didactic and critical, or speculative. In didactic texts, the purpose is instruction on wise living, which is nearly always cast in terms of a father teaching his son. Scholars debate the original settings of these instructions, be it within the home, schools, or the royal court, though it is likely that there was a certain fluidity between these settings. The critical texts are more indeterminate than the didactic. They are not all speculative but typically reflect on a traditional doctrine or idea within the didactic texts to evaluate or comment on it.

For the above reasons, it is infelicitous to draw up a tight definition of wisdom literature. Instead, general characteristics can be identified that aid in understanding the purpose and perspective of wisdom texts both for Israel and its neighbors.

1. **Humanistic**. This literature focuses on humanity and the world. There is nothing anti-religious in this, for an underlying assumption of faith in the Lord or the gods permeates the text. Creation, its order, and humanity's experience are prime concerns. Within this purview lies an interest in nature, animate and inanimate, and "creation theology." The story of origins does not dominate the creation theology of wisdom literature; rather, the importance falls upon the character of creation and humanity's experience of the world.[3]

2. **International**. The wisdom books do not center upon the unique national story of Israel, but they can be applied on an international scale within any geopolitical state. Without a doubt, this international interest is worked out within the framework of the fear of God. Wisdom, nevertheless, works and is valuable in any nation or empire. This is evidenced by the sharing of wisdom between royal courts and sages. Solomon gained an international

reputation for his wisdom and was visited by the Queen of Sheba, and he borrowed from the wisdom traditions of Egypt.

3. **Non-historical**. This does not mean reality was seen as unhistorical. Nor are its lessons exactly timeless, universal truths.[4] Rather, it means the sages of Israel did not investigate the Lord's history as it unfolded in the covenants of Abraham, Moses, and David. Unlike the other Old Testament writers, redemptive history was not their interest. Wisdom dealt with concrete issues of life as they are experienced generally and more universally. These lessons were handed down within the family or from historical sages (i.e., Solomon). Yet daily experience as it may arise in any time was the focus of wisdom's analysis.

4. **Eudaemonistic**. This characteristic refers to the expectation that wisdom works to bring well-being and happiness within life. Wisdom seeks success in both the avoidance of destructive folly and wickedness, and the attainability of uprightness for a better life in every sphere. Behind this expectation laid the commitment to a created order and to laws set by God that humanity could follow to their benefit. Hence, this is not irreligious or mechanically automatic, as if happiness was the only quest. Instead, an inherent morality rooted in God upheld the goodness of happiness. And a certain mystery of the divine activity meant a dynamic relationship with the environment of the world and a quest to further understand the created order.

These characteristics help lay out the family attributes within wisdom literature in general, as well as highlight how the wisdom books in the Old Testament compare to neighboring traditions. These features also illumine how such wisdom themes pop up in other areas of the Old Testament, like Deuteronomy, the Psalms, and Genesis. The wisdom books do differ from the Law and the Prophets, but they do not contradict or compete with them. As Murphy writes, "Ultimately, trust in the patterns of human experience was trust in God, who was responsible for the reality that confronted the sages."[5]

WHAT IS WISDOM?

In addition to sketching an outline for wisdom literature, we must ask, "What is wisdom?" And the answer must incorporate the Hebrew word(s) for wisdom and the concept of wisdom. The main word for wisdom in Hebrew is *hokmah*, which is "essentially a high degree of knowledge and skill in any domain."[6] Therefore, this word can be used not only for the wise person in general, but for those highly skilled in some trade or craftsmanship (Exod. 35:31; Isa 40:20), academic erudition (Jer 8:8; Eccl 1:16), and prudence in interpersonal matters (1 Kgs 5:9; Eccl 2:3). This sense can range from expertise, craftsmanship, astuteness, cleverness, and good sense. This cleverness is why *hokmah* can even in a few places include evil stratagems (2 Sam 13:3).

Yet for the sages, wisdom in its true sense is inherently righteous. The deftness of wisdom is further brought out in the dozen or so other words used synonymously with *hokmah* in parallel or related ideas. In English translation, these include understanding, knowledge, deliberation, shrewdness, discipline, cunning, prudence, strategy, competence, and ability.[7] The character of wisdom is also developed by its antonyms within folly terminology.

Nevertheless, the sages had a definite concept of wisdom. Wisdom can be defined as "the art of living well." First, wisdom is an *art* in that it is a skill and expertise acquired through study, practice, and discipline. In fact, the Hebrew word for "discipline" or "correction," *musar*, is fundamental to the practice of wisdom. *Musar* is authoritative correction that comes from a superior to an inferior, and so it includes punishment, reproof, and chastisement.[8] Accepting *musar* requires humility and repentance. The practice of wisdom is teachable, not wise in its own eyes, and reveres authority. Yet the art of wisdom comprises both intellectual and practical ability. Wisdom can analyze under a microscope, draw up blueprints, and solve riddles. But it can also put into practice its deep learning. The hands of wisdom can frame a house, sew a quilt, finely slice sushi, and bind a book. Wisdom is both the architect and carpenter, the designer and seamstress.

Second, wisdom is the art of *living*, which embraces job and home, all your interpersonal skills and relationships. Wisdom masters your family relationships and societal interactions. It equips you to deal with friend or foe, stranger and neighbor, policeman and criminal. This living perceives the created order and then operates within it while respecting one's own limits and the absurdities of the world.

Finally, wisdom lives *well*. This wellness, though, does not consist primarily in health and success, but in righteousness. True wisdom is pious and upright, seeking to walk in the path of righteousness and the fear of the Lord, without swerving into the alleyways of wickedness. Moreover, wellness does not connote freedom from all hardships, as it might to a modern audience. Rather, wisdom appreciates and expects the potholes of struggle, loss, suffering, and hazards. For sure, the sages reckon that wisdom usually produces wealth and protects from dangers, but this is due in part to wisdom's self-destructive polar opposite of folly. Whereas folly is inherently suicidal, wisdom creates life and improves one's pious enjoyment of it, even as a certain measure of hardship and suffering is still experienced.

Even though wisdom as the art of living well has a general consensus among the sages, this does not mean they speak with a monotone voice concerning wisdom. Varying perspectives and emphases rub up against each other among the sages. These differing voices converse within the wisdom books, as we shall see below. A simple example of this discussion is that where didactic wisdom literature tends to be more optimistic about wisdom, the critical literature teases out the limits of wisdom.

WISDOM LITERATURE
OUTSIDE ISRAEL

This dialogue among the sages also highlights another issue, which is what it means to author wisdom literature. In the ancient Near East, authoring wisdom literature consisted not just in originating new material, but also in collecting and editing proverbs from others. Proverbs were more open source than copyright material. The exchange of wisdom happened within a particular society, from generation to generation, and between nations.

In this regard it is helpful to survey some of the wisdom documents from Israel's neighbors. Even if it has its own distinct flavor, Israelite wisdom is not unique but it fits well into its ancient environment. As John A. Wilson states, "A general parallelism of thought or structure between Egyptian and Hebrew literature is common. It is, however, more difficult to establish a case of direct literary relation."[9] We will mention only a few works of Egyptian and Mesopotamian provenance that are more relevant for the biblical literature.

The wisdom instructions of Egypt are numerous and date from its early history. The Instruction of Prince Hor-Dedef, for example, dates from ca. 2600 BC. He was legendary for his wisdom, such that even though the text of this work is in poor condition, a sentence of it is quoted in a first-century-AD text.[10] The Instruction of King Merikare, dating to ca. 2100 BC, relays the tutelage of his father to the king. Much of the advice relates to Merikare's royal duties, including his religious obligations. The moral and traditional nature of wisdom is clear:

Shaped in the sayings of the ancestors.
Copy your fathers, your ancestors …
See, their words endure in books,
Open, read them, copy their knowledge,
He who is taught becomes skilled.
Don't be evil, kindness is good,
Make your memorial last through love of you.[11]

The acquisition of wisdom comes from books and ancestors that require study and practice; such learning becomes one's heritage and memorial.

Another early compilation of wisdom instruction is that of Ptah-hotep, which is set during the reign of King Izezi (ca. 2400 BC), though the manuscripts and language date from a later period. As the vizier to the king, Ptah-hotep requests that the king would appoint his son to be his successor, as he is old and near death. In the prologue, Ptah-hotep describes the evils of old age: "Oldness has come. ... The heart is forgetful and cannot recall yesterday. ... Good is become evil. All taste is gone."[12] Then, Ptah-hotep turns to his son for the purpose of "instructing the ignorant about wisdom and about the rules for good speech, as of advantage to him who will hearken and of disadvantage to him who may neglect them" (1.48). The first maxim spoken to his son resonates clearly with the humility of wisdom in Scripture.[13] "Let not thy heart be puffed-up because of thy knowledge; be not confident because thou art a wise man. Take counsel with the ignorant as well as the wise" (1.52).

The final Egyptian instruction to be mentioned is probably the most significant for the book of Proverbs. The instruction of Amenemope dates likely to the twelfth century BC and holds the strongest case for direct influence on the book of Proverbs, particularly Proverbs 22:17–24:22. As Miriam Lichtheim concludes, "It can hardly be doubted that the author of Proverbs was acquainted with the Egyptian work."[14] And while Fox does not doubt this claim, he argues for a mediated influence, positing that Amenemope was translated into Hebrew.[15] Nonetheless, Amenemope opens with its claims, "Beginning of the teaching for life, the instructions for well-being ... so as to direct him on the paths of life, to make him prosper upon the earth; to let the heart enter its shrine, steering clear of evil."[16] The ideal wise man for Amenemope is the "truly silent man ... who accepts God's will in serenity and trusts in his justice."[17] The affinity this has with the fear of the Lord is unmistakable. The advice of Amenemope is diverse, ranging from the dangers of anger to greed to veneration of the gods. As one couplet states,

> Better is poverty in the hand of the god,
> > Than wealth in the storehouse;
> Better is bread with a happy heart
> > Than wealth with vexation. (9:5–8)

Likewise, the theme of proper speaking and the evils of too many words persist through this work. "If a man's tongue is the boat's rudder, the Lord of All is yet its pilot" (20:5–6). And even though the life-prospering benefits of wisdom are undeniable, Amenemope cautions against arrogance and encourages the limits of man's wisdom: "God is ever in his perfection, man is ever in his failure" (19:14–15). Fox's conclusion is apt: "Amenemope's impress on Israelite Wisdom … was deep and wide."[18]

The wisdom literature from Mesopotamia is also varied and includes fables, theodicy, and instructions, both didactic and critical. We will mention only two. First is the instruction of Shuruppak, dating from ca. 2500 to ca. 1800 BC. The setting for this Sumerian work is the ruler Shuruppak advising his son Ziusudra, who was the hero of their flood story, like Noah. The counsel he gives his son is mainly ethical and practical in nature, and in the form of short prohibitions. "Do not vouch for someone; that man will have a hold on you. … Do not buy a prostitute; she is the sharp edge of a sickle."[19] Shuruppak's interests are in secular life and social behavior, and he deals little with religion.

The second work, Ahiqar, is an Aramaic text set during the reigns of Sennacherib and Esarhaddon of Assyria (704–669 BC). The text dates later, but it was widely translated and revised. Ahiqar shares many affinities with Proverbs and Ecclesiastes and may have some direct influence; he is mentioned in the book of Tobit (1:22). Ahiqar was a vizier in the royal court of Assyria, who escaped a plot against him and then delivered a series of wise counsels. His advice covers many topics both of a practical and religious nature. In one place, Ahiqar seems to personify wisdom as a prized lady to the gods.

> Wisdom is from the gods.
> Also, she is precious to the gods.
> Rulership is hers f[oreve]r.
> She/it has been placed in heaven,
> Because the lord of the holy ones has exalted her.[20]

This passage is fragmentary and difficult, yet it is the only extrabiblical text where wisdom has been personified. Numerous other parallels with Proverbs are found in Ahiqar. To give one more example, "I have lifted sand, and I have carried salt; but there is naught which is heavier than grief."[21]

These few samplings from wisdom literature help acclimate us to the ancient environment in which the books of Job, Proverbs, Ecclesiastes, Psalms, and Song of Songs were taught and circulated. They also help us appreciate the creational theology of biblical wisdom, where the Lord shares his wisdom not with Israel alone but with all humanity, which in turn encourages us that the ancient wisdom still holds value for us who live in a distant time and place.

PROVERBS

Proverbs exemplifies didactic wisdom, as it positively advocates wisdom for life. The book of Proverbs also exhibits its international flavor as it is an anthology of different authors. Even though much of the book is associated with Solomon, other parts are explicitly credited to Agur, Lemuel, wise men, and the men of Hezekiah as collectors. Both Agur and Lemuel are unattested elsewhere, so we do not know their identities. It is possible that they are non-Israelite, especially Lemuel from Massa, which was near Moab.

The structure of the book is arranged into six parts, with the final section being a four-part appendix. Discerning a flow and organization in the opening discourses in 1:8–9:18 is relatively easy, but the rest of the book? It can seem like a random, willy-nilly bunch of isolated proverbs stuck together like strangers on a bus. While these chapters do not evince a tight, thematic structure, this does not reveal carelessness. Rather, by using various literary devices and thematic links, the proverbs in chapter 10 on form smaller clusters and groups by associative thinking. These literary devices include repetition of words and phrases, wordplays, numerical sayings, paronomasia (play on sounds), inclusios, chiasms/inversions, and catchwords, to name a few. Additionally, by taking isolated proverbs and sitting them next to each other, new levels of meaning are created. By itself, the proverb may mean one thing, but its placement before and after other proverbs adds further depth to its meaning that can amplify and clarify. And by doing this, Proverbs accomplishes one of its key goals: to make you think.

The proverbs are more than moral tidbits; they are musings that are supposed to make you ponder, ruminate, and contemplate. Like a stone rolled down a river, we are to turn them over and inspect them top to bottom, backward and forward. Wisdom takes effort, study, and practice; it cannot be spoon-fed. A good example of this sprouts from Proverbs 26:4–5:

> Do not answer a dullard in accord with his folly,
>   Else you will become like him.
> Answer a dullard in accord with his folly,
>   Else he will think himself wise. (NJPS)

One wonders about the right course of action. Do you answer the dullard according to his folly or not? The point is it depends on the situation. Sometimes you should, and sometimes you should not—it takes wisdom to know when. Taken together the force becomes, "it is dangerous to respond to a fool (v 4), but the wise have a duty to speak up (v 5)."[22]

Even though the wisdom book authors agree that wisdom is the art of living well, each book speaks with its own accent or perspective.

Proverbs teaches from the angle that wisdom really works. This could be considered optimistic, but a more accurate way to analyze this is through the deed-consequence nexus, or the intrinsic retribution principle. The deed-consequence nexus means that the Lord built into his world the natural consequences fitting one's behavior. Hence, in Proverbs 6, the youth is warned against laziness: "A bit of sleep, a bit of slumber … and your poverty will go as a vagabond" (Prov 6:10–11, my translation). Poverty is portrayed as the built-in consequence for sloth. The diligent labor of wisdom, however, yields wealth (Prov 10:15–16). Evil deeds produce negative results, while upright acts bring forth rich blessings. This nexus does have a certain automatic nature to it, but it is not impersonal or mechanical; rather, the nexus is part of God's created moral order and upheld by his providence (Prov 3:12, 33; 5:21; 10:3). Therefore, overall, Proverbs stresses that intrinsic retribution works so that one can be assured of the benefits of wisdom and have no doubts that folly is the highway to death.

Finally, one of the standout features of Proverbs is the personification of wisdom as Lady Wisdom, who is contrasted with Mistress Folly (Prov 8–9). As a literary feature, personification takes some abstract concept or wholistic object and condenses it into a person to make it more vivid, appealing, or understandable. Proverbs 8 personifies a divine attribute, wisdom. Lady Wisdom is not a type or representation of Christ. Lady Wisdom does not instruct us on the Trinity. Rather, this divine attribute is personified so that we might share in it. The Lord desires us to use his wisdom for life. This personification is a powerful way, then, to invite and encourage us to seek and grow in God's wisdom. In fact, Lady Wisdom calls us to love her (Prov 8:17). Romantic imagery is employed to make Lady Wisdom all the more attractive and enticing. The Lady lists her excellencies to woo us to her. She is public and accessible (Prov 8:1–5). She is crowned with every talent: truth, righteousness, fear of the Lord, understanding, and might (8:6–14). Her pragmatic expertise covers government, justice, administration, and business. All the systems of human society depend on her (8:15–21). Yet Lady Wisdom is not all business and no play. She was the Lord's first creation and a witness to all his creative wonders (8:22–30).[23] Lady Wisdom was a young girl dancing before the Lord and delighting in humanity (8:30–31). She is delighted in the Lord and all that is his. This is the aesthetic side of Lady Wisdom. And those who behold her find similar delight, for who can gaze upon Lady Wisdom and not fall in love? Therefore she says, "Whoever finds me finds life and obtains favor from the LORD" (8:35).

Diametrically opposed to Lady Wisdom is Mistress Folly (9:13–18). The personification of folly as the mistress builds on the characterization of the Illicit Lady in earlier chapters (Prov 2:16–19; 5:3–14; 7:4–27). The Illicit Lady refers to an actual type of woman, a seductress and adulteress. She is a married woman who is constantly on the hunt for more paramours. Yet where the adulteress embodied the lethal danger of sexual temptation, Mistress Folly personifies the lure of all temptation, folly, and licentiousness. Mistress Folly is a temptress, seductive and unlawful. She copies Lady Wisdom by calling out from the rooftops—she plagiarizes, poaches, and pirates. She is a profane imitation of Lady Wisdom, a knockoff, a cheap replica. Moreover, the mistress is selling illegitimate pleasures: "Stolen water is sweet, and bread eaten in secret is pleasant" (Prov 9:17). Her seduction is not merely pleasures, delights, and indulgence, but gratification in the unlawful and prohibited. The lure is to relish in evil or sin itself. The wages of folly, therefore, is death: falling into the depths of Sheol or hell.

Together these two women embody the deed-consequence nexus in Proverbs. Wisdom is a tree of life to those who lay hold of her. Folly is a downward escalator into the pit, the land of no return.

JOB

The book of Job is regularly called a theodicy. Yet if by "theodicy" one means an answer to that age-old dilemma, "Why do bad things happen to good people?" then the label does not fit very well. The answer to human suffering is glaringly absent. But if it is taken to mean the vindication of divine goodness amid the existence of evil, we come a bit closer to the mark. Still, we do not quite hit it. For even though human suffering persists as a theme in the book, the pressing question is who is wise. Every character claims wisdom, but the conclusion asserts that the Lord alone is wise and dispenses wisdom as he sees fit. The application consists not in an explanation of suffering, but in human repentance and submission before the all-wise God.

In fact, the central issue in Job is not suffering in the abstract but the deed-consequence nexus, the retribution principle. Traditional wisdom asserts that sin leads to suffering, righteousness to prosperity. (Even Proverbs asserts this.) The supremely upright Job, however, is suffering beyond comprehension. How does one figure this? Job's three friends are confident of possessing the right answer: Job suffers, so he must have sinned. They read the retribution principle backwards. If sin leads to punishment, so suffering must mean you have sinned. For them, all suffering can be explained by sin. Yet it is precisely the friends who get rebuked. They were wrong; you cannot read the retribution principle backwards. Job argued for a more complex answer, that more nuance is needed. In this regard Job was vindicated, but he still did not get an answer for his suffering.

Additionally, the deed-consequence nexus highlights Job's tension with Proverbs, in two ways. First, Proverbs paints simple and clean that wisdom leads to life and folly unto death. Job does not argue with this in general, per se, but he affirms that reality is more complex. There is more to the story. Particularly, one cannot reverse the nexus into a consequence-reveals-the-deed equation. There is suffering that cannot be explained by human behavior. Second, in Proverbs, Lady Wisdom sings of her accessibility; she is public and attainable by humans. Job does not doubt that humans can have some measure of wisdom, but he wrestles with a wisdom that is above him, one mysterious and inaccessible. Hence, in his famous poem (Job 28), wisdom cannot be found. "From where, then, does wisdom come? ...

It is hidden from the eyes of all living" (Job 28:20–21). He concludes that God alone knows wisdom, and that for humans, to fear the Lord is wisdom. In the dialogue between Proverbs and Job, the complex nature of wisdom in this world gains focus.

Yet this message of Job cannot be divorced from the drama of the book. A very deliberate frame contextualizes the debate between Job and his friends. The theme of this drama is trial by ordeal.[24] In the ancient Near East, kings could wage war or compete in contests by champion instead of the whole army. David and Goliath exemplify such a battle. The Philistines and the Israelites fought through their champion representative. The ordeal of the battle vindicated the true victor. These ordeals could include various types of contests, like a battle of the wits[25] or wrestling. The lords or kings would prove who was better by competition between their champions.

This motif colors the drama of Job. The story opens upon the champion, the blameless Job in his vast wealth—evidence of his wisdom. The great King, the Lord, is enthroned in his royal court as the sons of God report in. The Lord initiates a contest with the Accuser (*ha satan* is the Hebrew transliterated, meaning "the accuser"): "Have you considered my servant Job, that there is none like him on the earth, a blameless and upright man, who fears God and turns away from evil?" (Job 1:8). The Lord claims Job as his champion. The Accuser spits back a challenge, which amounts to, "Job only loves you for your money!" Job is not truly upright and wise, for he loves God only for his blessings. If the blessings are removed, Job would curse God. This is the challenge. Does Job love God or only God's blessings? Is Job wise only for its wealth, or will he cling to wisdom amid suffering? To pass this test, Job must submit to the suffering while holding onto the Lord and his wisdom.

The first round of the contest kicks off with a single day of bankruptcy and bereavement. Every son and daughter are dead. Job, though, bows the knee: "The LORD gave, and the LORD has taken away; blessed be the name of the LORD" (Job 1:21). Job passes the first trial. The Accuser, though, wants a second attempt: "Skin for skin! All that a man has he will give for his life. But stretch out your hand and touch his bone and his flesh, and he will curse you to your face." (Job 2:4–5). The Lord is confident in his champion; the Accuser can torment Job as long as he spares his life. Soon, festering boils chew on Job from head to toe, and nothing eases the agony except to scrape the open wounds with a broken piece of pottery. Job's pathetic trauma pushes his wife to defect to the Accuser's team: "Do you still hold fast your integrity? Curse God and die" (Job 2:9). Job, however, will not follow his bride; he will not forsake his Lord so easily. With Job abandoned by his wife, Job's three friends visit him in the hope of providing some well-needed comfort. And with their arrival commences several rounds of disputation and argumentation.

Yet for all their advice, the three friends make the same basic point. Somehow Job sinned, so if he will just repent, everything will return to normal. The backward retribution principle is the way to understand Job's trial. Job is the only one to blame for his agony. Job, though, will not capitulate to this argument. He defends his uprightness; he insists that sin is not the explanation. Additionally, Job begins to demand an audience with the Lord. Even more so, he wants his day in court to plead his case before the Lord, in order to prove his uprightness and to establish that his affliction has some other reason than sin. And without much delay, the Lord grants Job his request. From within the tempest, the Lord speaks to Job:

> Who is this who darkens counsel,
>   Speaking without knowledge?
> Gird your loins like a man;
>   I will ask and you will inform Me." (Job 38:2–3, NJPS)

To gird up one's loins is like strapping on a Sumo's mawashi. The Lord Almighty steps into the ring with Job for a wrestling of wits.

In the first round, the Lord lays out a contest of knowledge by pelting Job with questions about creation. The Lord laid the earth's foundation; he adorned the sea with clouds as a garment. Does Job comprehend the expanse of the earth? Can he number the clouds with wisdom? Let him who arraigns God respond! Job can squeak out a few, mere lines:

> See, I am of small worth; what can I answer You?
>> I clap my hand to my mouth.
> I have spoken once, and will not reply;
>> Twice, and will do so no more. (Job 40:4–5, NJPS)

The Lord, however, is not going to let Job off so easily. He must go a second round, which is a test of power: "Have you an arm like God?" (Job 40:9). The Lord fashioned Behemoth, but Job cannot even snare it by the nose. The Almighty molded Leviathan, yet Job is unable to pierce its scales. If Job is powerless against mighty beasts, how can he stand before the Lord? Job failed in knowledge and flunked in power, which are the two ingredients of wisdom. The Lord alone is truly wise; Job is not. Hence, Job bends the knee in submission: "Therefore, I recant and I relent, being but dust and ashes" (Job 42:6, NJPS). He withdraws his complaint and repents for uttering things too wonderful for him.

Yet it is precisely as the humble and vanquished one that Job triumphs over the Accuser. Satan's challenge was that Job would curse and forsake God in his suffering, that Job only loved the Lord for his blessings. But in his misery and dust, Job remained faithful in love and devotion. The conquest of Job comes in his humiliation, which in turn vindicates him over his friends (42:7). They did not speak the truth about the Lord. Reading the retribution principle backward is not wise. Not all suffering can be explained by sin, but the reason for suffering is not given. Rather, the surpassing and transcendent wisdom of the Lord is crowned as supreme over all. In the words of the wise Elihu:

> The splendor about God is awesome.
>> Shaddai—we cannot attain to Him;
> He is great in power and justice
>> And abundant in righteousness; He does not torment.

Therefore, men are in awe of Him
Whom none of the wise can perceive. (Job 37:22–24, NJPS)

ECCLESIASTES

The name Ecclesiastes comes to us in English from the Latinized form for the Greek translation, and it means "a member of the citizen's assembly."[26] In Hebrew, the name of the book is Qohelet, which, though debated, means "one who presides over or speaks in an assembly." "Public teacher" or "professor" would be fitting English translations.[27] Since Qohelet is the title or name for the author of this book, it will be used here for both the book and the author.

Who, though, is Qohelet? Traditionally, Solomon was posited as the author, for Qohelet does take on a Solomonic persona (Eccl 1:1). But Qohelet never claims to be Solomon. There are two insurmountable problems with Solomonic authorship. First, the language of the book aligns with post-exilic Hebrew as we find it in Ezra, Nehemiah, and Chronicles. To use an analogy, if someone told you they had discovered a new sonnet by Shakespeare, but the language more resembled a modern rap song, you would question its authenticity. Similarly, the classic biblical Hebrew of Solomon's day does not match the Hebrew of Qohelet. Second, the social world expressed in Qohelet fits best within the Persian period and its economic and civic structures.[28] Therefore, a general window for Qohelet falls between 500 to 300 BC.

The message of Qohelet interjects his voice within the dialogue between Job and Proverbs. He does this by going on a quest. The quest is to search and probe by wisdom all that happens under the sun (Eccl 1:13), which is an explicit task of using common revelation (wisdom) and not special revelation (Torah). Yet Qohelet crystalizes his quest with a question: "What profit is there for man in all his toil by which he toils under the sun?" (Eccl 1:3, my translation). As a commercial term, "profit" here refers to a benefit with a true and lasting value, to an enduring advantage. And as the next verse states, this profit must avail beyond death; "a generation goes, a generation comes." By his work, what profit can man attain to survive the grave? Qohelet's answer was given before the question: "Absurdity of absurdities."

The precise usage and connotations of the Hebrew word for "absurd" here, *hevel*, is best captured by Fox: "The essence of the absurd is a disparity between two phenomena that are supposed to be joined by a link of harmony or causality but are actually disjunct or even conflicting. ... The quality of absurdity does not inhere in a being, act, or even in and of itself ... but rather in the tension between a certain reality and a framework of expectations."[29] That is, Qohelet expects wise labor to bring about profits, particularly life. This is the traditional voice of the sages: wisdom yields life. But Qohelet counters, All die! (3:19). The fool and wise man, even the animals, have the same fate. Qohelet takes issue with the deed-consequence nexus, the retribution principle, as it works out in reality. Again, Fox:

> Basic to Qohelet's thinking are certain assumptions about the way reality should operate. His primary assumption is that an action and a fitting recompense for that action are cause and effect; one who creates the cause can justly expect the effect. ... At the same time that he cleaves to this expectation, he sees that there is in reality no such reasonableness, and his expectations are constantly frustrated.[30]

As a matter of justice, Qohelet expects wisdom to yield lasting profit that will survive death, but reality does not match this expectation. Hence, absurdity for Qohelet carries with it connotations of injustice, irrationality, frustration, and pain. Wisdom cannot earn profit beyond death—frustrating!

Qohelet's quest also explains why he takes on the persona of Solomon in chapters 1–2, which he drops for the rest of the book. If anyone should be able to obtain ultimate profit by wisdom, it should be Solomon under the Mosaic law, which upheld the retribution principle. Yet after building an Edenic paradise by wisdom (2:1–11), Qohelet's conclusion is absurdity: no profit under the sun (2:11). And what buries this profit? There is one fate for all, fool and wise alike (2:15). There is no remembrance for Qohelet, and his heir may be a fool who will squander his fortune. Memorials and children were common ways in the ancient Near East that men tried to attain immortality. These, however, do not work for Qohelet—there is no forever remembrance, for both fool and wise are forgotten (Eccl 2:16). The Lord put eternity in man's mind, but man cannot figure out what God is doing from beginning to end (Eccl 3:11).

Qohelet's Scriptural presuppositions peak out now and again. God will judge the wicked and the righteous (Eccl 3:17). He believes that it will go better for those who fear the Lord (Eccl 8:12). Yet by wisdom, from common grace, one cannot know if man's spirit goes upward and an animal's spirit sinks into the earth (Eccl 3:21), for beasts and people have the same fate, so that humans will know that they are but beasts (3:18).

Therefore, Qohelet lists off the numerous absurdities in life that show the breakdown of the retribution principle. In the place intended for righteous judgment, there is wickedness (3:16). He who loves money is never satisfied by it (5:10). Some have money but never enjoy it (6:2). The righteous sometimes perish in their righteousness, while the wicked can prolong life with wickedness (7:15). The race is not always won by the fastest, the wise do not always have the bread, and sometimes the strong lose the battle (9:11). Accident and tragedy can spring on anyone at any time. The expected result often is not attained. How well Qohelet describes our everyday lives.

Qohelet's critical take on the retribution principle, though, does not make him a complete skeptic or hedonist. He clearly prizes wisdom as better than folly (Eccl 2:13). Wisdom is a good inheritance; it helps one succeed, and its protection is like that of money. In no way does he advocate the abandonment of wisdom. Yet to counter an exaggerated optimism, Qohelet exposes the limits of wisdom. You can be the fastest and still lose. "A little folly outweighs massive wisdom" (10:1, NJPS). The wise remains in the morgue as a constant reminder of his mortality. What is good is to know God's lot that he has given humankind, to do good and enjoy one's toil as long as one lives (2:24; 3:12–13; 8:15; 9:7–9). This includes remembering the Creator in one's youth, as the day you die is your own personal day of the Lord. As humans, we may know next to nothing about what the Lord is doing from beginning to end, but one conclusion is firm: "Fear God and keep his commandments," for judgment is sure (12:13). In this way, Qohelet adds his Amen to Proverbs's and Job's commendation of the fear of the Lord, even as he tells us the rest of the story about the limits of wisdom and the absurdity of life.

SONG OF SONGS

Strictly speaking, the Song of Songs, or the Song of Solomon, does not belong to either didactic or critical wisdom literature. The book is love literature, which is a well-known classification in the ancient Near East. Yet since the Song deals with humanity and the world with respect to sexuality, it is appropriate to survey it here.

The title of the book, "The Song of Songs," is the typical Hebrew construction for the superlative—the best or most sublime song ever. The superscription credits the book to Solomon, but none of the speakers in the book are identified as Solomon. Rather, they are anonymous. One debate surrounding the Song is whether it is a story of courtship, wedding, and marriage or a collection of love poems. The strongest evidence argues against a story and favors an artistically arranged collection of poems.[31]

The Song does extol the love and sexual pleasure between a man and woman. With its many echoes of Eden, the created goodness of love is praised and the poetry revels in the beautiful attraction between the woman and the man. The Song is first of all a celebration, an enjoyment, before it does any teaching or instruction. The pure delight of sexual love, though, does not flow unhindered. The marriage bed at times is blanketed with frustration, disappointment, and unfulfilled desire. "I opened to my beloved, but my beloved had turned and gone" (5:6). The man came and left before the woman was fulfilled. Even as the Song relishes in the bliss of sexual love as it was created, it acknowledges the disharmony injected by the fall and it longs for renewal, for greater unity. "Many waters cannot quench love, neither can floods drown it. ... Make haste, my beloved" (8:7, 14).

The major issue of the Song, however, is whether it should be interpreted allegorically. In the history of Christian interpretation, the allegorical reading of the Song holds the dominate position. Even Jewish exegesis allegorized it concerning the Torah. Though the allegory is spun in many directions, the basic sketch centers around Christ and his church. Nevertheless, the Song's affinity with other ancient love literature and the natural reading of the text substantiates that it should be understood as love poetry for the marriage bed and not as an allegory. This is not to deny that by analogy lessons can be mined about the covenant between God and his people, which is often likened to marriage (Ezek 16; 23; Hos 1–3; Eph 5). Yet it is enough and good that God preserved for us a book of the Bible where we can uprightly delight in sexual love within marriage.

PSALMS

Like an aerial view of a country reveals only its basic features, so a survey of the Psalms shortchanges its true majesty. Therefore, in this section I opt instead to supply you with tools for fruitfully trekking through the book yourself, equipping you with reading strategies so that the individual psalms are more accessible for your spiritual journey.

The book of Psalms is a collection of songs and hymns. Its name in Hebrew is the Book of Praises, which honors its flavors of worship and doxology of the Lord. The timespan of the collection is massive, as Psalm 90 is credited to Moses while others date to exilic and postexilic times (Pss 89; 126; 137). David wrote the greatest number of the psalms, approximately seventy-three. This is the Hebrew number; the first Greek translation of the Psalms, the Septuagint, adds more. This brings up the issue of titles, which has been much debated. The best solution is probably that psalm titles are not original but are early and reliable additions concerning authorship and historical setting. Even if this is the case, many psalms do not have a title, or the title consists merely in a name (e.g., "of David") or an obscure musical reference. With this absence of historical context, scholars turn to genre.

The definition of a genre varies, but most scholars talk about a genre as a literary type, a category of literary composition with commonalities in structure, mood, and content. Genre also includes function or purpose and the author's intention for the text as a whole. Genre can locate a psalm in the life of Israel's worship or calendar, such as a gate liturgy or an enthronement hymn. The genre of the psalm, then, becomes a reading strategy and map for how to understand the psalm and its goal. Genres elucidate meaning and can communicate how one experiences and conceives of the world, and so can be hugely important.

This being said, a few qualifications are in order. First, sometimes it is difficult to identify the genre of any given psalm, as it may not fit well into an established genre. If this is the case, the psalm should not be shoved into a genre against its will. Second, a genre classification is not a rigid cookie-cutter mold, but an elastic band that the author can stretch according to his imagination and purpose (though it does have a snapping point). Third, genre is not the only interpretative tool used to unlock a psalm. A genre helps color in the setting of the psalm, but the content of the psalm is chief, and its relationship to surrounding psalms is important, too.

For length, only three genre classifications will be probed here. They are broader, overarching categories that enjoy more consensus among scholars. As is no surprise, scholars disagree on the number of genres and subgenres and how they relate to each other, but these three will orient us to the topic.

Hymn of praise

This classification is defined by its exuberant praise to the Lord, for who God is or for what he has done. The stance of this genre is orientation; life is going well. These hymns have a basic three-part structure: call to praise, reason for praise, and conclusion with a renewed call or exhortation to praise. The reason for praising God can vary from historical acts, the identity of God, the deeds of God, or his kingship.

Consider these examples.

Psalm 117

Call (v. 1)	Praise the LORD, all nations! Extol him, all peoples!
Reason (v. 2)	For great is his steadfast love toward us, and the faithfulness of the LORD endures forever.
Conclusion (v. 3)	Praise the LORD!

Psalm 33

Call (vv. 1–3)	Shout for joy in the LORD, O you righteous! ...
Reason (v. 4)	For the word of the LORD is upright. ... (vv. 4–19 go on to extol the Lord's word and his promise to save)
Conclusion (vv. 20–21):	Our soul waits for the LORD; he is our help and our shield.

These hymns summon us to worship the Lord and list reasons why he is worthy of our praise. The infused gratitude within the hymn centers the congregation upon the Lord himself as their highest good. As Sigmund Mowinckel states, "The core of the hymn of praise is the consciousness of the poet and congregation that they are standing face to face with the Lord himself, meeting the almighty, holy and merciful God in his own place, and worshipping him with praise and adoration."[32] The world out there may be burdened with many dangers and needs, but within the presence of the Lord, all is well and the Lord is good.

The doxological focus of the hymn of praise influences other types of psalms, and its features are widely spread across the Psalter. Subgenres related to the hymn include annual festival psalms (Ps 81) and remembrance songs (Ps 105), and some scholars will link royal and enthronement psalms to the hymn of praise, though these two often receive their own classification.

Lament

The second major classification of the Psalms is the lament, which is the most common type. The laments can be individual-focused or corporate-focused, and due to David, the lament can center on the royal office. The key burden of the lament is to petition, complain, or confess to the Lord for deliverance from distress. The stance of the lament is disorientation; life is not well. The causes of the distress are manifold, but three basic causes are enemies, the psalmist himself (sin or sickness), and God.

The structure of a lament typically has five parts: (1) an entreaty (plea to God), (2) the lament proper (complaint), (3) a confession (sin or trust), (4) the petition for God's help, and (5) a promise (to praise, express confidence, or bless). In fact, the structure of many laments aligns nicely with the form of the vow as it was practiced in the Old Testament, which grounds the laments both in daily piety and worship in the sanctuary.[33] The first example is an individual lament of David.

Psalm 28 (NJPS)

Entreaty (vv. 1–2)	O LORD, I call to You; my rock, do not disregard me. ...

Lament (v. 3)	Do not count me with the wicked and evildoers
	    who profess goodwill toward their fellows
	    while malice is in their heart.

Petition (vv. 4–5)	Pay them according to their deeds. ... May He tear them down. ...
Confidence (vv. 6–7a)	Blessed is the LORD, for He listens to my plea for mercy. ...
Promise/Plea (vv. 7b–9)	I will glorify him with my song. ... Deliver and bless Your very own people.

Here we can see how David's individual petition and confidence in the Lord translates into a corporate concern in the final two verses, which relates to his royal office. Likewise, the location of the parts of the structure have a fluidity to them, as their order can be mixed up. We can witness similar dynamics in a corporate lament.

Psalm 12 (NJPS)

Entreaty (v. 2a)	Help, O LORD!
Lament (vv. 2b–3)	For the faithful are no more; the loyal have vanished from among men. ...
Petition (v. 4)	May the LORD cut off all flattering lips every tongue that speaks arrogance.
Lament (vv. 5–6)	They say, "By our tongues we shall prevail ..."
Confidence (vv. 7–9)	The words of the LORD are pure words. ... You, O LORD, will keep them.

These corporate laments could be used on a national fast day in response to some defeat, famine, or plague, or in conjunction with a festival and a penitential rite. Either way, the human soul is casting itself upon the Lord in faith that he would hear and help when an evil threatened them. Subgenres related to the lament are imprecatory psalms (Ps 137), lawsuit or ordeal psalms (Ps 26), and protective or confidence psalms (Ps 27).

Thank offering or thanksgiving

The final classification that we will survey is the thank offering song, which comes from the Hebrew word for the thank offering sacrifice, which also can mean thanksgiving (Lev 7). These psalms could have been the verbal accompaniment to the sacrifice, though they are not confined to this. The thank offering song is also related to the lament and the vow. In a lament, the psalmist vows to worship the Lord if he answers his cry. The thank offering is offered up in the payment of his vow, so the previous prayer is often referenced in the song. The rough structure of the thank offering plays out in three parts: (1) address to praise, (2) recounting deliverance, and (3) renewed call to praise.

Psalm 116

Address (v. 1)	I love the LORD because he has heard my voice. ...
Recounting (vv. 2–11)	Because he inclined his ear to me. ... The snares of death encompassed me. ...

Praise (vv. 12–19)	What shall I render to the LORD
	        for all his benefits to me? ...
	I will offer to you the sacrifice of thanksgiving
	        and call on the name of the LORD.
	I will pay my vows to the LORD
	        in the presence of all his people.

These thanksgivings are marinated in the emotions of rejoicing, gratitude, and delight in a specific work of God. As Mowinckel summarizes, "It seeks to give honor and praise to God for some definite benefit and *thank* him for it."[34] Other thank offering psalms include Psalms 66, 118, and 138. A key related thanksgiving psalm is the victory song, where the Lord is praised for a distinct victory (Pss 18; 68; Exod 15; Jud 5).

In addition to these three overarching types of psalms, other genres include psalms of confidence (Pss 23; 91), remembrance psalms (Pss 78; 105; 106), wisdom psalms (Pss 1; 73; 111), and royal psalms (Pss 2; 45; 89; 110).

As is evident from the genres, though, the psalms are located within the very life of Israel in covenant with her Lord and God. Therefore, the essential tools for reading Psalms is the story of Israel with God, particularly the covenants. The things we have studied in previous chapters are the strongest aids in reading the Psalms. The Abrahamic covenant seals the Lord's unbreakable fidelity and kindness to his people and forms their confidence to pray and sing to the Lord. The Mosaic covenant lays out the sin and curses that summon the people to confess and to desire righteousness. Particularly, the Mosaic legislation inculcates the theology of worship within the tabernacle/temple and during the pilgrim feasts. And special weight goes to the Davidic covenant, as David and his royal heirs permeate the Psalter. The book of Psalms has a general progression from lament to praise, and it is the hope in God's anointed king that moves this progression along, as the life of the people is wrapped up in the life of the king. The dominance of the king colors the book of Psalms as messianic.

Finally, the beauty of the psalms shines in that every human emotion and experience finds a place within them. As a sort of summary of the whole Bible, Psalms connects us to creation and to heaven, to the fall and to salvation. By their poetry, the psalms are human prayers and songs that are intended to be re-prayed and re-sung by God's people through history. In the psalms we can locate the struggles of our individual lives and see how our experiences link us to God's people as a whole and show us that we are not alone. Indeed, as the psalms connect us to the king and vice versa, so they unite us to our beloved Savior, the true Davidic king, who so often took the psalms upon his lips. As we pray and sing the psalms, we are reminded that

Christ did so first. Therefore, may we trek through these psalms and learn them intimately, one by one.

STUDY QUESTIONS

1. What are the general characteristics of wisdom literature?

2. What was the definition given for wisdom?

3. What is the deed-consequence nexus, or retribution principle?

4. Who is Lady Wisdom in Proverbs?

5. How does Job overcome in his trial by ordeal?

6. What does Qohelet mean by his conclusion "Absurdity of absurdities"?

7. Discuss how Proverbs, Job, and Qohelet are in dialogue and have their own voice.

8. What are the three overarching genres in the book of Psalms?

9. In what key way do the psalms direct us to Christ?

1 0

THE GOSPELS

Bible Reading:
Matthew, Mark, Luke, John

Upon the newly consecrated walls of Jerusalem, Nehemiah took his stand with eyes on the horizon, waiting for the return of the king. By the time we reach the Gospels, Nehemiah has long been in the grave, but his posture of faithful waiting was alive and well in Judea. When we first meet Zechariah in the temple—the first scene chronologically in the Gospels—we see in him the same posture of faithful waiting we saw in Nehemiah. Four hundred years have passed since the temple's rebuilding, but the spiritual thirst for God's full restoration has remained. The world, however, has changed greatly.

The mighty Persian Empire toppled to Alexander the Great, who introduced a potent influence into Judea: Hellenization, the spread of Greek ideas and culture through the Mediterranean and Near East world. During the Hellenistic period, the size of the Jewish diaspora grew, and Jews both inside and outside of Palestine wrestled with Greek culture, either by resistance or accommodation. Though some Jews were more Hellenized than others, all felt its sway. Moreover, as we saw with Ezra and Nehemiah, the tension between having the temple and being under foreign rule continued to fester and blister. Under the Ptolemies (301–198 BC), the situation in Palestine was

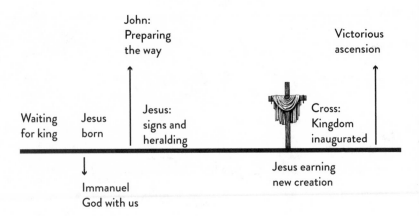

Chart 8: New Covenant, Gospels

relatively peaceful. But in Egypt, the Jewish population expanded and flourished in Alexandria, where one of the most significant religious developments took place: the translation of the Old Testament into Greek.

Whatever peace was enjoyed in Palestine ended when Antiochus III took control of Palestine for the Seleucids (198–167 BC). This flared a rivalry between two families in Judea, the priestly family of Oniad and the house of Tobias, who had the roll of collecting taxes. The Oniad Jason purchased the high priesthood from Antiochus IV and accelerated Hellenization in Jerusalem by changing its structure to resemble that of a Greek city state.[1] With support from the house of Tobias, Menelaus paid a larger sum to Antiochus IV to purchase the high priesthood from Jason, and he intended to intensify Hellenization. This more extreme Hellenization created a division within the Jewish population between the Hellenizers and the Hasidim, or holy and pious ones. When Antiochus IV came to Jerusalem to install Menelaus, he plundered the temple, tore down Jerusalem's walls, and outlawed Jewish religious practices, including Sabbath, food laws, and circumcision (169–167 BC).

Even though some Jews supported Antiochus IV, his new laws were too much for the Hasidim, who sparked the Maccabean revolt under the priest Mattathias and his son Judas. Judas Maccabee ushered in what is called the Hasmonean period (167–63 BC). The Hasmonean descendants of Mattathias ruled Jerusalem as high priests and won independence from the Seleucids. In fact, Aristobulus I (104–103 BC) even took for himself the title of king. Even though the Hasmoneans revolted against the Hellenization of Menelaus in order to revive traditional Jewish practices, they were themselves heavily Hellenized. In fact, it is

GOVERNORS OF JUDEA AD 6–62	
Coponius	6–9
Marcus Ambibulus	9–12
Annius Rufus	12–15
Valerius Gratus	15–26
Pontius Pilate	26–36
Marcellus	36–41
Herod Agrippa I	41–44
Cuspius Fadus	44–46
Tiberius I. Alexander	46–48
Ventidius Cumanus	48–52
Antonius Felix	52–60
Porcius Festus	60–62

during this time that the Pharisees began to coalesce to oppose the Hasmonean high priests, who were aligning with the Sadducees.

When the Roman general Pompey arrived in Jerusalem in 63 BC, he was welcomed by a civil war between two Hasmoneans, Hyrcanus II and Aristobulus II. Pompey sided with Hyrcanus and confirmed him as high priest, but Hyrcanus was soon deprived of civil rule. After the turmoil of the next two decades, both in Rome and Judea, Herod was declared king of the Jews by the senate (40 BC), and he solidified his power over the next three years. Herod "the Great"[2] was a client king of Rome and was known as a friend and ally of the Roman people. Even though Herod was religiously Jewish, he was descended from Edomite stock. He did not have much goodwill among the Jews, but with skill and an iron fist, he ably kept the peace between Rome and the Jews.

The reign of Herod sets the stage for the opening of the Gospels. First, under Herod the Jews were newly under the dominion and taxes of Rome, after being under Jewish Hasmonean rule for nearly a hundred years. Ezra's complaint of slavery throbbed with fresh vitality. In fact, after Pompey entered the temple, the extrabiblical book Psalms of Solomon was written, in which the author hoped for a righteous Davidic king-messiah to deliver the holy land.[3]

Second, Herod's massive building programs included the grand rebuilding of the temple, which was highly loved by most Jews and increased the feeling of national pride. However, Herod also constructed numerous pagan temples filled with images around Judea that infuriated the Jews. This was part of his skill as a ruler; he could delight with one hand and enrage with the other.

Third, the peace and prosperity Herod ushered in was carefully held together by his violent control. Herod zealously guarded his royal position and would snuff out any whiff of opposition. Hence, Herod massacred the infants in Bethlehem in Matthew 2, which is the only place he appears in Scripture. Herod had no qualms at burying a son who appeared threatening, which earned him a reputation. In an obituary for Herod called the Acta Diurna, Augustus reportedly said about Herod, "Gentlemen, it is better to be Herod's pig than to be his son."[4]

Finally, under Herod Romanization was added to the Hellenism of the past several centuries. Even though Greek and Roman culture had similarities, particularly from a Jewish point of view, Roman culture was a newer outside influence. To begin with, the Roman world was very hierarchical, glued together by honor and shame within patron-client relationship. The personified city of Roma was honored as a goddess. And the emperor was considered the paterfamilias of the entire empire, which became full-blown emperor worship after the death of Augustus. Thus, loyalty to Rome and its law was a matter of piety. Rome took over the heritage of Alexander the Great, which

is why Greek remained the lingua franca and Greek culture domi-
nated in the east. The Pax Romana, however, made Rome's power
felt everywhere.

The Pax Romana was a period of relative peace and great prosperity brought in by Caesar Augustus. As Strabo wrote about Augustus,
"The Romans and their allies have never enjoyed such peace and prosperity as that provided by Caesar Augustus from the point when he
acquired absolute dominion."⁵ Yet this peace was held together by the
Roman army and law. As Ferguson writes, "If for Greece the measure
of all things was man, for Rome the measure of all things was law."⁶ A
key foundation of the Pax Romana was Rome's elimination of pirates
from the Mediterranean so that trade could flourish. Likewise, the
totalitarian grip of Rome would squash any riot or uprising. The times
may have been prosperous and peaceful, but the Roman garrison and
taxes meant little freedom.

Back in Palestine, with the death of Herod the Great, Rome
changed its governmental structure. When Herod died in 4 BC (Jesus

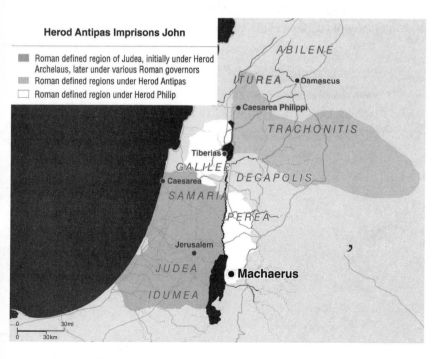

Herod Antipas Imprisons John

▨ Roman defined region of Judea, initially under Herod
  Archelaus, later under various Roman governors
▨ Roman defined regions under Herod Antipas
☐ Roman defined region under Herod Philip

ABILENE

ITUREA   ● Damascus

● Caesarea Philippi

TRACHONITIS

Tiberias ●

GALILEE   DECAPOLIS

● Caesarea

SAMARIA

PEREA

Jerusalem
●

JUDEA   ● **Machaerus**

IDUMEA

0   30mi
0   30km

was born a few years before this), Rome divided his realm up between his three sons. Herod Antipas was made the tetrarch of Galilee and Peraea, who remained in power from 4 BC to AD 39. Herod Antipas is the one who kills John the Baptist and holds a trial for Jesus. The tetrarchy of Iturea and Trachonitis was given to Philip. Herod's son, Archelaus, inherited the ethnarchy of Judea, Idumea, and Samaria. However, his short reign ended in AD 6, when Judea was transferred to direct Roman control, governed by a Roman prefect (Pilate's office).

JEWISH LIFE IN THE FIRST CENTURY

Notwithstanding all the outside influences, though, Jewish life and society within Palestine and outside had its own distinct character. By the first century, the Jewish population had grown and spread throughout the Roman Empire. Some estimates register that seven percent of the Roman population was Jewish.[7] We do not know the exact character of Judaism within the diaspora communities, for it could change greatly from one locale to the next. Some diaspora communities could be very Hellenized and syncretistic, while others could be zealously devoted to Pharisaical customs. Similarly, some Jewish communities had good relations with the local authorities, while others were persecuted.

Yet due to the favor of Julius Caesar and Augustus, Herod the Great had secured several privileges for the Jews. The Jews could freely practice their religion, being exempted from the necessity of worshipping the Roman gods, and they could regulate their communities by their law. Particularly significant was the protection for messengers to transport the half-shekel temple tax from diaspora communities to Jerusalem, which helped contribute to the enormous wealth of the temple in the first century AD. Other privileges, which were granted more locally and sporadically, were Sabbath protections, kosher meat markets, and exemption from military service.

Judaism, then, benefited from many privileges granted under the Roman government, but these privileges did not necessarily translate into the Jews being respected. Some Gentiles were attracted to Judaism enough to become God-fearers or even proselytes (see below), but "most cultivated Greeks and Romans expressed a negative attitude toward Jews."[8] Not only was circumcision considered gross and highly offensive to the Greeks and Romans, but Jewish ways were strange and base to their standards. A good example of this comes from the Roman historian Tacitus. Tacitus blames the Jews' Sabbath practice on their laziness. He describes the Jews as regarding the rest of humankind with the hatred of enemies, and comments that converts to Judaism do so "to despise the gods, to disown their country, and set at naught parents, children and brethren." Tacitus summarizes: "All their other customs, which are at once perverse and disgusting, owe their strength to their very badness. ... The Jewish religion is tasteless and mean" (Histories 5.5). This hostile prejudice, though, was not uniform across the empire. Local communities varied drastically within the Roman world. Ferguson concludes that in places where Jewish customs were unfamiliar, anti-Semitism flared, but where they were more familiar, attitudes were more favorable.[9]

Within Palestine, Jewish society and life was marked by the existence of several different parties or sects. Particularly noteworthy for the New Testament are the Pharisees and the Sadducees. These two are by no means exhaustive, and there were even subgroups within them. Furthermore, complex religious, social, and political issues interact within the parties and make it difficult to determine the lines of inclusion. Nevertheless, famed ancient Jewish historian Josephus describes the Jews as having three basic sects of philosophy (Antiquities 18.12–25).

First, the Pharisees were characterized by their zeal for the law and the tradition of the elders in keeping this law. They lived frugally and were keenly devoted in all matters of purity, worship, and Sabbath. With a few exceptions, the Pharisees believed that everything happened by fate or providence, that the soul survived death, and that the afterlife included a bodily resurrection as well as eternal rewards and punishments. They also interpreted the law in light of custom. The

Pharisees tended to dominate in the synagogue, were more middle class, and enjoyed more support from the populace. The academic offices of scribes and lawyers seem to have favored Pharisaic ideas. This most likely explains why Jesus conflicted with the Pharisees so often. Yet Pharisees still could be found among the nobles, had seats in the Sanhedrin (the Jewish ruling council), and were supported by wealthy landowners.

Second, the Sadducees are associated more with the upper class and the priests. Josephus says that few were Sadducees but that they were of the highest dignity. Where the synagogue housed the Pharisees, the Sadducees centered around the temple. This is a generalization and should not be taken to mean that all priests were Sadducees or vice versa. According to Josephus, the Sadducees read the law without custom, rejected fate and the resurrection, and believed souls perish with the body. [10] Moreover, as they belonged to the ruling class, the Sadducees were more likely to hold to the status quo and to cooperate with the Romans to retain power and peace. [11]

Third, Josephus mentions the Essenes and describes them as being more fervent than the Pharisees. Like the Pharisees, the Essenes believed in the immortality of the soul, the resurrection, and eternal rewards for righteousness. The Essenes lived in their own communities and held to varying ideas that the Jerusalem temple was defiled or illegitimate. The Qumran community was likely one expression of these Essene ideas. Josephus also praises the Essenes as surpassing all other men by being addicted to virtue and righteousness. Some Essenes were monastic and ascetic, while others married. It is possible that "Essene" is a more general term to describe numerous sects that lived apart from society and shared many similarities.

Even though Josephus names three sects, he does add a fourth, which he attributes to Judas the Galilean as being the founder. This sect is more political and are basically the Zealots. Josephus writes that "these men agree in all other things with the Pharisaic notions; but they have an inviolable attachment to liberty" (*Antiquities* 18.23). They believed it unlawful to pay taxes to Rome, and Josephus credits them as making the nation "grow mad with this distemper" and revolt from the Romans.

This brief tasting menu of the different Jewish parties is designed to fill in a partial background for reading the New Testament. Yet as readers, we need to remember that social and religious classes or parties are complex and often

HIGH PRIESTS AD 6–37

Annas son of Seth	6–15
Ishmael son of Phiabi	15–16
Eleazar son of Annas	16–17
Simon son of Camithus	17–18
Joseph son of Caiaphas	18–37

have porous or stretchy boundary lines. As Saldarini states, "Great care must be taken not to impose modern concepts and rigid systems on antiquity."[12] This sampling, though, allows us to get a better feel for Jewish life in Palestine and the world that Jesus and his disciples belonged to. In addition, this background enables us to appreciate more fully the context into which Jesus was born.

THE BIRTH AND KINGDOM OF JESUS

What was the nature of Jesus' kingdom? What kind of king would he be? How did the popular concepts of the coming Messiah align with Jesus' own conception? The answers to these questions are brought out by the Gospels.

The year is within two years of Herod the Great's death, 7–5 BC. Herod's carnage in Bethlehem well fits with the succession paranoia at the end of his life, in which he had three of his sons executed. For two decades, Caesar Augustus had been successfully ruling Rome. Coins with his image could be found in Jewish pockets. Temples dedicated to him dotted the empire. The titles he bore multiplied in number and prestige. He was addressed as the Imperator and the Savior of the World. The title of Pontifex Maximus, which meant he was the high priest of the state religion of Rome, was granted to him. About this time, the Senate declared Augustus the "Father of the Country" and set up in his honor an altar in Rome called the Pax Augustus, the peace of Augustus. Moreover, since Julius Caesar was deified post-mortem, "Son of God" rested upon Augustus. Before Gabriel revealed to Mary that her son would be called the Son of God, Augustus was addressed as the same. The peace of Augustus may have covered the land, but for many Jews he was still an unwelcome dictator. Therefore, in Nazareth matters were not so peaceful.

Due to some historical ambiguity, we are not able to date precisely this first census,[13] but we do know of Quirinius. When Quirinius ordered a census, a wave of Jewish discontent erupted into little revolts across the country.[14] And one of the leading rebels was Judas the Galilean, whom Josephus credited as the head of the Zealot movement. In fact, Judas preached that taxation was slavery, so the Jews should express their liberty by refusing the census and rioting instead. The imperial decree that was issued demanded that people be registered, but registration served the purposes of taxation. As part of Rome's governmental administration, taxation required regular censuses. This is the event that Luke brings to mind as the setting for the birth of Jesus. On the way to Bethlehem, then, Joseph and Mary likely passed on the road picketers and rebels decrying how it was sinful to be registered, how they should not submit to Rome's taxation. These new parents were armed with the knowledge that this boy to be born would be David's greater Son; he would be greater than Moses. When Moses was born, his birth was marked by acts of civil disobedience. The midwives lied to Pharaoh; Moses was hidden in the reeds. But Joseph's first act as father, before Jesus was born, was to register to pay taxes. Jesus' birth is marked by obedience to the state. Something is different about this child.

Earlier on, when the angel appeared to Joseph, he relayed that the boy was to be named Jesus, "for he will save his people from their sins" (Matt 1:21). Jesus is the Greek form of the Hebrew name Joshua—a strong name for a leader, one who could destroy the enemies of God's people. Yet the angel does not mention enemies. In the Old Testament, the word for "save" almost always refers to God delivering Israel from their hostile foes or physical distresses. "Save" is not normally paired with sins. The angel, though, clearly states that Jesus will save the people from their sins. The political zeal in the air does not seem to align with the message about Jesus from the angels.

In fact, each Gospel in its own way contrasts the public's expectation and preconceived ideas about the Messiah with what type of Messiah Jesus reveals himself to be. In the first century, there was no one stable concept of the Messiah. Several messianic figures floated about within the current ideas: a Davidic Messiah, an Aaronic Messiah, the greater Mosaic-like prophet, and even a Melchizedek figure. Yet within these various hopes, one expectation was constant: that the period ushered in would resemble the Solomonic age with its political and geographical features. As Talmon writes, "[the messianic era] is seen as a sublime reenactment of the favorable conditions which obtained in the idealized period of the united monarchy under David and Solomon."[15] The historical realities remembered under Solomon were idealized and expected to come to fruition. Lurking just under the surface of Pharisaic ideas, the tendencies toward zealotry against Rome were consistent with these messianic hopes. The Gospels, however, simultaneously embrace the Old Testament promises concerning the Messiah and push against popular expectations.

In Luke, with the spirit of Elijah, John the Baptist would make the people's hearts ready for the coming of the Lord. Gabriel piles honorable descriptions on Mary's boy: the Son of the Most High, the throne of David, the Holy One to reign forever. Mary sings of her enemies being scattered and the humble ones being exalted. Zechariah praises the Lord for the horn of salvation raised up in the house of David to deliver them from their enemies. The angel tells the shepherds, "a great joy that will be for all the peoples. For unto you is born this day in the city of David, a Savior, who is Christ the Lord." The angelic choir harmonizes, "Peace on earth," even as riots spark over taxes. How can these headlines not ignite the Solomonic desires of the people? Yet Luke closes the joyful scene with something unsettled.

All who heard the shepherds were disturbed and amazed, while Mary treasured these things up in her heart (Luke 2:18–19). The glory of the angelic music clashes with a baby lying in a barn.

In a similar fashion, Matthew lays out every step of Jesus' early life to paint him as the new David and new Israel. Jesus' genealogy links him to the promises of Abraham and David. Conceived by the Spirit, they shall call his name Immanuel ("God with us," Matt 1:23). Following a star from the east, the magi lay royal gifts before him as the Messiah, while Herod seeks to eliminate him as a political threat. After sojourning in Egypt, Joseph returns to Nazareth to fulfill Scripture, "Out of Egypt, I called my son" (Matt 2:15). Within the motif of a second exodus, adorned with lofty images of Isaiah, there is no doubt that Jesus is the Messiah, both the Davidic king and the greater-than-Moses prophet.

When Jesus comes of age, though, the manner of his ministry differs from the common public hopes—even from those of his forerunner, John the Baptist. At Jesus' baptism, John clearly acknowledges him as the greater one: "I need to be baptized by you" (Matt 3:14). He also identifies Jesus as "the Lamb of God, who takes away the sin of the world" (John 1:29). While this is sacrificial imagery and not a royal title, it indicates that John knows something of Jesus' unique destiny. But later, after John has been imprisoned and Jesus is well into his ministry, John's confidence has turned to doubt: "Are you the one who is to come, or shall we look for another?" (Matt 11:3). The ministry of Jesus was not what John expected from the Messiah.

In Luke 4, Jesus begins his messianic ministry as the promise from Isaiah 61 is fulfilled in his reading, "The Spirit of the Lord is upon me … to proclaim good news to the poor; he sent me to proclaim liberty to the captives" (Luke 4:18). The Nazarenes begin to foam at the mouth with praise and expectation for Jesus, but he cuts their excitement off at the knees. He knew they were going to ask for a sign, but he refuses, and the Nazarenes try to toss him off a cliff.

The Nazarenes had false expectations for the Messiah. In fact, if you take Isaiah 61 in a sociopolitical way, then Jesus has to be judged a failure. There is no account of Jesus freeing any prisoners; instead, he left John the Baptist in prison to be beheaded. The twelve disciples and Jesus held money, some of which was given as alms, but he did not move anyone up the socioeconomic ladder. Peter and John quit being fishermen to follow Jesus. Jesus made people poorer, not wealthier—just ask Zacchaeus. If "poor" and "good news" have financial referents, then Jesus did not fulfill Isaiah 61. He preached more against the evils of money and the virtues of poverty. Hence, when Jesus asked the Twelve what the crowds think of him, they respond with John, Elijah, or one of the prophets (Matt 16:14; Luke 9:19). The political, royal messianic ideas popular among the people did not match what they saw in Jesus. On one occasion, being swept up with excitement, the crowd approached to force Jesus to be king, but he hid out on the mountain, refusing to have any part of it (John 6:15). Consistent through all the Gospels, the theme resounds that Jesus will define his own messiahship and will not suffer the public to impose their definition upon him.

This discrepancy between Jesus and the populace raises the question about the kingdom. The melody of Jesus' preaching and teaching was the kingdom of God. Matthew favors the name "kingdom of heaven," but this is synonymous, as heaven is merely a more pious circumlocution for God. If Jesus announced the coming of the kingdom, then what is the kingdom? Whatever it is, clearly the nature of Jesus' messiahship and the makeup of his kingdom are related.

The simplest and most accurate definition of the kingdom comes from looking at the end of the story, the goal of Christ's work. Spoiler alert: the kingdom of God is the new heavens and new earth. The kingdom of Christ is new creation. The final, eternal realities of the majestic new Jerusalem woven in full color in Revelation 21–22 show the kingdom in its fullness.

As Jesus' time drew near to the cross, his teaching and preaching began to clarify this definition. In John 14, Jesus forewarned his disciples that he was going away to prepare a place for them before his return. The Olivet discourse and the parables of the latter days all direct the disciples to a time when they must be alert and awake when the Son of Man comes on the clouds of heaven to separate the sheep from the goats and to grant the upright eternal life. Equally clear, however, is the fact that the kingdom is present in and with Jesus. After his resurrection and upon the ascension, all authority is given to Jesus and he takes his seat at the right hand in heaven (Matt 28:18; Luke 22:29). Likewise, the presence of the kingdom was revealed in Jesus' ministry, as he said, "If it is by the finger of God that I cast out demons, then the kingdom of God has come upon you" (Luke 11:20). This tension between future and present is often referred to as the "already but not yet" nature of the kingdom. In his resurrection, Jesus obtained the kingdom fully, but some of its blessings are manifest now while others await his second coming.

The new creation essence of the kingdom further elucidates the earthly ministry of Jesus, beyond his preaching. While the Lord Jesus did not free political prisoners, he did perform miracles. And his miracles were signs and portents of his salvation. It is helpful to think of his miracles in three ways. First, all of his miracles revealed the identity of Jesus, but some of them were more exclusively revelatory, like walking on water, turning water into wine, calming the sea, and the transfiguration. Secondly, many of the miracles focus on healing, such as restoring the blind, deaf, and crippled, raising the dead, or healing the leper. Such ailments reflect the common curses that hobble humanity, even the curse of death, all of which entered the world through sin. To ultimately slaughter death, sin must be dealt with. Therefore, early in his ministry, Jesus healed a paralyzed man by declaring his sins forgiven. These healings point us to the resurrection when the last cancer and defect will be eradicated, and they signal Jesus' power to deal with sin. In the words of Hebrews, Jesus appeared once to bear sins, and he will appear a second time to save those waiting for him (Heb 9:26–28).

Third, others of Jesus' miracles stressed the defeat of demons and the evil one.[16] The text of the Gospels clarify that Jesus set his sights on Satan. Hence, this theme leaps out of the starting gate with Jesus in the desert parrying Satan's three temptations. And once he is back within civilization, Jesus unsheathes his sword upon the demons. In Mark, Jesus' first miracle is silencing the impure spirit who calls him out as the Holy One of God (Mark 1:24–25). In Matthew, Jesus calms the stormy sea, which imitates the divine warrior motif of the Old Testament, and then he sends the Gadarene demons into a heard of pigs and drowns them (Matt 8:23–34). In his own way, Luke stresses the demon-conquering power of Jesus. After escaping the lynch mob of Nazareth, Jesus enters the synagogue of Capernaum to rebuke an impure demon (Luke 4:35). This word for "rebuke" comes from divine warrior contexts of the Old Testament, where it refers to the verbal assaults of the Lord upon the forces of evil and chaos. The Lord blasts the chaotic sea and it becomes dry (Ps 106:9; Nah 1:3). The Lord blasts the nations that roar, and they flee as chaff before the storm (Isa 17:13). And twice in Zechariah 3 the Lord blasts Satan. Jesus, then, blasts the demon with the power of his voice as the divine warrior. This motif in Luke hits a crescendo upon the return of the seventy disciples from their mission trip, when Jesus declares, "I saw Satan fall like lightning from heaven" (Luke 10:18).

These three characteristics of Jesus' miracles echo the original promise to Eve that her offspring would mortally wound the serpent. They make manifest that Jesus had come to remedy the original curse of sin and the agent of its coming, Satan. He came not to be served, but to serve and lay down his life as a ransom for many (Matt 20:28), to pour his blood out for the forgiveness of sins (Matt 26:28). And it is for this reason that once Peter declares Jesus to be the Christ, each Synoptic Gospel beats the drum of the cross. Jesus is not a messiah who will enjoy earthly honor and prestige, but shame and death.

Ruins of Capernaum

As Christians enculturated to the language and art of the cross, it is difficult to appreciate the radical offense of crucifixion to first-century sensibilities. First, the Messiah was the holy servant of God, and the holy belonged to the inviolable glory of God, untouchable by the curse. Second, crucifixion was the epitome of cursed shame and wretched judgment (Deut 21:23). Upon the rack, scum-of-the-earth criminals were stripped naked and tortured in ways only limited by the imagination of their executioners. As a grotesque banner, their bodies were exposed and displayed as those cursed by the gods and men as warnings for all to heed.

The holy cannot be judged in such a way, yet here was the Christ, trudging toward the condemning cross. To the first-century psyche, the combination of death, especially on a cross, and Christ would be like a spark to mental gunpowder, blowing up their neural networks. This is why Peter so quickly flew off the handle to rebuke Jesus when Jesus said he would be killed (Matt 16:22; 20:19). To mention Messiah and death encroached upon the blasphemous. Yet Jesus would not budge; he was the suffering Messiah destined for slaughter.

John surfaces this paradoxical nature of Jesus' messiahship in his own vivid style, which begins with a pun. In John 3, Jesus speaks about how the Son of Man, who descended from heaven, must also be lifted up. Yet the more common use of being "lifted up" carries the sense of exaltation, glorification. The Son of Man must be glorified. There is nothing odd about this—until Jesus likens this uplifting to Moses lifting up the bronze serpent in the wilderness. The bronze serpent was a figurine of cursed snakes that poisoned the sinful Israelites. It was an image of the curse looked to in faith to be healed from that very curse. Jesus' exaltation, then, was being lifted up as a curse. The Father glorified his name in Jesus as he was lifted up to draw all people to himself and to cast out the ruler of this world (John 12:28–32). The cross becomes both the defeat of the evil one and the way for the Son to die for the salvation of all who believe in him.

The "already" presence and blessings of the kingdom, therefore, include Jesus entering his kingdom through death and resurrection, which then rains down the presence of the Holy Spirit for the forgiveness of sins and the formation of the church. Luke exhibits the expansion of the kingdom as the preaching of repentance for forgiveness in Christ's name (Luke 24:46–49). Matthew describes it as the disciples going forth to make disciples through baptism and teaching (Matt 28:18–20). This triumphant progression of the kingdom, however, never advances beyond the cruciform pattern. Being a disciple entails self-denial and cross-bearing to imitate the crucified, now exalted Christ. Jesus forewarns how his people will suffer for him, for it is enough for the disciple to be like his teacher (Matt 10:25). And as servants awaiting the return of our Master, disciples will eagerly remain alert for the coming of the Son of Man and the resurrection (John 5:28–29).

The "not yet" aspects of the kingdom encompass all the glorious realities not enjoyed in the present. The ability to look upon the Savior and King for everlasting life (John 17:24). The resurrection of the unjust and the just (John 5:29). The judgment of wicked unto eternal punishment (Matt 25:46). And the everlasting life for those who believed in Christ (John 6:47).

By the end of the Gospels, Jesus had shown how the Law, the Prophets, and the Psalms all speak about him. He is the Davidic Messiah, but his throne resides in heaven and not in earthly Jerusalem. He did not come to change the political order or to improve the economy; rather, he rendered things unto Caesar to show that these earthly kingdoms with their wealth are passing away. Jesus was both priest and sacrifice, as he became the Lamb of God who took away sins in the pouring out of his blood to inaugurate the new covenant. And Jesus was the prophet greater than Moses, who taught with greater authority than all the scribes (Matt 7:29). Jesus did not allow the populace or his disciples to define his messiahship or his kingdom. Instead, with his face set toward Jerusalem, Jesus would not swerve from the path of the cross for our salvation. And with equal power and fidelity, Jesus will not lose a single soul given to him by the Father, but will raise up each one on the last day.

THE GEOGRAPHY OF JESUS' MINISTRY

When it comes to the dates and places of Jesus' ministry, honesty requires us to admit there is much we do not know. From a strict chronological point of view, the Gospels raise more questions than they answer. To begin with, Matthew locates Jesus' birth in a general window, before Herod the Great's death (7–5 BC). The dating of Luke's infant narrative adds more wrinkles. In agreement with Matthew, Herod is king when Zechariah receives notification of Elizabeth's pregnancy, but roughly fifteen months later when Mary's due date arrives, Quirinius is governor of Syria, which according to Roman history dates to AD 6–7. How this works is unclear.[17] Furthermore, we have no precise age for when Jesus began his ministry; Luke says, "about thirty years of age" (Luke 3:23). "About" indicates that Luke rounded up or down, but which way and by how many years we do not know. Could

Jesus be as young as twenty-six or as old as thirty-four? By modern rounding standards, this is possible, but Luke's rounding technique is unknown. Jesus' ministry has been assumed to have lasted three years, but this figure has been computed from John's Gospel that puts Jesus in Jerusalem for three Passovers (John 2:13; 6:4; 12:1). Yet it would be an unfounded assumption that these were the only three Passovers during Jesus' ministry. All we can say is that Jesus lived to be at least thirty, and his ministry seems to have lasted about three years. Allowing for a larger spectrum within ancient rounding, this bookends a period for Jesus from 8 BC to AD 35.

Such dating imprecision, or apparent contradiction, aggravates our modern historical sensibilities. But this uncomfortable sensation should alert us to the cultural shock of the ancient world. As moderns, our lives are ruled by the clock and calendar; we know the minute and hour we were born. Watches and phones schedule our daily routines. Chronology monopolizes the discipline of history. But rewind the calendar back a mere fifty, one hundred, or two hundred years, and, depending on where one lived, this was not the case. In the Roman period, the composition of a historical narrative was not organized solely based on chronology; rather, logical or thematic concerns may take preference. For example, the Roman historian, Suetonius, stated this about his account of Augustus: "After this summary of Augustus' life, I shall fill in its various parts; but the story will be more readable and understandable if, instead of keeping a chronological order, I use a topical arrangement" (*Lives* 2.9). Besides, narratives by necessity have to be selective, and such selection follows the author's purpose. For example, John confesses that his goal is for readers to believe that Jesus is the Christ (John 20:31), but he honestly admits Jesus did a great many more signs and deeds, which he did not include, for they would fill the world with books (John 20:30; 21:25). Luke, likewise, states his purpose that Theophilus may be certain of the matters he learned (Luke 1:4). John wrote for faith, Luke for assurance.

Luke adds further information about his writing process and product. He gives his credentials for writing, saying he "followed all things closely for some time past" (Luke 1:3). This phrase implies a focused and diligent dedication to learning and mastering the material. Luke also mentions eyewitnesses and ministers of the word, which discloses his personal access to such authorities. In the ancient world, and even today to some extent, it was thought that you could not write a proper history without having access to eyewitnesses. A good and reliable history required that you had experienced the events or had interviewed eyewitnesses. Luke, then, composes a factual account based upon the testimony of those who were companions of Jesus. Additionally, Luke labels his product a "narrative," which means an orderly description of facts, events, actions, and words. He describes his narrative as precise and orderly (v. 3). However, Luke does not make his organization explicit. The sequence from birth to death and ascension is obvious enough, but within his book, many sections seem to be more thematically organized.

Sea of Galilee

The chronological tensions we sense, either within a single Gospel or between Gospels, should not trouble us as being erroneous or untrue. Each Gospel writer, using his own sources and memory, and carried along by the Spirit, composed a factual, historical account of Jesus' ministry in a manner that served their pastoral and theological purposes. According to the best standards of the day, it was not dishonest or manipulative to rearrange events from a chronological order to a thematic one. Rather, it served to reveal the meaning and significance of the events for the reader's clarity.

Despite certain limits concerning a timeline for Jesus' life, the Gospels do present a unified portrait of his ministry and death. The Synoptic Gospels (Matthew, Mark, and Luke) record Jesus' activity primarily in Galilee and the Decapolis. After returning from Egypt, Jesus grew up in Nazareth, as the city was considered his hometown (Matt 13:45; John 1:45). In Mark 6:3, Jesus is called the son of a carpenter, but this word can refer to a craftsman who works in a variety of materials from wood to stone. A general contractor may be a better modern comparison. At some point, likely near the beginning of his ministry, Jesus relocated to Capernaum (Matt 4:13), which functioned as his home base for his itinerant ministry. As a small fishing village nestled on the northern end of the Sea of Galilee, Capernaum was home to Peter's mother's house, and it lay near the border between Antipas' and Philip's tetrarchies. Matthew or Levi may have been a toll collector at this border crossing (Matt 9:9).

Branching out from Capernaum, Jesus crisscrossed Galilee extensively and found himself on both sides of the Sea of Galilee. Luke mentions Jesus ministering in Judea (Luke 4:44; so John 3:22), and each Synoptic mentions Jews following him from Judea, but none of this southern ministry is explicitly narrated, save in the environs of Jerusalem. The unusual practice of Jesus was to preach and teach in the local synagogues, particularly on the Sabbath. His most well-known open-air teaching is the Sermon on the Mount in Matthew or the Sermon on the Plain in Luke, though no specific location is given for either. Another frequent setting for Jesus' teaching was around the table, a particular favorite for Luke. The Synoptics also do not locate the mountain where Jesus was transfigured, other than being within the vicinity of Caesarea Philippi. Even the address for the feeding of five thousand is unlisted, beyond being on the east of the Sea of Galilee.

Simply put, the Gospels are not intended to be travel journals. Rather, the Synoptics are presenting the person and work of Jesus to reveal him as the Messiah. This interest in Jesus' identity surfaces also by the focus of his destination: Jerusalem. Often, the Gospels have been called passion narratives with long introductions. Luke has Jesus set his face toward Jerusalem in 9:51. Matthew has his crosshairs on the holy city in 16:21, and Mark in 8:31. Even though Jesus is all over the map in his early ministry, a clear trajectory soon emerges, aimed directly at Golgotha.

In contrast to the Synoptics, John's Gospel focuses on Jerusalem from the outset. For example, Luke doesn't locate Jesus in Jerusalem in all of chapters 3–18. In John, though, Jesus cleanses the temple shortly after he turns up the cheer with more wine in Cana (John 2:13). After

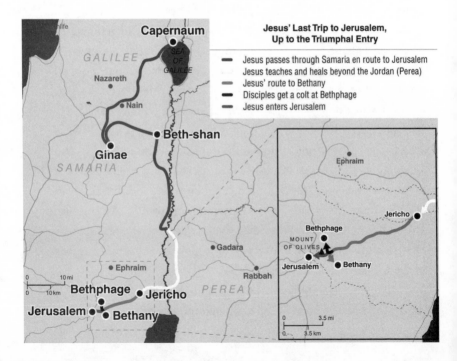

sharing a conversation with the Samaritan woman, Jesus returns to Jerusalem for a healing and Sabbath debate in John 5. The grand Feast of Booths forms the setting for the events of 7:1–10:21. At the Festival of Rededication, the Jews pick up stones to put an end to him (10:22–39). A few short miles east of Jerusalem, the little town of Bethany witnesses the raising of Lazarus. By the opening of chapter 12, it is six days before the fateful Passover, with Jesus again enjoying the hospitality of Mary, Martha, and Lazarus. After his royal procession into the capital, Jesus washes his disciples' feet and nestles down for his long, Last Supper table talk (13:1–17:26). The final blueprint of John's Gospel, then, places Jesus in or near Jerusalem in every major event save two: the Samaritan woman (John 4), and the bread of life discourse (John 6).

This geographical divergence between the Synoptics and John should not trouble our historical sensibilities. The Mosaic law required that every Israelite male present themselves before the Lord at his temple three times a year for the pilgrim feasts (Deut 16:16), though first-century women and children often made the trip as well.[18] In order to fulfill all righteousness, Jesus trekked up to the city of David at a minimum of three times per year, while spending the rest of his time ministering in the other regions of Galilee and the Decapolis. This tri-annual habit provides a straightforward explanation for how the Synoptics can focus on his Galilean ministry while John favors Jesus' visits to Jerusalem. In fact, the two different approaches grant us as readers a fuller portrait of the extraordinary ministry of Jesus.

JESUS' FINAL WEEK

If the times and places of the Gospels lead us down some thorny paths, then the events of Jesus' final week drive us to a barbed-wire fence. Aligning the affairs leading up to the trial and crucifixion has been a notoriously difficult problem, yielding many negative assessments of the Gospels by scholars. Joseph A. Fitzmyer concludes this debate in the following way: "The upshot is that we cannot answer the question when the historical Jesus ate the Last Supper or whether he ate it as a Passover meal. ... No attempt should be made to harmonize the Synoptic and Johannine traditions."[19] His point is well taken. As we saw with the birth of Jesus above, Matthew and Luke did not write in a way to harmonize their accounts. Yet even with Fitzmyer's valid conclusion, a basic outline of Jesus' final days shines through, adorned with rich theology. A couple of preliminary points are necessary.

First, it is regularly assumed for both the Old Testament and the first century that a day began at sunset and went to the following sunset. Yet Milgrom has argued convincingly that this is an erroneous assumption. In the Old Testament, the day clearly began in the morning with sunrise. In the postexilic period, some evidence may point to an evening start of the day, but it is ambiguous. Milgrom concludes, "In any event, the sacrificial service at the Temple never changed; until the destruction of the Temple in C.E. 70, the day began in the morning."[20] Sadly, the misunderstanding of an evening start to the day taints many reconstructions of the New Testament.

Secondly, the calendar for Passover and the Feast of Unleavened Bread from the Old Testament ought to be firmly set before us. According to the law, this first holy pilgrim feast fell in the first month (named Abib or Nisan).[21] These two feasts were held together, with Passover being day one and the Feast of Unleavened Bread following for the next seven (see table). Passover was on the fourteenth of the month. The first day of the Feast of Unleavened Bread was a festival Sabbath on the fifteenth. The weekly Sabbath did not factor into these days, and so it could fall wherever it landed. Finally, Nisan 16 was the first barley offering and the day of firstfruits, when they started counting fifty days, as it was practiced in the Second Temple period (Lev 23:10).[22] In the New Testament, this eight-day festival is often referred to as a whole, as either the Passover or Feast of Unleavened Bread.

	Thursday Nisan 13	Friday Nisan 14	Sabbath Nisan 15	Sunday Nisan 16
Old Testament Law		Passover: Lamb killed, eaten in evening	Unleavened Bread: Festival Sabbath	Firstfruits: Barley offering, begin count to Pentecost
New Testament Events	Supper begins in the afternoon; Synoptics label as Passover. At night, they eat supper and go to Gethsemane. Jesus is arrested, tried, and beaten. Peter denies him.	**6 a.m. to 12 p.m.:** Pilate trial(s) **12 p.m. to 3 p.m.:** Jesus on the cross, lambs killed in the temple. **3 p.m. to sunset:** Jesus buried, Passover eaten after sunset.	High Sabbath = weekly, same day as festival.	Before sunrise, women go out to the empty tomb.

Table 6: Passion Timeline

With these as background, the final week of Jesus comes into greater focus. In order to fulfill the royal prophecy of Zechariah 9, Jesus proceeds into Jerusalem riding upon a donkey. Each Gospel records his triumphant entry, as the crowds chanted Psalm 118 in exultation to the King. From John 12:12, this parade happened five days before Passover; the Synoptics do not date it. During these days, Jesus stayed the night out in Bethany and spent his days teaching in the temple (Luke 21:37–38). The debates with the Sadducees and Pharisees, the cursing of the fig tree, and the parables of the last days all transpire within this time. Then, Jesus has his disciples prepare a meal for them all in a large room in Jerusalem. The Synoptics clearly present this as a Passover meal. John, though, dates it before the Feast of Passover (John 13:1).

Garden of Gethsemane

During this last supper, Jesus institutes the Lord's Supper, Judas leaves to betray him, and Jesus' teaching goes late into the evening. As darkness has settled over the land, Jesus and the eleven disciples exit Jerusalem to pray on the Mount of Olives in the garden of Gethsemane. The snoring disciples awaken when Judas shows up with a small battalion of soldiers and temple officers to arrest Jesus. As the night wears on, the priests have plenty of items to check off their to-do list. They shuffle Jesus around between Caiaphas and Annas, during which time Peter denies Jesus three times and Jesus is beaten. By sunrise, the high priests gain a hearing with Pilate. The trial and mocking of Jesus before Pilate unfolded over the course of the morning, for by noon Jesus had been strung up to be crucified.[23] Some scholars doubt everything in the Gospels could be done in such a short span of time, but this fails to take into consideration that the priests were in a hurry and their only concern was the mere appearance of justice.

With Jesus marching out to Golgotha bearing his own execution device, John remarks that it was the Day of Preparation, which refers to the time when the lambs were brought into the temple, sacrificed, and then eaten after sundown. According to ancient rabbinic sources, the priests began to slaughter the lambs at noon. So, as Jesus stumbles outside the city, the Passover lambs are led into the temple. As the throats of the lambs are slit, the blood of Jesus drips down the cross. Between noon and three, the blackness of the day of the Lord drenches the whole land. As the clock strikes three, the temple curtain tears in two. Jesus knows the end has arrived, saying "My God, my God, why have you forsaken me?" and "It is finished." Then giving up his spirit, he dies. The earth shakes and rocks split open like eggs. Even the bodies of dead saints are raised and appear to many after Jesus' resurrection (Matt 27:52–53). After being well acquainted with the day of the Lord imagery of the Old Testament prophets, Jesus' death is unmistakably the Lord pouring out his fury—on his Anointed One.

Once Jesus has willingly laid down his life and the sun has returned, the disciples face an urgent task. Being the Day of Preparation, the bodies have to be buried before sundown. Joseph of Arimathea has secured Jesus' body from Pilate, so he wraps the cold cadaver in linen and quickly embalms him. A new tomb close to a garden was close by, so Joseph laid the corpse down and closed the great stone door. As the Sabbath rolls in, the women and disciples rest according to the commandment. The ladies, though, are not satisfied with Jesus' preparation for burial.

At the crack of dawn, a few of the women hurry out to the tomb to pay their last respects and finish up the funeral. Yet to their shock and dismay, the grave is open, revealing only clothes, no body. Fear and uncertainty flood into the hearts of the ladies, as if they just rammed an iceberg soon to be inundated by the frosty deep. An angel guarding the tomb tells them, "Do not be afraid, for he is risen!" The promise of Jesus has come to pass. He was handed over to the chief priests, crucified, and on the third day, he rose from the dead. (The three days are not to be taken as a seventy-two-hour period. Jesus died Friday at about 3 p.m. and by Sunday sunrise had donned his new body. This does not cover a full forty-eight hours, but part of Friday, all of Saturday, and part of Sunday, rounding out to three days.)

The Kidron Valley, with Jerusalem on the right and the Mount of Olives on the left

Nevertheless, as the risen King, Jesus meets with his disciples to shore up their weak faith and disclose how everything in Moses, the Prophets, and the Psalms are fulfilled in him. In his second volume, Luke says these resurrection appearances lasted forty days. Having been made both Lord and Christ, Jesus commissions his apostles, once they receive the Spirit, to announce forgiveness of sins to all nations, baptizing them and making disciples of them, even to the end of the age. They will see Christ return in the same manner as he was taken up from them: in a cloud of glory.

STUDY QUESTIONS

1. What is Hellenization?

2. Describe how Romanization influenced Judea.

3. What were the four sects within Jewish life?

4. What is the kingdom of God?

5. How did Jesus' miracles reveal the nature of his kingdom?

6. How did the popular expectation for the Messiah differ from what Jesus taught?

7. How do John and the Synoptic Gospels differ in their accounts of Jesus?

8. How did Jesus' time on the cross show forth the day of the Lord?

11

THE ACTS OF THE APOSTLES

Bible Reading: Acts

Can you imagine what they had seen? What profound mysteries they had heard made clear? Since the baptism of John, the apostles had followed Jesus around in the dust of Galilee. John confesses that all the acts of Jesus could make the world obese with books, and the apostles had read these unpublished books. Yet quick on the uptake is not an expertise the disciples could juggle. The Gospels do not laud the apostles with tales of heroics and sagas of superhuman faith; rather, they frankly narrate the apostles as men with clay feet. If we judged Jesus by the fealty of his followers, he would not have made it into the history books. If it was not for the resurrection, the Jesus-movement would have ran out of fuel on the runway. The resurrection, though, did not repair all the flaws of the disciples or shore up what was lacking in their education. The Risen Lord was clear that they needed something extra. The apostles had to remain in Jerusalem until they were clothed with the power from the Father, the Holy Spirit. And it is within this holding period that Acts opens its gates.

An ancient writing technique for a two-volume work was to link them with a hinge. The hinge repeated the material at the end of volume one at the beginning of volume two. The ascension and com-mission of Christ at the close of Luke is retold at the opening of Acts. By duplicating this information, Luke sketches out the map and key for his second volume. Specifically, Luke's prologue offers five guid-ing considerations.

First, Luke tells his patron, Theophilus, that in his first book he dealt with everything Jesus *began* to do and teach (Acts 1:1). If Luke's Gospel is the beginning of Jesus' work, then Acts is the rest of Christ's work. This means that volume two has been misnamed. This book is not "The Acts of the Apostles," but "The Rest of the Acts of Christ." Or, since the enthroned Christ labors through the Holy Spirit, "The Acts of the Spirit." The apostles preach and teach, but it is Christ laboring through the Spirit using these blemished men.

Second, before his ascension Jesus stresses the necessity of the Holy Spirit's coming. He has been telling them about this promise of the Father since John baptized him, and now it is only a few days off. This underscores the significance of Pentecost, as we will see below, and it ties together the imagery of baptism with the Spirit.

Third, once clothed with the Spirit, Jesus commissions the apostles to be his witnesses. Eyewitness testimony ranked as the most superior form of evidence in the ancient world. The Lord, therefore, grants the world firm proof about the resurrection and salvation of Christ through apostolic preaching. The eyewitness preaching further adds a forensic element. Testimony is given in court, and if one snubs the exhibition of the truth, then a condemning verdict is rendered. To accept the preaching is to be saved, but to reject it leaves one in sin.

Fourth, the apostles will be Christ's witnesses in Jerusalem, in Judea, in Samaria, and to the ends of the earth (Acts 1:8). This verse summarizes the theme of the book and forms its outline. These four regions foreshadow the movement of the gospel out from Jerusalem. Hence, Acts launches in Jerusalem, expands out to Judea (Acts 5:16), travels to Samaria (Acts 8:5), and finally concludes in Rome (Acts 28:16), the epicenter of the known world.

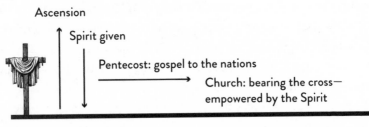

Fifth, Luke issues one final clarification about the definition of the kingdom. This clarification arises from the hazy and muddy thinking of the apostles. They asked Jesus, "Will you at this time restore the kingdom to Israel?" (Acts 1:6). This is a question about theocracy, the defeat of Rome, and the dawning of a Solomonic utopia. The disciples yet fail to grasp that Christ's kingdom is not of this world. Christ, thus, answers them by ignoring their question. The sense of ignoring the inquiry is a mild form of rebuke, like when a teacher responds to a dumb question, "I am not even going to answer that question." Rather, Christ responds to reform their thinking, "It is not for you to know the times and seasons" (Acts 1:7). This phrase about times and seasons refers to the end of history when the new world will be ushered in with the coming of Christ in glory. Jesus focuses their question about the kingdom upon the consummation. This is confirmed when Jesus disappears into the cloud and the apostles stand there gawking. Two angels suddenly appear and tell them, "This Jesus ... will come in the same way as you saw him go into heaven" (Acts 1:11). Christ's second coming will alone bring the kingdom in its fullness, which the Father has marked on his secret calendar.

These five points prepare us to understand the upcoming story, but there is one more matter to address. About 120 disciples had

Day of the Lord

New heavens
and new earth

Chart 9: The Acts of the Apostles

crammed themselves into a room in Jerusalem to pray and wait, when Peter stands up and commands, "One of these men must become with us a witness to the resurrection" (Acts 1:22). Peter cites the Old Testament both concerning the apostasy of Judas and the need to fill his office. The qualifications for the replacement read as a definition for the apostolic office. First, more than one man meets the qualifications, but they do not ordain thirteen apostles. The number must stay as twelve, which displays the symbolic value of twelve connecting Old Testament Israel to the New Testament church. The new people of Christ are constituted upon the twelve apostles.

Second, the qualifications limit the office bearer to the specific historical period of Jesus' earthly ministry. There are three qualifications. One, it had to be a man who accompanied Jesus. Many women stayed with Jesus for the duration of his ministry. Mary Magdalene's devotion proved stronger than the men's on the morning of the resurrection, yet this particular office was only open for one of the men. Two, the duration of partnering with Jesus was from his baptism to the ascension. The entire earthly ministry of Jesus had to be experienced by the apostle. Any person born in another time and place does not make the cut (Paul is an exception to this; see the discussion in the next chapter). Three, the apostle had to have seen Jesus in his resurrected glory.

This definition of the apostolic office has several ramifications. It shows the necessity to fulfill the Old Testament promises continues in Acts just as they were prominent in the Gospels. The limiting of the number to twelve reveals that the word "apostle" is not always used in a technical manner as defined above. In Acts, and other New Testament books, "apostle" can be used in a more general sense of messenger, sent one, or minister (John 13:16; Acts 14:14; Heb 3:1). Rather, to clarify the twelve official apostles, they will sometimes say "the Twelve" (John 20:24; Acts 6:2; 1 Cor 15:5). In other passages, the exact referent of "apostles" has to be determined by context, though it is not always clear. Nevertheless, the apostolic twelve remain the foundation for the New Testament church.

PENTECOST

With the apostolic vacancy filled, Luke next signals that he has been keeping track of the calendar. Pentecost marks the fiftieth day after Passover, which is the Old Testament feast named "Feast of Weeks/Harvest."[1] Yet this is after Luke has said the ascension came forty days after the resurrection (Acts 1:3). The Old Testament festival calendar forms the template for the New Testament acts of redemption. Jesus died on Passover; he rested in the grave on the Sabbath of Unleavened Bread; he was raised on the day of firstfruits. And now, on Pentecost, the Father sends the Spirit of Christ.

Pentecost is significant here for two reasons. First, Pentecost was a joyous feast celebrating the beginning of the wheat harvest as God's guarantee of the full harvest. The full harvest followed months of hot, laborious work. Yet the Lord called his people to worship as his guarantee that his blessing would fill their barns. The giving of the Spirit is Christ's pledge to gather in the full number of his people. Second, in the intertestamental period, Pentecost is linked with the giving of the law at Sinai and God's glory filling the tabernacle. This is because Pentecost came in the third month, when Israel arrived at Sinai (Exod 19:1). And Luke strongly alludes to the Sinai events.

Pilgrims from across the Mediterranean and Near Eastern world swarmed to Jerusalem like ants on a hill. Good estimates place Jerusalem's regular population around 25,000; during the pilgrim feasts, it could swell to 150,000-plus. Elbow room in the streets was a rare commodity.

In this context the events of Pentecost in Acts unfold. As rivers of crowds inch along outside, 120 disciples are praying in a crowded upper room. Suddenly, a loud roar came from heaven like a mighty wind and filled the room. Divided tongues like fire appeared over each person's head, as if crowned by a torch. Then, all the disciples were filled with the Holy Spirit and began speak in foreign languages. In the Old Testament, a distinct idiom was used to describe the glory cloud filling the tabernacle (Exod 40:34–35; 1 Kings 8:10–11), and the same idiom appears in Acts 2:4 for the Spirit filling the people. The Spirit of glory fills not the room or temple, but the living stones of the redeemed saints. At Sinai, the Lord revealed himself in a single pillar of fire atop Sinai and crowning the tabernacle. At this final Pentecost,

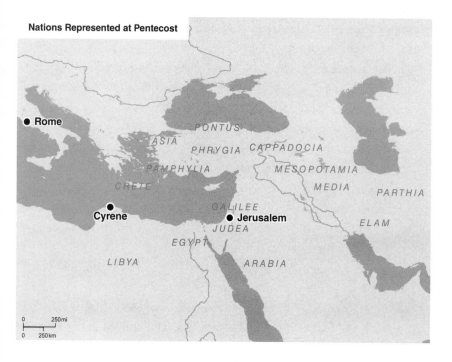

Nations Represented at Pentecost

the Spirit is manifest not in one flame but in many flames. The prophets promised that God would put his Spirit within his people and write his law on their hearts, and this promise has reached its fulfillment. Sinai was the ratification of the old covenant, so Pentecost ratifies the new covenant inaugurated in the blood of Christ.

The sign of the Spirit's coming on Pentecost matches perfectly the international goal of the new covenant. The disciples spoke foreign languages. The phrase "to speak in a tongue" is merely the Old Testament idiom for speaking a language different from your mother language. These Galilean fishermen started speaking in Persian and Phrygian. Thus the thunderous roar from heaven called all the pilgrims to attention for them to focus on hearing the mighty deeds of God in their own dialects.

The amazing sounds of Pentecost, though, leave most people perplexed and others mocking. Therefore, Peter mounts his podium to deliver his famous Pentecost sermon. Peter's sermon is noteworthy for many reasons, one being it sets the pattern for apostolic preaching in the book. All the other sermons in Acts follow the same basic template of Peter's first sermon in order to show the consistency of the apostolic teaching.

The recipe for this teaching has three main ingredients. First, from beginning to end, the focus is on Jesus as the glorified Messiah, resurrected and ascended. Peter says, "God has made him both Lord and Christ, this Jesus whom you crucified" (Acts 2:36). Second, the apostles show from the Old Testament how God's promises are fulfilled in Christ. For example, Peter quotes Joel to explain the Spirit's gushing forth, cites Psalm 16 for the resurrection, alludes to 2 Samuel 7 for God's enduring oath to David, and quotes Psalm 110 for the exaltation of Jesus as Lord and Christ. Third, Peter finishes with a call to repentance, faith, and baptism.

After the sermon, we witness the development of the church. The newly baptized believers form a new community, one devoted to the apostolic teaching, the breaking of bread (Luke's term for the Lord's Supper), the fellowship, and the prayers. The church is not some later development of formalism imposed upon the free charisma of the Spirit. Rather, the Spirit organizes the believers to be a committed community, with structure, sharing, and numbered membership. This is another theme that Luke develops across his second volume.

THE GOSPEL IN JERUSALEM AND JUDEA

After Peter's grand sermon, a pattern emerges in Acts for the next handful of chapters: preaching, opposition, and church life. For example, in chapter 3, Peter heals a crippled man and delivers another sermon that magnifies Christ from the Old Testament. The sermon causes an uproar. The priestly authorities drag Peter and John before them and order them not to speak in the name of Jesus any longer. The apostles must obey God rather than men, but the first blow of opposition has been dealt: censorship. After being excused from the Sanhedrin, the narrative returns to the church's prayer for boldness and the saints' generosity in sharing their possessions.

Not all is well within the household of God, though. External opposition is no surprise, but internal conflict is another matter. Two members of the church, Ananias and Sapphira, keep back money for themselves but lie about it. When their sins are exposed, they are met with swift judgment from the Lord—death. As Satan sees the church expanding, he tries to gain a foothold, but God prevails. And with this the pattern is set to repeat.

The ministry of the apostles again drives them to preaching in the temple. The infuriated high priest has lost all patience, so he puts the entire apostolic clan behind bars. But you cannot chain down what God wants free, so an angel emancipates them to resume their temple preaching. When the high priest is shocked with the liberty of the apostles, he is not ready to give up. After a trial, the temple authorities reiterate their censorship with a flogging and a release. The fresh blood running down the apostles' backs does not suppress their courage, for they go forth praising the Lord for the honor to suffer for the name of Christ and are committed to keep preaching Jesus as the Christ. The narrative shifts back to the church, where another problem has surfaced.

The dispute concerns the treatment of Hellenistic widows. The Hellenists are those Jews who could not speak Aramaic but mainly Greek, while the Hebrews are those who were untrained in Greek but spoke Aramaic or Hebrew (Acts 6:1). The Hellenists accuse the Hebrews of favoritism and inequity because the Hebrew widows were receiving more than the Hellenist widows.

Now, this is only the accusation; the text gives no indication if this was true or not. The apostles, though, sense their limitations and priorities. They must remain devoted to preaching and prayer and cannot be distracted by serving tables. This phrase "serving tables" most likely does not refer to a literal waiting on tables, but is rather an idiom for overseeing accounts, like a treasurer or secretary. This work was to oversee and organize the church's duty of dispersing money and provisions for the needy. The people respond positively as they put forward seven godly men.

We come now to the beginning of another cycle. One of these men, Stephen, full of wisdom and the Spirit, regularly preaches and reasons in the synagogue of the Freedman, which is made up of people from the regions of Cyrene, Alexandria, Asia, and Cilicia (Paul's home territory). All the brain power of the synagogue, though, cannot better Stephen's reasoning about Christ from the Old Testament, so they resort to underhanded methods: false witnesses and trumped up charges. Without delay, Stephen is standing, with angelic face, before the Sanhedrin on trial for teaching that Jesus will destroy the temple and change the Mosaic customs.

Stephen's speech in Acts 7 is one of the most beautiful and rich passages in all of Scripture, as he masterfully weaves together passages and themes of the Old Testament to show forth Christ and to condemn his audience for their stiff-necked unbelief. It would take a book to list off all the fine delicacies of Stephen's oratory, so just a few of his themes will be mentioned.

First, Stephen is accused of speaking against the holy temple (Acts 6:13). Stephen, therefore, demonstrates that the place of God has never been confined to a single building, to a handmade temple, but that the Lord makes himself known wherever his people are. The God of glory appeared to Abram in Mesopotamia; Sinai was the place of worship after the exodus; the temple did not stand until Solomon. The true place of God is his believing people.

Second, Stephen shows how Israel of old regularly stood against the saviors raised up by God. The brothers sold Joseph into slavery, who became their savior from famine. The Hebrews wanted nothing to do with Moses, who would lead them out of Egypt. Stephen fashions Joseph and Moses after the image of Christ.

Third, Stephen teases out how Israel's rejection of Moses perverted the tabernacle into a tent of idolatry. And this is the prophetic punch in Stephen's discourse. The high priests' rejection of Jesus, the Righteous One, and their veneration for the temple makes them just like the idolatrous generation in the wilderness. "You stiff-necked people, uncircumcised in heart and ears ... And they killed those who announced beforehand the coming of the Righteous One, whom you have now betrayed and murdered, you who received the law as delivered by angels and did not keep it." In the manner of an Old Testament prophet, Stephen just condemned the august body of priests and Pharisees as law-breaking idolaters. It is no wonder why they could not suffer him a syllable more. With plugged ears, they stampede at Stephen and stone him outside the city. Mob justice will silence the preaching of the name of Jesus. Before he breathes his last, Stephen squeaks out a final few words: "Behold ... the Son of Man standing at the right hand of God. ... Lord Jesus, receive my spirit. ... Do not hold this sin against them." The holy presence of Christ is revealed not in the temple, but with Stephen as rocks pummel the life from him.

The murder of Stephen brings to the surface several noteworthy issues for our story. For one, a new character is introduced, Saul, who will soon become the leading figure of Acts. Second, the blood of Stephen is also the crescendo of the external opposition. Censorship sprouted into imprisonment, which budded into flogging, which bore the fruit of execution. The opponents who killed Jesus are now in shape to murder his witnesses. The people of Jesus now have the privilege to follow their Lord even to the death. Finally, Stephen's death raises a question with the church. The risen Christ exhorted the apostles to use their passports, but they have racked up no miles. All the previous missionary work has unfolded within Jerusalem and its bedroom communities. The apostles are only speaking with fellow Jews; no Gentiles have been brought into the conversation at this point. What does this say about the church? Well, the Lord has the tendency to help his people with a push. The persecution led by Saul and ignited by Stephen's death is this push. The threat of afflictions scatters the saints, and as they flee across Palestine the gospel is being preached.

GOSPEL TO THE SAMARITANS AND BEYOND

The spread of the gospel beyond Jerusalem, though, is not apostle-led. The Twelve remain in the city of David, while one of the seven men ordained to serve tables wanders into foreign territory. Stephen's co-worker, Philip, crosses over to the Jews' hated cousins, the Samaritans. He begins preaching the gospel, and they receive the word. Philip even starts baptizing the Samaritans. Word gets back to headquarters, "The Samaritans have believed and been baptized." Peter and John are dispatched to investigate, and sure enough, their faith and baptism are real, and so the Spirit must be given. Normally, baptism is the sign of having the Spirit; here though, the sign and reality are disconnected to show that the Samaritans have been made full members of the new covenant. Philip baptized, so the apostles have to lay on hands for the Spirit. This marks the next step on the map of Acts 1:8. The gospel has reached Samaria—check. Soon we will see another similar check mark.

The Lord has a special second mission for Philip. He directs Philip to set himself along a deserted stretch of road between Jerusalem and Gaza. An uninhabited place is a strange place for evangelism, but soon the entourage of a VIP comes around the corner, a wealthy and high-ranking Ethiopian eunuch. The man is clearly a God-fearer. God-fearers were non-Jews who partially converted to Judaism, but they did not go the full way by accepting circumcision and the dietary and purity laws. (By contrast, proselytes were Gentiles converts who took on the full yoke of the Mosaic law.) According to the law, the genital mutilation of the eunuch prevented him from becoming a full convert (Deut 23:1). This eunuch, though, could afford his own copy of Isaiah, and providentially he is stuck on a passage he does not yet know is about Jesus (Isa 53:7–8).

Philip runs over to his chariot and, hearing the man reading Isaiah, asks if he knows what it means. The eunuch invites him to explain it, and Philip, beginning with Isaiah 53, unfolds how all of Scripture speaks of Christ. With eyes opened to Christ, the eunuch's first question could not be more telling. "See, here is water! What prevents me from being baptized?" He was prevented from full status in the old covenant, but in the new covenant this law was no longer a hindrance. Baptism is a better sign of inclusion in Christ, for it can be applied to women and even eunuchs. As the eunuch arises from the baptismal waters, he is a full member of Christ. Philip's work is done, so the Spirit beams him away to Azotus.

After the baptism of the eunuch, who journeys on to the ends of the earth, we come to the famous account of Saul's conversion on the road to Damascus. For our purposes, we will focus on Christ's purpose for Saul (Acts 9:15–16). Saul, later known as Paul, will be Christ's chosen instrument to carry his name to the Gentiles, kings, and Israelites. He will be the servant of the gospel to the nations. And in his world travels, Saul will suffer much for the name of Christ. The irony is rich. The persecutor Saul, who drove the gospel out of Jerusalem, will actually bear the gospel to far-off places. In fact, after

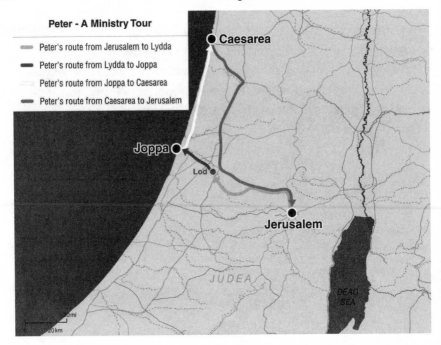

Peter - A Ministry Tour

— Peter's route from Jerusalem to Lydda
— Peter's route from Lydda to Joppa
— Peter's route from Joppa to Caesarea
— Peter's route from Caesarea to Jerusalem

Caesarea

Joppa

Lod

Jerusalem

JUDEA

DEAD SEA

a brief stint of preaching, "Wanted" signs are posted in Damascus for Saul's head. Once Barnabas introduces him to the apostles, Saul spends some time in his hometown Tarsus, so that Peter can enjoy his final major scene.

Up to this point, with the exception of the Ethiopian eunuch, the gospel had only been shared with other Jews (Acts 11:19). The Samaritans had Jewish blood in them, so this was not too big of a leap for the saints. Cornelius, though, is a Roman from Italy; he does not have the slightest link to the noble line of Abraham. As a God-fearer, Cornelius is a pious believer in God, for which the Lord is about to answer his prayers in a way he could never have imagined.

As Cornelius sends for Peter, the Lord is making preparations on the other end. Peter's dream of a sheet lowered down to earth filled with animals marks a tectonic shift from the old covenant to the new, one foreshadowed in the story of the eunuch. The shift has to do with dietary laws. Mosaic dietary laws functioned not only to regulate Israel's purity to enter the temple, but also to distinguish them from the nations. In Peter's dream, the four-cornered linen sheet, which was white in color, represents the earth in a state of purity, so that all the lobsters and frogs and other formerly unclean things were declared pure. As the voice from heaven states, "What God has declared pure, do not call ritually impure" (Acts 10:15, my translation).

Yet this change does not come easily for Peter. In the vision, Peter cannot fathom letting impure meat touch his tongue. And upon arrival at Cornelius' home, Peter's nausea is still swirling. "You know how unlawful it is for a Jew to join or visit a foreigner, but God has shown me not to call common or impure any person" (Acts 10:28, my paraphrase). Peter does not want to be in a Gentile's house; it feels wrong to his conscience. As he begins preaching, another surprise is just around the corner. The apostle's sermon continues in the normal way about Christ and his resurrection, but as soon as Peter mentions forgiveness, he is interrupted. The Spirit cuts Peter off by falling upon the believing household of Cornelius. The Pentecostal signs for foreign languages and praising God are exhibited in an uncircumcised family of Italians. The last stop on the map of Acts 1:8 has been reached.

Peter's reaction is telling: "Can anyone withhold water for baptizing these people?"(10:47). In other words, "They have the Spirit, I guess we have to baptize them." With the Samaritans, it was the opposite. Philip baptized so that the Spirit had to be given. Here the Spirit rushes upon them, so baptism has to be administered. These unique repetitions of Pentecost do not just mark steps on the map, but they are pushing the apostles to pass their comfort zones. Just as he was unwilling to eat lobsters, Peter was not ready to accept the Gentiles as full members of Christ. The Jews struggled to compute the Gentiles being saved without keeping all the rules of Moses. This is clear, as Peter returns to Jerusalem and is rebuked by the circumcision party for eating with uncircumcised folk. If the Gentiles kept the law, maybe, but without the law, never. Peter has to retell the whole story, and he ends with, "Who was I that I could stand in God's way?" (Acts 11:17). Peter admits that his hand was forced by the Spirit, and the Jerusalem church agrees: God has granted repentance unto life to the Gentiles. The ethnic prejudice against the Gentiles was not easy for the Jews to get over.

GOSPEL TO THE ENDS OF THE EARTH

Nevertheless, with the gospel having broken another barrier with the household of Cornelius, the time has come for the church to be more proactive. In Acts 12, another wave of persecution sweeps over Jerusalem, as Herod Agrippa I kills James the apostle and intends to do the same to Peter. After Peter's angelic jailbreak, the narrative opens at the church in Syrian Antioch, where a group of teachers are instructed to send off Barnabas and Saul. The active pursuit of missions is the divine order. Here is where the missionary journeys of Paul commence. From Acts 13:4 to 14:28, the first so-called missionary journey of Paul occurs. Barnabas and Paul sail first to Cyprus and then spend the rest of their time evangelizing south-central Asia, before retracing their steps and returning to their home base in Syrian Antioch.

From this first journey, Paul's method of missions is set forth in clear terms. He first visits a population center, typically a larger city with a synagogue, so Salamis, Pisidian Antioch, Iconium, Lystra, and Derbe. Next, Paul would stop in the synagogue and preach, a sample of which is given in Pisidian Antioch (Acts 13:16–41). This longer sermon is remarkable due to its similarity to Peter's earlier sermons. Paul reasons from the Old Testament, rehearses Israel's history, mentions John the Baptist, and even cites Psalm 16 to prove the resurrection of Jesus. The preachers have changed, but the apostolic gospel remains the same. After preaching to the Jews, unbelieving friction sparks opposition, so that Barnabas and Paul turn to the Gentiles (Acts 13:46). Persecution often drives Paul and his companions to the next city. In this instance, hostile Jews of Pisidian Antioch chase Paul and Barnabas all the way to Lystra to stir up trouble. Finally, after this initial evangelism, Paul returns to the cities in order to appoint elders and to commend the new believers to the grace of God (14:23).

Paul organizes the mixed body of Jews and Gentiles under elders as a local congregation. This first missionary journey displays the apostolic method for building the church through preaching the gospel.

Yet when Barnabas and Paul land back home in Syrian Antioch, a quarrel is rumbling through the churches, threatening to crack the foundation. The circumcision party, who gave Peter grief for Cornelius, has emboldened their dogmatism: "Unless you are circumcised according to the custom of Moses, you cannot be saved" (Acts 15:1). In his muted style, Luke writes that "no small dissension arose." An avalanche of contention swept across the church. The issue is salvation, which does not get any bigger. The dispute is whether keeping the law of Moses is a necessary condition to be saved (Acts 15:5). From the previous stories, God's verdict stands clear. The Ethiopian eunuch was saved through faith and baptism. The voice from heaven declared all foods pure, repealing the dietary laws. The Spirit filled the household of Cornelius without a care in the world for them being uncircumcised.

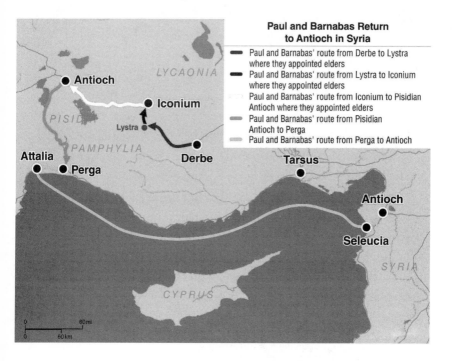

Paul and Barnabas Return to Antioch in Syria

- Paul and Barnabas' route from Derbe to Lystra where they appointed elders
- Paul and Barnabas' route from Lystra to Iconium where they appointed elders
- Paul and Barnabas' route from Iconium to Pisidian Antioch where they appointed elders
- Paul and Barnabas' route from Pisidian Antioch to Perga
- Paul and Barnabas' route from Perga to Antioch

With the theological altercation at a standstill, a resolution had to be reached. The Antiochian church dismisses Paul, Barnabas, and others as delegates to Jerusalem. All the living apostles and elders assemble in Jerusalem as a high court to reach a solution. Witnesses are called to provide evidence. Peter receives privileges of the floor first. With a reminder of Cornelius, Peter argues that the Holy Spirit made no distinction between the Jews and Gentiles, having cleansed all their hearts by faith. The Jews have never been able to bear the yoke of the law, so why put it on the Gentiles? He concludes, "We will be saved through the grace of the Lord Jesus, just as they will" (Acts 15:11). Silence stuns the assembly. Barnabas and Paul take the floor next to summarize all the gracious wonders of their missionary journey, all of which happened apart from the law.

The final speaker to take the stand is James, the brother of Jesus, who had become the head of the Jerusalem church. He reaches his conclusion quickly: "We should not trouble those of the Gentiles who turn to God" (Acts 15:19). The law is not necessary for salvation—no circumcision required. The grace of God wins the day. James does propose, though, a few items of abstention for the Gentiles (Acts 15:20). It is important to note here that the topic is not table fellowship between Jews and Gentiles or Jewish sensibilities. Nor is there any reference here to the Mosaic law or the regulations found in Genesis 9. Rather, the topic remains what is necessary to be saved. James argues it should include abstaining from "the pollution of idols, that is sexually immorality, strangled and blood" (my translation). The last three items are examples of the first, idolatry. James is not concerned about adultery here. He is not giving dietary laws. Rather, strangling and blood played a role in pagan sacrificial practice, and sexual immorality was rampant in the feasts that followed sacrifices. In short, James only advocates one abstention necessary for salvation: idolatry. In the first century, the Gentiles were by nature polytheists. Adding a new god to their pantheon to venerate was not a hard step: Jesus, Zeus, and Artemis. Worshiping God alone to the abandonment of other gods was more of a challenge. Therefore, James finishes by saying that yes, the Gentiles are saved by grace, but they must cease all idolatry, along with the pagan practices often associated with sacrificial rites and celebrations. And James' motion passes without dissent. The quarrel has been resolved. The Mosaic law is not necessary for salvation. By God's grace and through faith in Christ, both Jews and Gentiles are saved.

With the Jerusalem Council's clarification of the gospel, it is time once again to spread the good news, both to comfort the troubled congregations and to bring it to new fields. Silas and Barsabbas join Paul and Barnabas to bring the Jerusalem letter to the saints in Antioch. After much rejoicing, Paul has the itch to get back on the road again. He plans to revisit the churches he planted on the first missionary journey, but he and Barnabas cannot agree about taking Mark along. The impasse propels Paul to pick a new team. Silas will be his partner in the ministry for his second trip.

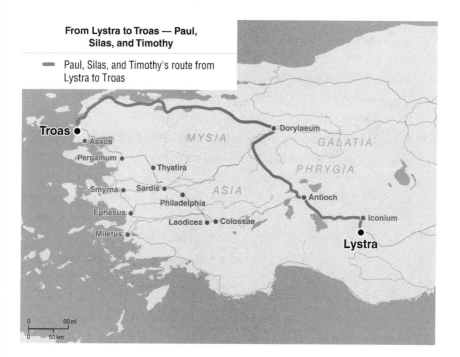

From Lystra to Troas — Paul, Silas, and Timothy

Paul, Silas, and Timothy's route from Lystra to Troas

PAUL'S SECOND
MISSIONARY JOURNEY

Paul's second missionary journey commences in Acts 15:40 and ends in Acts 18:22. Paul forgoes the sea initially for the inland route. The first part of this expedition entails revisiting the churches to deliver them the good resolution of the Jerusalem Council. And in Lystra, Paul adds a third man to his ministry team, Timothy, who must have been fairly young at the time. By the time they reach Troas to receive the Macedonian call, a fourth member has enrolled with Paul. Passages that use "we" begin in Acts 16:11, which has traditionally been understood as Luke entering the story to speak from firsthand experience.

The squad of four catch a boat to Samothrace to reach the Roman colony of Philippi. With a slight variance from the norm, Philippi does not seem to have a large Jewish community. The "place of prayer" down by the river could refer to a synagogue, but more likely it is a less established meeting place for Jews to meet and pray. Either way, Paul first seeks them out and shares the name of Christ with some women on the Sabbath. The Lord opens the heart of Lydia, a businesswoman dealing in the expensive trade of purple. Once her entire household is baptized, Lydia's house becomes the hotel for Paul and his companions.

As we have come to expect, however, wherever the gospel sweetens the air, persecution soon blows in. Paul and Silas land themselves in jail after performing an exorcism that costs some their business. They sing hymns while in prison to the delight of the Lord, who rattles the foundations of the prison and bursts open its doors. The jailer, whose duty was to guard the prison, reaches for his sword to kill himself, but Paul restrains his hand. Here, the gospel does not liberate the prisoners, but it keeps every criminal safely in his cell chain-free. After the jailer's household is saved, morning dawns with a full prison. Once the magistrates release the two, Paul and his crew say their final encouragements to Lydia and the saints to get back on the road again.

The next two documented stops in the travel journal are Thessalonica and Berea. The stay in Thessalonica lasts barely a month, as a group of hostile Jews ignite a mob to banish the team from the city. These sons of Belial even chase Paul to Berea, where the Jews are more honorable. The intensity of this violence forces Paul's team to split up. Paul is smuggled out to Athens, while Timothy and Silas remain behind. The brief stays and hasty exits, however, did not hinder the Paul and his crew from planting two new congregations.

The Acropolis in Athens

While waiting alone in Athens, Paul's spirit is provoked by the ubiquitous idols, and he manages an opportunity to address the philosophers hanging around the Areopagus. The Areopagus was the center of Greek reason and honor, the ivy league of prestige and philosophy. For this reason, Paul's address to these Epicurean and Stoic brainiacs is a model of wise accommodation. Unlike his previous recorded sermons, Paul does not begin or focus on the Old Testament, but reasons from creation and natural law to lead his audience to the problem of sin and the need for repentance in the face of coming judgment (Acts 17:30). The final judgment cannot be mentioned without bringing up the Judge, the man of God's appointment certified by his resurrection from the dead! Sin, judgment, and Christ—all the essential ingredients of the gospel are present, even without citing the Old Testament once.

The astute philosophers are tracking with Paul until he mentions the resurrection. These Greeks could believe all sorts of odd myths, but this is one idea that they cannot except. In a play by the famous Athenian poet Aeschylus, whose sculpture was in the theatre of Dionysus, a character named Apollo says, "When the dust has soaked up the blood of man, once he has died, there is no resurrection."[2] This was a crucial tenet of Greek philosophy, that death cannot be overcome with resurrection. Most scoff and dismiss Paul, but a few want to hear more and end up believing in Jesus.

After his stay in the heart of the Greek world, Paul finds himself farther south in Greece but in a city with strong Roman flavors, Corinth. The Roman army had buried the old Corinth in 146 BC, and it remained largely fallow until 44 BC, when it was reestablished as a Roman colony and as the capital of the senatorial province of Achaia. Inhabited by many retired Romans soldiers, the city maintained its Roman feel despite being surrounded by Greek culture. Corinth was also a crucial business hub that conducted trade from all around the Mediterranean world. Moreover, Paul's time in Corinth grants us probably the most firm date for his ministry. The antagonistic Jews drag Paul to court before the proconsul Gallio, who is known from Roman history to have been in office during AD 52.[3] Gallio's ruling on the matter sets a precedent that Christianity was an internal debate within Judaism, and so was no concern to the Roman courts (Acts 18:15).[4]

Paul's season in Corinth also gains him two more companions, Aquila and Priscilla. This husband-wife team travels with Paul's crew to Ephesus, where they remain while the rest of Paul's team sets sail for home. They reach Antioch in Syria to report all the great deeds of the Lord and to conclude the second missionary journey (Acts 18:22).

PAUL'S THIRD MISSIONARY JOURNEY

As one eager to be on the move, Paul's third globe-trotting gospel operation launches without delay. As with his second expedition, he chooses the inland route across Galatia and Phrygia, presumably revisiting the churches planted earlier. This plops Paul down in the great city of Ephesus, where he decides to make his base of operations for about the next two years. Ephesus is also where the last unique Pentecostal sign recorded in Acts occurs. Paul finds some disciples who have only heard of the baptism of John and are ignorant of the Spirit's Pentecostal outpouring (Acts 19:1–2). Paul tells them about Jesus, baptizes them, and lays hands upon them for the Spirit.

As Paul ministers daily in the hall of Tyrannus, the success of the gospel in urban Ephesus does not go unnoticed. Between Paul's miracles and the saints burning up magic books valued at 50,000 silver drachmas,[5] a businessman named Demetrius is provoked. In order to defend his silversmithing trade, Demetrius ignites a mob against the church with cries, "Great is Artemis of the Ephesians." In this swell of zeal, two of Paul's companions, Gaius and Aristarchus, get swept into the theater and held captive for two hours by further chants for Artemis. Providentially, the town clerk senses the danger of this uproar under Rome's no-tolerance policy with riots and ends it. Thus the assembly heads home, and no permanent damage to Paul's team or the church is mentioned.

Terrace house in Ephesus

This mayhem, though, did put fuel in Paul's tank to get back on
the road. His travel plans foreshadow the rest of the story. Not unlike
Jesus who set his face toward Jerusalem, Paul maps a path through
Macedonia, Achaia, Jerusalem, and finally to Rome. "I must also see
Rome," he says (Acts 19:21). Once Paul reaches Corinth, he winters
there during AD 57–58, and he turns around for Jerusalem with nine
others (Acts 20:4), who most likely accompanied him with the collection for the Jerusalem church, though this is not mentioned in Acts.
Retracing his steps through Macedonia, Paul's company reaches Miletus,
outside of Ephesus, where he delivers his masterful farewell address to
the Ephesian elders. In a hurry to reach Jerusalem by Pentecost, the
fellowship puts out to sea, and soon they reach the shores of Palestine,
which essentially puts the period on Paul's third missionary journey
(Acts 21:7).

DESTINATION ROME

After this, Paul is dead set on winding up in Rome, but his route must take him through Jerusalem, despite numerous prophetic warnings that severe suffering awaits him in the holy city (Acts 21:4, 11–12). Refusing to be deterred, Paul and his fellowship touch down on the home turf of James, the head of the Jerusalem church. For unknown and questionable reasons, Paul agrees to pay all the sacrifices for four men who had taken Nazirite vows. While in the temple making the offerings, Paul is recognized and falsely accused of bringing a Greek into the temple, but this charge explodes into a mass of zealotry that blows Paul out of the temple and locks the temple gates. Before hostiles can slit Paul's throat, the Roman soldiers salvage him from the crowd and take him into custody.

Paul's arrest carries us to the last section of the book of Acts: Paul's trials and defenses. In this subdivision, Paul retells his conversion story twice; he stands trial before the Sanhedrin, Felix, and Agrippa II; and he makes his appeal to Caesar that buys him a stormy boat trip. This is a beautiful and rich portion masterfully composed by Luke, yet it is fitting to put up on the chalkboard the unified purpose and message of both Paul and Luke in these trials and apologies. To begin with, the charge against Paul is a bit fluid and imprecise, which is partly Luke revealing its false character. The charge starts out accusing Paul of teaching against the law and the temple and bringing a Greek into the temple to defile it (Acts 21:28). The resurrection gets added to the mix before the Sanhedrin. Claudius describes the charge as being about matters of their law (Acts 23:29). Tertullus' opening argument highlights Paul stirring up riots, leading a sect, and attempting to profane the temple (Acts 24:5–6). Festus summarizes the case as points of dispute about their own religion concerning Jesus who was dead, but whom Paul asserts is alive (Acts 25:19). The Jewish priests are seeking Paul's death sentence.

From these accusations, Luke makes evident that the priests believe they, not Paul and members of the Way, are the rightful heir of the Old Testament. Jesus followers are an apostasy that must be cut off. The core issue focuses on whether Jesus and his preacher Paul are the true successors of the ancient covenants or if the temple aristocracy is. This is the brunt of the force aimed at Paul, and the logic of his rebuttals is tight.

The first premise Paul labors to establish is his past credentials under the law as a faithful expert and zealous activist. When he retells his Damascus trip epiphany, Paul lays out the fervor with which he sought to protect the sanctity of the law against the Way (Acts 22:3–5; 26:4–11). In setting forth his Old Testament orthodoxy, Paul additionally makes clear that the resurrection beats at the heart and hope of the twelve tribes. The way of worship laid down by the Law and Prophets sought to attain the resurrection (Acts 23:6; 24:14–15, 21; 26:6–8). Paul's Pharisaic heritage, so robust with the resurrection hope, certifies that he is not a divisive sect or religious faction.

Paul's second premise concerns his encounter with the risen Christ. He narrates this fully before the crowd outside the temple and Agrippa II (Acts 22:6–16; 26:12–19). He believes two things from his encounter. First is that Jesus of Nazareth is both Lord, the supreme authority to be obeyed, and Christ, the fulfillment of the Old Testament promises. Second is that the resurrection is a fact. Paul's zealous persecution was backward; true fervor followed the Way of Jesus Christ. His speech basically amounts to saying, "I was just like you, but then, my eyes were opened by the Christ himself" (Acts 22:3, 13; 26:18).

Paul's third premise concerns his obedience to Christ. Having received this revelation and commission, his every activity has only been to remain in step with it. Going forth from Damascus, to Jerusalem, to Judea, and even to the Gentiles, Paul has only been a witness for Christ so that Jew and Gentile may receive forgiveness of sins and a place among those sanctified by faith in Christ (Acts 26:16–20). For Rome, and against the false charges of the priests, Paul has carried out his ministry without stirring up a crowd (Acts 24:11–12). As Paul concludes with Agrippa II, "I stand here testifying both to small and great, saying nothing but what the prophets and Moses said would come to pass: that the Christ must suffer and that, by being the first to rise from the dead, he would proclaim light both to our people and to the Gentiles" (Acts 26:22–23). Ironically, Paul finishes in the same spot where Stephen concluded, whom he approvingly watched his blood splatter: those who reject Jesus, the Righteous One, prove themselves idolaters, while the way to the resurrection comes only by faith in Christ. Luke fashioned Paul's apology before the courts of men to resound through the ages that the Way are the true heirs of those ancient covenants, which are yes and amen in the resurrected Jesus.

Alas though, Paul had appealed to Caesar. The various civil authorities of Palestine could discover no chargeable offense in Paul and would have released him, but the appeal had to be processed (Acts 23:29; 25:20–21; 26:31–32). Paul had set his crosshairs on Rome, and now, under the watch of a Roman centurion, he will hit his target. The travel log of Paul's sailing trip at first seems like a jumble of nautical technicalities, and Luke does speak like a captain with all the technical jargon in this chapter. Yet in the eyes of a resident of the first century, Paul is an accused criminal on appeal to Caesar; the final verdict has yet to be rendered. And the gods had a tendency to intervene to remove the guilty party.

In ancient times, the sea was particularly good at exacting justice on the guilty. Sea voyages and storms were epically strewn across the old myths and poems; the daily superstitions of salty dogs were monopolized by the fear of divine justice and capriciousness. For Paul to slip through the teeth of the courts only to be waylaid at sea by a typhoon, nothing could be more obvious—the gods were after justice. If our modern responses are skeptical, the natives of Malta could not be more frank: "No doubt this man is a murderer. Though he has escaped from the sea, Justice has not allowed him to live" (Acts 28:4). "Justice" here is a reference to a goddess who was the daughter of Zeus and punished criminals if they escaped human justice. She was a mighty and relentless goddess who wrathfully wielded the weapons of revenge and death.

The viper's poison did not stop Paul's heart, and the sea failed to swallow a single passenger. In fact, Paul sets up a safe landing as a sign of God's salvation. He tells the starving sailors, "Take heart, men, for I have faith in God that it will be exactly as I have been told" (Acts 27:25). Yet the all men must stay aboard for there to be salvation (Acts 27:31). Finally, Paul gives the passengers a Lord's Supper sign: "I urge you to take food, for this is for your salvation, for not a single hair of yours will perish from your head" (Acts 27:34, my translation). God performs a miracle at sea, as all 276 safely landed upon the sandy beach. And such a salvation vindicated Paul as the Lord's upright servant. Justice did speak, but it was to approbate a witness of Jesus Christ. As God told Paul, "You must stand before Caesar" (Acts 27:24). Even where human strength cannot avail, the Lord carries his preachers to the end of the earth.

Therefore, the final scene of Acts pictures Paul under house arrest in Rome. In keeping with his missionary habits, he reaches out to the Jews first, some of which believe, some of which do not. Notwithstanding the

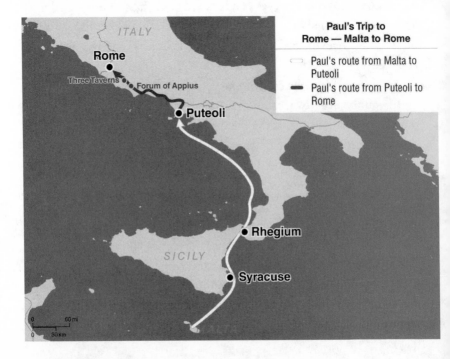

Paul's Trip to Rome — Malta to Rome

⌐ Paul's route from Malta to Puteoli

━ Paul's route from Puteoli to Rome

closed ears or the short leash of Rome, the last apostle of Jesus Christ did not lose courage, but remained proclaiming the kingdom of God and the truth of Jesus Christ will all boldness and without hinderance. The final act of Christ by the Spirit has reached cruising altitude. All that remains is for this altitude to be maintained until the time of the Father comes with the return of the Resurrected One.

STUDY QUESTIONS

1. Where did Christ sends his apostles to be his witnesses?

2. What are the qualifications for an apostle as given by Peter?

3. What is the significance of Pentecost?

4. Describes some of the issues that faced the early church in Acts.

5. How did the apostles drag their feet in going to the Gentiles? What pushed them along?

6. What problem did the Jerusalem Council deal with?

7. How did the sea voyage vindicate God's message through Paul?

1 2

PAUL AND HIS EPISTLES

Bible Reading:
Romans, 1–2 Corinthians, Galatians, Ephesians,
Philippians, Colossians, 1–2 Thessalonians,
1–2 Timothy, Titus, Philemon

Between the narratives in Acts and his thirteen letters, more ink has been spilled on the apostle Paul than any other biblical figure—perhaps even more than Jesus. This flood of literature has created no small amount of controversy. In Acts, whenever Paul enters a synagogue, disputes seems to swell around him, and these disputations have only ballooned since his death. We cannot deal with all of them here, but to make us more capable readers of Paul, a handful of issues should be teased out.

First, is Paul even an apostle? Paul had to defend his apostleship in his life. A tension can even be felt in the pages of Acts, where we learn so much about Paul. As was pointed out in the last chapter, when looking to replace Judas the apostles were looking for a man appointed by Jesus and who was with Jesus from John's baptism until the ascension. Paul does not fit. Besides being an opponent of Jesus, he was too young and on the wrong team to be an apostle. Moreover, the apostolic number was limited to twelve in connection with the tribes of Israel.

One point in his favor, however, is that on the road to Damascus, the risen Christ met Paul and commissioned him as an eyewitness to testify to everyone about what he had seen and heard (Acts 22:14–15). A commissioned eyewitness of Jesus' glorified body—this is the pure essence of an apostle. To kneel in the presence of the King and to be told, "Go, preach what you have seen and heard." And Paul himself felt the strain between the clarity of his call and his status relative to the Twelve. In 1 Corinthians 15, Paul recounts the Lord's resurrection appearances and says that Jesus appeared to all the apostles and "last of all, as to one untimely born, he appeared also to me" (1 Cor 15:8). The abnormal time of his birth refers to him missing the historical window. Paul senses that he is a gracious exception to the rule. Hence, he might be called "the last apostle."[1]

Paul's status as the thirteenth apostle further fits with the numbering of the tribes of Israel in the Old Testament. There were actually thirteen tribes, since Joseph received a double portion in Manasseh and Ephraim. The tribal lists always include twelve, frequently excluding the tribe of Levi, because its inheritance was in the sanctuary instead of the land. The symbolic twelve with an exceptional thirteenth is already well established in the Bible. Therefore, sealed by the Damascus appearance, Paul speaks the truth as he takes the official title of apostle for himself in nearly every one of his letters.

The next ingredient in any meet-and-greet with Paul is his upbringing and background. Paul's biography starts in Tarsus, the leading city of the region of Cilicia, where he was born with both Roman citizenship and Tarsus citizenship. Paul's Roman citizenship likely stems from his father or grandfather earning citizenship for loyal service to Rome, when they were leading campaigns in the region. Citizenship in Tarsus may indicate family wealth, as local citizenship belonged to landowners of means, and Paul admits to knowing abundance (Phil 4:12). Such dual citizenship granted Paul a fairly high social status, though his precise rank is unclear. This higher rank is evidenced in Ephesus when his friends, the Asiarchs, kept Paul from entering the theater.[2] The Asiarchs were among the most socially elite people in Ephesus, holding some of the highest political positions. To rub friendly shoulders with them indicates that Paul's status was high.

Paul's impressive Greek and Roman credentials, though, were added to by his gleaming Jewish heritage. Of the tribe of Benjamin, his pedigree makes him a Hebrew of Hebrews—the gold standard. His family ensured that his education matched his ancestry. Paul, though born in Tarsus, was educated in Jerusalem (Acts 22:3). Paul's family could even afford the prep school of Gamaliel, where he flourished as an outstanding student (Acts 22:3; Gal 1:14). This background means Paul most likely had the Torah memorized, along with the Psalms and large sections of the Prophets and other Old Testament books. It further suggests his language prowess in Hebrew, Aramaic, Greek, and likely Latin, being a Roman citizen. Paul's trade, according to Acts 18:3, was that of a tentmaker, but the meaning of this Greek word is uncertain. It could include a range of activities from sewing fabric together (leather or goat-hair material), constructing other parts of the tent, putting the tent up, or building a structure like a tent. The term may even be linked to the theater, stage equipment or setup. Either way, the work seems to be more technical and something done in a city. Popular images of Paul sweating away while sewing in a marketplace may be a far cry from reality. Nevertheless, being a leading student of Gamaliel, Paul was foremost a scholar, a Pharisaic scribe with a trade skill on the side. That the Sanhedrin employed Paul to persecute members of the Way (pre-conversion) shows that he was a religious officer of the high court (Acts 8:1; 9:1–3).

Paul was an upper-class Jew with status and capability in the Greco-Roman world and was privileged with the highest caliber of education (Acts 26:24; 2 Pet 3:15–16). In fact, Paul's privilege makes his labor even more meaningful. Physical labor was not universally regarded as shameful; it was a matter of station. For artisans and craftsmen, your manual labor was good and proper, as it fit your place in society. Upper-class members, however, were free from such sweat and toil by the employment of servants. To dig holes as an upper-class person was shameful, as it was below one's station. And Paul's status was twofold. As a scholar, Paul should have been sponsored by a wealthy benefactor. As an apostle, he had the right to be supported by the church. Yet he willingly forewent both these rights to labor so that the gospel may be free and so that he might imitate the humility of Christ (1 Cor 4:10–12; 9:3–6). Paul happily chose what was beneath him in order to more fully embody the gospel.

Nevertheless, to be more accurate, Paul's labor to support himself was not practiced in every city. This issue appears to be more poignant with the Corinthians, where he refused their support (2 Cor 11:8–9). Due to the Corinthians' worldly view on patron-client relationships, Paul would not accept their gifts. But in churches not hampered by such views, Paul accepted support, like from the Philippians (Phil 4:15–17). In Ephesus, Paul's daily preaching in the hall of Tyrannus may have been supported by the giving of others. Furthermore, while in prison, his daily needs would most likely have been supplied by others. Rather, we should understand Paul as open to do any work that was culturally below him for the sake of the gospel. But if the church's generosity properly freed him to preach more, he would not hesitate to devote more time to the gospel.

LETTER WRITING

Another key feature in getting to know Paul is his letter-writing ability. There is no way to appreciate Paul's writing, though, without defining what it meant to be literate in the ancient world. In our day, we use literacy for the ability to read and write within a more literary, non-oral culture. The Roman world, and the ancient world in general, was an oral culture, where writing materials were pricey and owned by the privileged. Moreover, to be well spoken was how one gained more honor. In fact, there was little social mobility in the Roman world, but one slight chance of improving your station was through oration. If a craftsman could afford to send his son to be tutored by a rhetorician, then he could use his oratory craft to better his situation.

The talents of reading, writing, and composing form the necessary background to the letter writing of Paul. Having been privileged with a superior education, Paul could do all three. Luke explicitly presents him as a talented orator in Athens and before Agrippa II, though Paul was not interested in refined sophistry (Acts 17:22; 26:1–2).[3] The Pharisaic scribal training would have inculcated him with both memorization and reading talents. He does ask for parchments to be brought to him (2 Tim 4:13). And his signature with his own hand is the customary authentication to all his letters (2 Thess 3:17).

Yet even with these talents, the typical way to compose a letter in Greco-Roman society was through a secretary or amanuensis. Paul admits to using an amanuensis in Romans 16:22, and it is implied elsewhere when he mentions writing a greeting in his own hand (1 Cor 16:24; Gal 6:11; Col 4:18). He probably employed a secretary for all of his letters.[4] The role of the secretary in Greco-Roman practice could vary from transcribing dictation word for word to composing the letter. Additionally, Paul lists several co-authors in his letters: Silas and Timothy (1, 2 Thess); Sosthenes (1 Cor); and Timothy (2 Cor, Phil, Philm, and Col). These coauthors are to be distinguished from the secretary, as they composed together with a secretary.[5] Paul also employed letter carriers, who were guided on how to read the letter (Col 4:7). Paul's authorship, then, includes his use of coauthors and secretaries (plus his sources), but he officially signed his name in order to take responsibility and to impart his authority and office.[6] Although Paul's rhetorical devices and style reveal his concern for the importance of his letters, he is not concerned with a polished smoothness like his contemporary sophists would have been.[7] As Richards concludes about Paul's letters, "While not in the same class as the premier rhetoricians of the classical age, they demonstrate a rhetorical sophistication that would have earned him respect as a persuasive speaker and letter writer."[8]

The normal practice of secretaries rings critical as one judges the similarities and differences between Paul's epistles in vocabulary, style, and content. Such apparent discrepancies between letters can be accounted for by the use of co-authors and secretaries. Another factor in varying styles links to local or regional rhetorical techniques. What was considered the "best style" fluctuated from Corinth to Athens to Ephesus. The secretary may have helped Paul accommodate to the local style. Nonetheless, this brief introduction to Paul and the first century makes us more mindful of not imposing modern ideas or expectations upon him and his epistles. Rather, we can analyze the data of the text within its own historical setting.

We should also mention purpose and genre. What was Paul's purpose in sending out correspondence? Our modern treatment of Paul tends to view his letters as theological treatises, ethical manuals, or spiritual devotionals, but none of these do justice to his epistles. To begin with, Paul is writing to congregations as their pastor and apostle, most of which he planted and personally knew well. The exceptions to this are Romans and Colossians. He is also writing to them to aid their Christian faith as a congregation. The Pastoral Epistles and Philemon are addressed to individuals, but it is clear from the letters that Paul expected them to be read to the congregation. Hence, his letters are first of all pastoral, holding together in harmony the authority of his office and his personal love for the people. Paul's purpose is to build up churches in the faith of Christ.

Within this focused goal, the rich theology of Paul blooms not as abstract speculation into esoteric matters but as pastoral theology rooted in Old Testament interpretation for the life and faith of the saints. Likewise, Paul's moral exhortations are not cast as a timeless code of human morality, but as wise ethical truths applied to the life and culture of particular congregations. His wisdom holds value for all times and places, but it cannot be simplistically cut and pasted without the careful work of history. Similarly, the spiritual vitality of Paul's epistles is in the concrete issues of human life and society. Paul's heavenly mindedness sings in harmony with how faith expresses itself in love for the imperfect saints of one's local congregation.

THE EPISTLES OF PAUL

Similar to our survey of the Old Testament prophets, a thorough introduction to any particular epistle of Paul requires more time and space than we have here. Since most Bible readers seem more familiar with the content of Paul's letters than their historical settings, our introductory remarks will focus more on the latter. Furthermore, even though there is a general Greco-Roman culture in the first century, the local cultures of any particular city could vary significantly. Ephesus was a different place than Corinth. Hence, any examination of an epistle must take into consideration the local culture and history of that city or region. The order of our survey will be canonical, but the table on the next page posits a reasonable chronology of the letters.

Romans

Often lauded as Paul's magnum opus, Romans receives pride of place in the English Bible's ordering of the New Testament epistles. Yet from Paul's point of view, Romans was his get-to-know-me letter, as he did not plant the churches in Rome, nor had he visited them in person. This explains why the greeting section extends over so many verses; Paul wanted to solidify the numerous personal connections they shared as strangers. The apostle wrote and sent this letter from Corinth, where he wintered for three months in AD 57–58 during his third missionary journey. He mentions the collection he is taking to Jerusalem, to which the saints of Achaia and Macedonia contributed (Rom 15:25–27). Paul also reveals his plan to head for Spain after Jerusalem while stopping in Rome so they may help him. He indicates no certainty of his imprisonment, but he does ask for their prayer to be delivered from opposition in Judea (Rom 15:30–31). In fact, Paul hopes to make Rome his new home base for his further missionary work in the west (Rom 1:13; 15:24). Paul is eager to meet the Romans, whom he has been praying for, face to face, to impart to them a spiritual blessing, and to announce the gospel in Rome (Rom 1:11–15).

The unfamiliarity between the apostle and the house churches in Rome help color in the background for the contents of the letter. At the close of his thanksgiving introduction, Paul states his goal of preaching the gospel in Rome, and then announces this gospel: "I am not ashamed of the gospel. ... For in it, the righteousness of God is revealed from faith to faith, as it is written, 'The righteous shall live by faith'" (Rom 1:16–17). Simply put, Romans is Paul's fuller exposition of the gospel to saints he has never met. This explains the more systematic presentation. No pastoral fires must be quenched, and no individual issues have to be addressed, per se. Paul wants to establish his apostleship and gospel to bless the saints in Rome and gain their assistance in his further ministry.

APPROXIMATE DATES FOR PAUL'S EPISTLES

48	Galatians
51	1 Thessalonians; 2 Thessalonians
54–57	1 Corinthians; 2 Corinthians
57–58	Romans
58–62	Ephesians; Philippians; Colossians; Philemon (Prison Epistles)
62–64	1 Timothy; Titus
65–66	2 Timothy

Hence, the logic of Paul's argument moves from law to gospel, from Old Testament to New Testament. All the Gentiles stand condemned under natural law; all Jews are condemned under Moses. Thus there is no distinction; all have fallen short. Salvation comes by propitiation in Christ's blood to justify all who believe in him. Moreover, this redemption by faith is revealed in Abraham who believed before circumcision to become the father of all who believe, Jew and Gentile alike. Paul expounds this justification through the first Adam/last Adam pattern of redemptive history. He also addresses the relationship between Israel and the Gentiles in salvation history in chapters 9–11.

After laying the doctrinal foundation of the gospel and Christ's work in the first eleven chapters, Paul shifts gears to the duty and life of the Christian. As living sacrifices, the saints are to use their varied gifts for the goal of love, even under the earthly authorities appointed by God. The issues of Christian liberty, with respect to diet and calendar, follow with the continued goal of love, righteousness, and peace in the Holy Spirit between Jew and Gentile. Paul signs off by showcasing his travel plans and missional goals and offering extended greetings and a benediction. The rather lengthy benediction intricately connects his opening thesis of the gospel of Christ to the glory of the only wise God through Jesus Christ forevermore.

1–2 Corinthians

Paul penned the letters of 1 and 2 Corinthians on separate occasions; yet it would be infelicitous to treat them separately, as they belong to the ongoing and emotional conversation between the apostle and one of his churches. In fact, one could argue that the letters are misnamed, as we know of a total of four letters written by Paul to the Corinthians. But a bit of history is in order to outline the drama of this relationship.

On his third journey, Paul spent around two years in Ephesus, which was a straight shot across the Aegean Sea from Corinth. During this period, there was no shortage of communication and updates between Paul and the church in Corinth. There was a letter from Paul to the church that is referred to in 1 Corinthians 5:9, to which they responded with a series of questions (1 Cor 7:1). Answering these queries and responding to a report delivered by Chloe's people, Paul wrote what we now have as 1 Corinthians, which dealt with a basketful of problems. After 1 Corinthians arrived and Timothy paid the church a visit (1 Cor 16:10–11), a serious issue erupted in the congregation, provoking an emergency visit by Paul he called "painful" (2 Cor 2:1). This visit did not turn out as Paul hoped, and instead of visiting again he wrote a "tearful" or "severe" letter delivered by Titus, which numbers as the third. Meanwhile, back in Ephesus, peril arose and pushed Paul out of the city and over to Troas (2 Cor 1:8), where he hoped to meet up with Titus for an update on Corinth (2 Cor 2:12–13). Distressed for both Titus and the Corinthians, Paul pushed on to Macedonia, where he finally met up with Titus and received the good news of the Corinthians' repentance over his tearful letter (2 Cor 7:5–9). Titus' report, though, was not all clean, as the so-called super apostles were working their damage. From Macedonia, Paul authored 2 Corinthians to defend his apostleship and to ready the church to give toward the Jerusalem collection. The four letters we know about, then, are an initial letter, a second (1 Cor), a third (the tearful letter), and a fourth (2 Cor).

Ruins of Corinth

The pastoral issues within the Corinthian correspondence clearly are varied and broad, from sexual immorality to worship matters to the resurrection. As Paul airs the dirty laundry of this congregation, one may doubt the sincerity of its faith, but Paul's confidence in Christ has no problem addressing them as saints, who will be sustained guiltless in the day of our Lord Jesus Christ (1 Cor 1:2, 7).

What is particularly noteworthy about both letters is Paul's astute perception of the local cultural dynamics and influences unique to the Roman colony of Corinth.[9] Both epistles indicate that one of these local dynamics hobbling the church concerns the interaction between oratory and social status. At this time in Corinth, eloquence as an orator could elevate your status and bring you honor. The congregation became addicted to this worldly striving for superiority and self-exaltation, causing issues of divisions, judging others, criticism of Paul, and infatuation with the super apostles. This is why Paul denies himself eloquence (1 Cor 2:1–2) and defends his apostleship with the credentials of suffering and weakness. Paul trumpets the weakness and foolishness of the gospel to counter their thirst for worldly honor and wisdom.

Galatians

Of the epistles we possess, Galatians appears to be the first written. The audience addressed does not fall to an individual or a specific city with any number of house churches, but to numerous churches within a large region. While Galatians could refer to those who were ethnically Galatian and residing in the northern part of Asia Minor, modern-day Turkey, we have no evidence placing Paul in these northern hills. More likely, Galatia denotes the Roman province in south-central Asia Minor and includes the cities of Lystra, Debre, Pisidian Antioch, and so on—where Paul planted churches during his first missionary journey. The letter was intended to be circulated around these congregations, or several copies could have been sent.

In the opening chapters, Paul recalls a bit of his history in defense of his apostleship, in which he mentions only two trips to Jerusalem to meet with the apostles. The first, brief visit, lasting only 15 days, aligns suitably with Luke's account in Acts 9:26–30. Luke writes in a general fashion that Paul met with the apostles (Acts 9:27), while Paul gets specific to swear that he greeted only Peter and James (Gal 1:18–19). After this layover, Paul shipped out to his hometown, Tarsus, in the region of Cilicia (Acts 9:30; Gal 1:21). The second trip comes after fourteen years with Barnabas and Titus, most likely when they brought relief for the famine in Judea (Gal 2:1; Acts 11:29–30). Upon the return to

Papyrus 46, one of the oldest existing
New Testament manuscripts (this fragment contains
the text of 2 Cor 11:33–12:9)

Antioch, Paul and Barnabas shipped off to plant the congregations of Galatia (Acts 13:4). Yet the joyful homecoming to Antioch was soured by controversy with the circumcision party, or the Judaizers (Acts 15:2). This is when Paul learns of the same ideas infecting the congregations of Galatia and writes to address them. This places Galatians before the Jerusalem Council and dates it to around AD 48.

The teaching of the Judaizers has plagued the churches with the necessity of circumcision. Faith in Christ is not enough, but the saints must also be circumcised to keep the law. This added condition, however, contaminates the true gospel of justification, not by the works of the law, but by faith in Christ. The infection of this false gospel summons Paul on a life-saving rescue mission. He is floored that they have so quickly twisted toward another gospel (Gal 1:6), and he bends over with labor pains, waiting for Christ to be formed in them (Gal 4:19). Paul, then, administers the truth of Christ's death and righteousness received by faith and powerfully demonstrated from the Old Testament. Since the Judaizers are distorting the gospel and putting the saints back under the cursed yoke of the law, Galatians is Paul's open-heart surgery of gospel defense. Like Romans, the gospel DNA is mapped with remarkable clarity.

Ephesians

With Ephesians, we come to Paul's Prison Epistles. After wintering in Corinth in AD 57–58, Paul landed in Jerusalem for Pentecost and was placed in Roman custody for nearly the next four years (AD 58–62). The first part of this was in Caesarea, the latter half in Rome. Paul stresses his imprisonment by mentioning it there times: "a prisoner of Christ Jesus" (3:1), "a prisoner for the Lord" (4:1), "an ambassador in chains" (6:20). Even though Paul could have written Ephesians during this four-year window, early testimony points to Rome, which enjoys a consensus by scholars.

Ephesians does not seem to address any certain malady or problem, hence the nonpolemical tone. Some evidence hints at it being a letter to be circulated among a number of churches, though early testimony agrees with the Ephesian identity of the recipients. In keeping with his custom, Paul expresses his thankfulness and prayers for the saints and covets their prayers for him and his gospel opportunities. This gratitude translates into a positive tone throughout the letter as Paul opens by gushing about the Father's electing love and closes with magnifying the incorruptible love of Christ.

The structure of the letter clearly reveals a regular pattern of Paul, which is the movement from indicative to imperative, or from grace to gratitude. In the first three chapters, Paul magisterially exalts God's great salvation as all of grace in Christ Jesus. After he has rooted the saints' faith in the finished work of Christ, Paul transitions in chapters 4–6 to how they should conduct their new lives in Christ. The salvation received by faith alone is lived out through love. Moreover, this movement elevates the unified theme of the book, "unity in the inaugurated new creation."[10]

Philippians

Moving down the cell block, Philippians is the next of Paul's prison epistles. With the mention of the imperial guard, Paul is again likely writing from Rome, AD 58–62. Paul planted the Philippian congregation during his second missionary journey (Acts 16), and without delay the congregation partnered with him financially (Phil 4:15–16). In fact, the occasion of the letter is another gift brought to Paul by Epaphroditus, who nearly died of sickness (2:25–30). Paul is sending the newly revived Epaphroditus back to Philippi with the letter and news of Paul (4:18).

The generosity and love of the Philippians seasons Paul's response with thankfulness and encouragement. He longs to communicate his satisfaction with the church and inform them how the gospel has advanced even in his confinement. Joy echoes throughout this brief epistle as Paul rejoices in his chains, the progress of the gospel, the Philippian prayers and partnership, and their obedience both in his presence and absence. He longs for the saints to rejoice with him (2:18; 4:4).

Amid all this rejoicing and encouragement, few problems are detectable. The only explicit issue is the personal dispute between Euodia and Syntyche, which some commentators take as having a deep divisive effect on the entire congregation, as he calls them to stand firm in one spirit (1:27). The topic of unity and sacrificial love is undoubtedly significant, yet it is uncertain if this is addressing a specific problem or is more general instruction. The happy tone of Paul does not seem to indicate a dire situation. Paul also mentions opponents who may be persecuting or bothering the church (1:28–29); warns against evildoers, who mutilate the flesh with circumcision (3:2); and calls out enemies of the cross (3:18–19). Whether these are the same or different parties is not clear, but there is a Jewish influence to each of them. Notwithstanding these issues, Paul's joy and encouragement coats Philippians in the sweetness of Christ's love and unity in happy suffering and service to the gospel.

Colossians

Strong evidence favors that Ephesians, Colossians, and Philemon were written around the same time, which again puts Paul in Rome. What is unique about Colossians, however, is that Paul did not plant the church or personally know them (Col 2:1). The city of Colossae lay at the southwest end of the Lycus valley, about 120 miles west of Ephesus and neighboring Laodicea. Paul's fellow brother and faithful minister Epaphras, who is from Colossae (Col 4:12), was the first to preach the gospel and pastor there (Col 1:7). Epaphras probably labored there during Paul's stay in Ephesus on his third journey (AD 54–57), when Paul sent out laborers to the surrounding areas.

Epaphras is now with Paul in prison in Rome, and he brought with him concerning news about the church. Epaphras is scared that this congregation will fall, which is why he asks for Paul's help and labors so intensely in prayer for them. Whatever the problem is, it does not cause Paul to doubt the faith or love of the saints, as he gives thanks for their faith and new identity in Christ. Yet the danger threatens the supremacy of Christ and so demands a serious rebuffing. This corrupting influence has come to be known as the Colossian heresy, though its exact nature is highly debated. The best guess describes this heresy as a folk religion, heavily colored with Jewish ideas and beliefs about the zodiac.[11] The so-called philosophers did not replace Christ per se, but they advocated the need for more than Christ. In addition to Christ, the saints needed to honor astral deities or angels, who governed fate and the seasons of life. Such veneration was paid by participating in ecstatic rituals, visions, ascetic dietary rules, and by keeping the Sabbaths and feasts of the Old Testament. These abasing practices of piety were sold in the name of humility, but the effect was an arrogant judging of others to elevate the self.

Over and against angel worship and legalism, Paul trumpets the surpassing glory of Christ, the image of the invisible God who is Lord over every rule and authority—even the angels. Having nailed sins to his cross, Christ effected forgiveness. Since the Colossians died with Christ, were buried with him in baptism, and have been raised with him to new life, they are free from the elemental laws and spirits of the world. With minds set on heaven—where Christ, their life, is seated—the new life of the saints is about putting to death what is earthly and putting on the new self, that is, Christ.

Colossians closes with a longer greeting section. Tychicus and Onesimus are identified as the letter carriers sent to encourage the hearts of saints. Paul sends greetings from Aristarchus, Mark, Justus, Luke, Demas, and Epaphras, names which also appear in Philemon.

1–2 Thessalonians

When we turn to 1 and 2 Thessalonians, we actually go back in time (and get out of prison) to just after Paul's second mission trip, not long after Paul first preached the gospel in Thessalonica. Paul's Thessalonian opponents chased him out of town and followed him to Berea, where Paul separated from Silas and Timothy to head for

Athens and then Corinth. Paul mentions this history in 1 Thessalonians 2:17–3:3. First Thessalonians, then, was written from Corinth after Timothy was sent out to check on them and return with an update. This dates the first letter to AD 51–52, and the coauthors include Paul, Silvanus (Silas), and Timothy.

Timothy's report on the saints of Thessalonica brought much joy and relief to Paul, who was worried sick about them. He gives thanks for their faith, love, and hope and how they became imitators of the saints by suffering for Christ. This casts 1 Thessalonians in a largely positive tone. By and large, despite the suffering, the Thessalonians are doing well in the faith. There are, however, a few issues to be addressed: sexual purity, resurrection comfort in the face of the death of beloved saints, the final parousia, and laziness.

Once his first letter arrives and produces fruit, another report of the Thessalonian's health gets back to Paul in Corinth, and he responds with another letter, with the same coauthors. Again, the overall fitness of the church is good, as Paul even takes the opportunity to boast about their faith and love in Christ amid the waves of continued suffering (2 Thess 1:4). Nevertheless, a couple of weaknesses persist. The first entails questions about Christ's second coming. The church is troubled by an idea circulating that the day of the Lord has come (2 Thess 2:2). Therefore, Paul clarifies that Christ will not return before the man of sin is revealed, but the only sure way to recognize the man of sin is that Christ himself will defeat him. The second ongoing and related ailment is sloth. Some in the congregation are unwilling to work, since they think Christ is coming back any day. The infection that was still minor in the first letter has metastasized into gangrene and now must be cut off. Paul, then, lays down the firm rule: keep away from brothers walking in idleness, for if anyone is unwilling to work, let him not eat (2 Thess 3:6, 10).

Both the Thessalonian letters sign off in significant ways for establishing the manner and function of Paul's letters. As in some of his earliest letters, Paul frankly states his habitual practice in signing off.

"I, Paul, write this greeting with my own hand. This is a sign of genuineness in every letter of mine; it is the way I write" (2 Thess 3:17). Even though Paul consistently employs a secretary in writing his letters, he always finishes them with his own handwriting. Like a wax seal, his John Hancock and penmanship certify the authenticity of his apostolic correspondence. Additionally, Paul adjures the church to have his letter read aloud to all the saints (1 Thess 5:27). By oath, he demands his letters to benefit the entire body of the church. Scholars will comment on how Paul's letters have liturgical characteristics to them, and this is not accidental in that Paul expected his letters to be read in worship. They were not merely personal letters, but also sermons. His letter writing was another aspect of his gospel preaching.

1 Timothy and Titus

Pairing these two epistles, rather than 1 and 2 Timothy, may seem like a mistake, but in terms of their historical occasion and function they are nearly twins. According to our information, Paul's imprisonment in Rome extended for about two years between AD 60–62, after which he was released. He enjoyed a few more years of free ministry before he was picked back up by the authorities and held in custody for another couple years, AD 65–66. According to church tradition, this second incarceration ended not with an acquittal but martyrdom. Between these two detentions Paul revisited some of his congregations in Greece and Asia and wrote to Timothy and Titus, who shared similar situations.

As Paul renewed his relationships with his old churches or planted new ones, he noticed that some of them were lacking in order. Their churches were a mess, and they needed some spring cleaning. Who better to do the dusting than his trusted coworkers? Therefore, Paul deposited Timothy in Ephesus and entrusted the churches of Crete to Titus. Paul gave both of these fellow workers the same job description. In both epistles, we find the qualifications for overseers and deacons and instructions for other matters of church life. The situations differed between Ephesus and Crete, so Paul accommodated accordingly. Yet he asked Titus to come to him in Nicopolis (Titus 3:12) and mentioned to Timothy that he was heading to Macedonia. As Nicopolis is not far from the region of Macedonia, it is probable that Paul wrote both letters close in time and place.

Paul also addresses Timothy and Titus with the same endearing title, "my true child" (1 Tim 1:2; Titus 1:4), which underscores another similarity between them. Both 1 Timothy and Titus are personal letters, addressed to individuals. Yet their shared goal of adding order to the church gives them a decidedly corporate feel. The letters are addressed to the respective ministers, but the congregation is intended to overhear their reading. The similarities of 1 Timothy and Titus further display Paul's consistent pastoral theology. In addition to addressing the offices of elder and deacon (1 Tim 3:1–13; Titus 1:5–9), Paul covers the interpersonal dynamics between the older and younger generations and the issues of widows, money, and false teaching. Personal piety for the apostle is concretely worked out within the relationships of the church society. Yet Paul is always relating his instructions to the gospel. In every other paragraph or so, the apostle cannot help but gush on about Christ (1 Tim 1:14–19; 2:5–7; 3:16; 4:10; 6:14–16; Titus 1:1–2; 2:11–14; 3:4–7). In addition to these explicit praises of Christ, the grace of the Savior seasons his every directive and administrative instruction. As Paul strengthens and builds the church, he never moves an inch beyond its one foundation, Jesus Christ.

2 Timothy

The canonical order of Paul's epistles is relatively harmless, but if a quibble could be raised it would be the placement of 2 Timothy. Written at the end of Paul's life, it unfortunately comes third from the end among his letters in the New Testament. A year or two has passed since Paul signed off on his first letters to Timothy and Titus. As for Timothy, we are not entirely sure where he is. It seems likely he is still in Ephesus, or at least in the nearby area. Paul, though, was picked up by the authorities. He is writing this letter from the inside of a jail cell in Rome, awaiting execution. As an old man in jail, Paul is all alone, save Luke. And the days of his waiting are cold and chaotic. It is circa AD 65 and the emperor is Nero, whose madness had reached epic proportions. There were revolts in Britain, Spain, and Armenia. As one ancient historian wrote, "Nero was now so universally loathed that no abuse could

ROMAN EMPERORS

Augustus	27 BC–AD 14
Tiberius	AD 14–39
Gaius	39–41
Claudius	41–54
Nero	54–68
Galba	June 68–Jan 69
Otho	Jan 69–Apr 69
Vitellius	Jan 69–Dec 69
Vespasian	July 69–79
Titus	79–81
Domitian	81–96

be found bad enough for him" (Suetonius, *Nero* 45). By this time, the Jewish revolts had started in Palestine. Bodies were piling up by the thousands, many of which were Christians. It was about this time that James the brother of Jesus was martyred in Jerusalem. Palestine is burning, Rome is in chaos, and Paul is in jail.

As these clouds swirl in the background, Paul is a father focused on passing on the family heritage to his true son, Timothy. The good deposit of the faith handed down from the ancestors, passed on to Timothy from his grandmother and mother, Paul entrusts to Timothy for safekeeping. The cold breath of death chills Paul's neck, and he longs to see his dear son before the Lord brings him home. If providence makes Timothy late, Paul needs to make sure the deposit is properly bequeathed to Timothy. And this family heirloom is the pattern of sound words in faith and love in Christ Jesus, which includes the ministry of the gospel for Timothy.

Paul's words eek out with groans. Death scratches at the door, brothers have abandoned him, and Timothy's arrival is uncertain. Yet amid these inclement temperatures, Paul finds warmth. Christ and his resurrection drape over Paul like a warm blanket. Maybe Timothy won't make it before winter. The scrolls and cloak might not reach Paul. Even more brothers may abandon Paul. But he is certain of one thing: Christ's love to bring him home. Christ is faithful to his promise. And just as Paul will be brought safely into his heavenly home, so Christ will preserve the same gospel consolation and truth through the generations. He will keep raising up Timothies to proclaim the sacred writings that are able to make one wise for salvation through faith in Christ Jesus (2 Tim 3:15).

Philemon

Philemon is another private letter meant for public reading. It is addressed primarily to Philemon, one of Paul's coworkers, and then secondarily to the church that meets in his home. The connections this letter possesses with Colossians are numerous. Paul is in prison, and a total of seven names are shared in common between the two letters. This would date Philemon to Paul's first Roman incarceration in AD 60–62. In fact, whereas Tychicus and Onesimus carry the Colossian correspondence, Onesimus seems to be entrusted with this note to Philemon, who also lives within the vicinity of Colossae. This implies that the two letters were sent together.

Either way, Onesimus is Philemon's slave—that much we know. Beyond that, the circumstances are not clear. Onesimus seems to have run away from Philemon, either going to Paul on purpose or running into him by happenstance. In any case, the two form a relationship, presumably one in which Paul led Onesimus to the Lord. Paul describes Onesimus as his "child" and "useful" to both Paul and Philemon (10–11). Therefore, Paul requests Philemon to receive Onesimus as he would Paul himself, and so refresh Paul's heart in Christ. Though brief, the letter is thick with substance about the sweet, potent, reconciling love of the gospel.

PAUL'S THEOLOGY

The very mention of Pauline theology plunges us into deep waters swarming with centuries of controversies. There is no debate, however, that Paul's thought is rich and complex. Peter's own testimony confirms the astuteness and profundity of Paul's letters: "There are some things in them that are hard to understand, which the ignorant and unstable twist to their own destruction, as they do the other Scriptures" (2 Pet 3:16). The very intricacy of Paul should make one skeptical and leery of one-dimensional portraits. Nonetheless, there are themes and emphases that run through and repeat in his letters, and it is helpful to highlight a few of these to see the consistency in Paul and the unity of his pastoral correspondence.

The primary message of Paul is the gospel of Jesus Christ. From beginning to end, Paul is all about Christ. The Father and the Spirit loom large for Paul—there can be no diminishing them—but Paul consistently understands and relates to the Father and the Spirit in and through Christ. As Paul ponders and exercises his ministry, Christ is both his pattern and goal. When it comes to morality and living out the faith, Christ's image tells the story. The church and worship have no other foundation than Christ. Paul relates faith, hope, and love to Christ. As Paul states in nearly every letter, he is an apostle and servant of Jesus Christ, and as such, his life, message, and work are all done in service to and for the glory of Jesus Christ, the Son of God the Father.

The next staple of Paul is the context in which he understands Christ, namely in light of the Old Testament or redemptive history. Given his background as a highly learned Pharisee, the pervasive presence of the Old Testament in Paul's mind is no surprise. He was raised on the Old Testament more than on mother's milk. The Old Testament pervades his epistles, especially Romans, Galatians, Ephesians, and Corinthians. Some may push back that some of Paul's letters possess few to no Old Testament citations, but we can explain this easily: he is able to be a Greek to the Greeks and engage communities with little Jewish influence. Besides, even when Paul does not reference a passage of the Old Testament, the theology and imagery of the Old Testament is never far below the surface. For example, in the grand Christ poem in Colossians 1:15–20, no citation of the Old Testament exists, but it is indisputable that his theology of creation, wisdom, and resurrection all sprout from the Old Testament. The poem shows us Paul's mind had marinated in the Old Testament.

Within Paul's dependence on the Old Testament, two more themes ought to be mentioned. The first circles Paul's title as the apostle to the Gentiles. The inclusion of the Gentiles was not merely the burden of Paul's apostolic office; he labored to show how the incorporation of the nations was both the fulfillment of Old Testament promises and the natural trajectory of God's plan of redemption. The second motif arising out of the Old Testament, which is fundamental for Paul, is the first Adam/last Adam parallel. The Adam scheme only appears twice in Paul's letters, Romans 5 and 1 Corinthians 15. Yet from these pregnant chapters Paul demonstrates that all of redemptive history, the whole of God's plan of salvation, consists in the first Adam, through whom came sin and death, and the last Adam, by whom comes righteousness and resurrection. In fact, the Adam scheme forms the backbone of Paul's covenantal theology, as it contrasts the covenant of works against the covenant of grace.

Further woven into Paul's dependence on the Old Testament and the Adam scheme are two more key Pauline tenets. The first is justification. Not only does Paul expound justification from the first and last Adam in Romans 5:12–19, but justification pervades Paul's explanation of Christ's salvific work for his people. This is not to say the gospel consists only in justification or to limit Christ's redemptive blessings to justification. Without a doubt, salvation is bigger than that. But the gift of Christ's righteousness to his people through faith is foundational to how Paul articulates his message concerning the Christian life.

The second tenet growing out of the Adam scheme is new creation. As this creation was consigned to death by the sin of the first Adam, so a new creation is born by the righteousness and resurrection of Christ. Circumcision and uncircumcision count for nothing, but new creation is everything. As the firstborn of the dead, Christ has invaded this dying age with the reality of new creation, so that to be united to Christ is to be a new creation. The heavenly mindedness of Paul never takes its eye off of new creation.

A final theme prevalent in Paul is an emphasis on Christian living. In almost every letter, readers can discern a dynamic between doctrine and practice: the indicative (doctrine) leads to the imperative (practice). That is, the indicative reality and truth of Christ lays the only foundation for pleasing the Father with good works. The exhortations issued by Paul always flow from Christ's work for us as a free gift. This dynamic shows itself in several ways. One, faith in Christ is necessary to pleasing God. "Whatever does not proceed from faith is sin" (Rom 14:23), and in Christ, all that counts is "faith working through love" (Gal 5:6). True obedience can only live united to Christ by faith. Two, since Christians are new creations in Christ, they are to put on the new self and its ways. By grace, Christ made us new, so the moral exhortations are to be who we are in Christ (Eph 4:22–24; Col 3:5–15). Three, the very structure of Paul's epistles often follow the movement from indicative to imperative. Romans 1–11 lays down what God has done in Christ, and chapters 12–15 set forth our duty in Christ. Similarly, Ephesians 1–3 is indicative, 4–6 are full of imperatives. Even at a passage level this happens. For example, in Philippians 2:1–4 Paul reasons that since we have encouragement in Christ, we should do nothing out of selfish ambition. By this dynamic, Paul keeps the saints rooted in the never-ceasing grace of Christ both for salvation and for living in love until Christ's return.

Many other important themes and topics of Paul could be listed, but these handful alert us to key doctrines near and dear to Paul's heart that he consistently inculcated in the churches by his letters.

For good or ill, debate will continue to swirl around Paul's theology, but appreciation of these points will clarify our reading of Paul and bring into greater focus the one indisputable interest of Paul: Jesus Christ and his eternal kingdom.

STUDY QUESTIONS

1. Explain how Paul was an apostle when he did not fit the criteria of Acts 1:21–22.

2. What was Paul's family and educational background? How did God use this background in Paul's ministry?

3. How did secretaries help write letters in the first century?

4. Where was Paul when he wrote Romans, and what was his purpose for writing?

5. Why was Paul so troubled over the Galatians?

6. Explain how 1 Timothy and Titus are similar.

7. What are some of the important theological themes for Paul?

13

GENERAL EPISTLES
AND REVELATION

Bible Reading:
Hebrews, James, 1–2 Peter,
1–3 John, Jude, Revelation

We come now to the last books of the Bible. Whereas previous chapters grouped books by relation (for example, the Gospels or Paul's letters), this one is sort of a grab bag. Scholars refer to this group of letters as the General Epistles. "General" is not negative, but rather refers to the non-specific addressees of most of these epistles. Whereas Paul wrote specifically to the Corinthians or to the house churches in Colossae, James speaks to the twelve tribes of the Dispersion and 1 Peter to the churches strewn across five large regions. Along with 1 John, Hebrews lacks a personal salutation. Jude and 2 Peter open with the equivalent to "Dear Christian." Second John addresses "the elect lady" and 3 John Gaius, making them exceptions among the group, but they are included to keep John's three short letters together. Jude addresses "those who are called" (1:1) and Revelation "the seven churches that are in Asia" (1:4).

The varied authorship, time, and place for the General Epistles increases the challenge of introducing them. Indeed, where Revelation is most likely the last written book of the New Testament, James probably dates the earliest. For this reason, a briefer presentation for each book will be given, focusing on matters of setting and theme. Then we will tease out several similar topics between the books that reveal a consistent picture of the Christian life in the early church.

HEBREWS

The authorship of Hebrews is one of the great mysteries of biblical scholarship. Origen posited Paul, Tertullian thought it was Barnabas, and Luther guessed Apollos. The stubborn truth remains: we simply do not know. So good is the author's anonymity, his encryption refuses to be cracked. However, a few personal attributes are discernable. He writes in Hebrews 2:3 that the great salvation first declared by the Lord was "confirmed to us by those who heard," which is a reference to the apostles. The author, then, is not an apostle, but one who learned from the apostles. Additionally, he knows Timothy, who is presumably Paul's Timothy, and he sends greetings from those from Italy (Heb 13:23–24). The problem with this phrase is that "those from Italy" could mean the author is sending the letter from Italy or that a group of Italians are with the author wherever he is located—another unknown.

The most definitive characteristic of the clandestine author is his smarts. Without question, his Greek skills surpass all the other New Testament writers. He could hide his name, but not his eloquence. Furthermore, his knowledge of Old Testament regulations concerning sacrifice, priesthood, and temple is off the charts. With ease, he moves backward and forward with eyes closed over the technicalities of holiness. His fluency with Greek rhetoric and mastery of ancient Judaism may seem like opposite talents, but he juggles them both without blinking.

Though the author, audience, and setting for Hebrews are hazy, its theme and purpose are clear as day. Just follow the author's use of the word "better." Jesus is the better mediator, better priest, and better sacrifice, and he inaugurated a better covenant. Whatever confusion one might have about Christ and the new covenant, both are exceedingly better than what came before. Why is the author stuck on the word "better"? Because the congregation he addresses is tempted (presumably) to return to Old Testament Judaism. Discontent with Christ, these saints are being pulled back by the tactile and olfactory lures of temple and sacrifice. The book of Hebrews is an urgent appeal not to return to Judaism, for if they fall away, they are crucifying again the Son of God and holding him in contempt.

JAMES

With a name like James, there are many possibilities for who could be behind this letter. It could be James the son of Zebedee or James the son of Alphaeus, both of whom have apostolic credentials. Yet few have the notoriety just to be called James without further identifiers than James the brother of Jesus and head of the Jerusalem church. Therefore, this James, whom we met at the Jerusalem Council in Acts 15, is most likely the author. The date of writing has traditionally been placed early. The fact that the letter makes no mention of the controversy surrounding circumcision and the Gentiles favors a pre-Jerusalem Council window. The early to mid-40s is a sound estimate for its date.[1]

The epistle possesses a distinctly Jewish flavor, but this should not be taken as excluding Gentiles. The saints he addresses are a mixed body of Jews and Gentiles, which makes his title for them further stand out. "The twelve tribes of the Dispersion" is a remarkable way to speak to the church. To begin with, the twelve tribes is an honorific title for all of Israel in covenant with God. Yet by the first century, the majority of the twelve were no longer in existence, as the destruction of the northern kingdom by Assyria lost them to history. The "twelve tribes" is not literal, but a metaphor for the church as God's full covenant people. Similarly, "Dispersion" originally referred to the state of exile, when God's displeasure was upon his people. In fact, the Messiah's work was to gather in the dispersed tribes. But James speaks as the servant of the Lord Jesus Christ to the Dispersion and calls them "brothers." By this, James is orienting our minds to the nature of the last days. Salvation has come in Christ, but the church—fulfillment and continuation of God's people from the Old Testament—awaits the crown of life. It matters not one's earthly address; the church is the Dispersion, since its homeland is not Palestine but heaven.

Genre-wise, James is often regarded as a hybrid between letter and wisdom literature. Just as the fear of the Lord undergirds Old Testament wisdom, so with James the essential starting point is faith in the Lord Jesus, faith that evidences itself with good deeds.

1-2 PETER

The letters of 1 and 2 Peter are written by the apostle Peter, the forward fisherman of Galilee. The dates of both letters are unknown, but if Peter was martyred in Rome in the 60s (as early church tradition tells us), they came before that. In the farewell of 1 Peter, he sends greetings from those in Babylon, which is actually a reference to Rome. This places Peter in the capital of the empire for the origin of the letter. Peter's second letter bears no geographical or personal details to put it on a timeline or a map. Presumably, he is still along the banks of the Tiber.

Peter intended his first letter to be circulated among the churches from the Black Sea in the north to the Mediterranean Sea. The five regions listed in its salutation comprise most of the territory of modern-day Turkey. Like James, Peter identifies the saints in terms of Old Testament exile theology: "To those who are elect exiles of the Dispersion" (1 Pet 1:1). Even though Christ has come with his imperishable salvation, his people remain exiles in this sin-cursed world, awaiting the revelation of Jesus Christ. His second epistle is addressed to "those who have obtained a faith of equal standing with ours by the righteousness of our God and Savior Jesus Christ" (2 Pet 1:1), which can apply to any believer. It was not necessarily intended for a specific group of churches.

In terms of contents, both letters seek to aid the saints in their lives of faith, particularly as a community of the Lord. 1 Peter's teaching is more general and overarching. He touches on the concrete realities of life, from relationships within the family to those in the broader society. In his second letter, Peter is more focused on the threat of false teachers and nature of the last days as we wait for Christ's glorious return. Either way, in both messages, Peter further demonstrates the apostolic teaching pattern of showcasing Christ and his grace for both faith and obedience, deeply rooted in the Old Testament.

1–3 JOHN

Little is known about the historical origins of the three letters of John. Some in the early church considered 2 John to be written by another disciple named John the Elder, but it was still more widely recognized as being from the apostle John. In fact, there is evidence that 2 John circulated as a sort of appendix to 1 John, which was universally accepted as being from the apostle, the son of Zebedee, who also penned the Gospel of John and Revelation. These letters were most likely written between AD 70 and 100, when John was ministering in and around the area of Ephesus.

The tone and message of these letters are overwhelmingly tender. John's letters may not be the giant of Romans or have the passion of Galatians, but they warm your soul like a comfy chair beside a fireplace on a cold day. This warmth radiates from several sources. First is the theme that glues together nearly every word and phrase: love— the love of the Father to send his only Son into the world, the love of the Son to be the propitiation for our sins, and the love we are to have for one another. God is love! Second, in 2 and 3 John the author calls himself "the elder," a title of endearment. With this, John presents himself as one with the people, who knows the people, and who shares in their frailty and joy. He is also able to impart loving wisdom. Third, John addresses the church as "the elect lady and her children," which echoes the Old Testament motif of Lady Jerusalem, the beloved wife of the Lord. This election recalls Jesus' words in John's Gospel, "You did not choose me, but I chose you" (John 15:16). It echoes the Father's election of a people and giving them to his Son—all the Father gave the Son come to the Son. Finally, John keeps his letters brief because he would rather talk with them face to face (2 John 12; 3 Jn 14). John's love images that of Christ himself as he longs to close the distance and be in their presence.

Yet John has a purpose behind his loving words. "I write these things to you who believe in the name of the Son of God, that you may know that you have eternal life" (1 John 5:13). The assurance of salvation and the certainty of life everlasting, this is where love aims. Faith expresses itself in love, and love turns around to bolster faith in Christ.

JUDE

Like others in the General Epistles, the original setting of Jude is obscure. Jude identifies himself as the brother of James, who was the brother of Jesus. This means Jude is Jesus' brother, a son of Mary and Joseph. Like 2 Peter, Jude addresses his correspondence to saints in general, "To those who are called, beloved in God the Father and kept for Jesus Christ." In fact, Jude shares many similarities with 2 Peter, particularly his warnings against false teachers. Indeed, Jude states up front his purpose: "to contend for the faith that was once for all delivered to the saints" (Jude 3), because people have crept in to pervert the grace of God. Jude gives a detailed description of the false teachers and their fate of judgment, and he calls the saints to build themselves up in the faith and to keep themselves in the love of God.

CHURCH LIFE IN THE GENERAL EPISTLES

Though the historical details of the General Epistles are sparse, the picture they paint about life in the church in the last days is detailed and clear. The dangers and maladies they address face us still today. And as the authors prescribe solutions, they all agree on the same medication, namely Christ Jesus and his grace to bolster our faith and love. For this reason, it is helpful to take the General Epistles as a whole and notice how their distinct voices harmonize. Particularly, we will notice five points of unity.

Let us first situate the New Testament church within Greco-Roman religious culture. In the first century, and in the ancient world in general, a religion had three main ingredients: temple, sacrifice, and priests. To be a recognizable religion, there had to be some sort of holy or sacred place, officiating priests or priestesses, and sacrificial or other rituals that embodied the religious experience. Additionally, religions regularly coincided with ethnic or family identity; you worshiped the gods of your people. Yet the New Testament church lacked all of these. There were no temples, but homes. Sacrifice was not practiced, nor any ritual around an altar. And instead of priests who performed esoteric rites, preachers and teachers expounded Scripture. Finally, adherents came from every ethnicity and social class. The church resembled more a philosophical school than a religion. Though the church borrowed much from the synagogue, it abandoned many Jewish idiosyncrasies, so society struggled to place the church in any of its existing categories. This was not just an effort for outsiders, but even within the church, believers labored to learn how to live together in this new and strange community called the body of Christ.[2] In light of this dynamic, the five points of unity of the General Epistles make more sense.

The relationship between old and new

How the New Testament church related to Old Testament Israel was a tense issue in the early church, particularly because often the local house church had been kicked out of the synagogue. The synagogue wanted to assert itself as the true heirs of the Old Testament over and against the church. Therefore, the apostles and teachers labored to show the continuity between the Old Testament and the New Testament in terms of the Old Testament's fulfillment in Christ. Hebrews dominates the field in this regard, as it shows how Christ is the true reality to which the Old Testament pictures pointed. The all-encompassing superiority of Christ demands that one cannot remain under the Aaronic priesthood, and that to return to it is eternally lethal. But Hebrews is not alone in this, as James takes a classic title for Old Testament Israel and tattoos it on the church made up of Jews and Gentiles: "the twelve tribes of the Dispersion" (Jas 1:2). Peter especially runs wild in this same manner, as he not only calls the saints the "elect exiles" but also lauds them as chosen race, a royal priesthood, and a holy nation—God's people (1 Pet 2:9–10). Peter also uses Old Testament events and figures like Sodom and Balaam to showcase the template for our lives in the last days (2 Pet 2:4–16). The General Epistles sing in harmony that there is not two people of God but one: Israel of old has blossomed in Christ alone to be the one people of God, the church, made up of believers from every tribe and language.

False teachers

One of the clear and present dangers for the saints are those who corrupt and deceive through false teaching. Each author labors to equip the saints against false teachers. John mentions a Diotrephes by name (3 John 9), and several times he sets off the alarm against antichrists (1 John 2:18–24; 4:2–3; 2 John 7). Jude and 2 Peter launch into a full diatribe against the lying prophets. Hebrews unleashes his Old Testament exegetical skill against those luring the saints back to Judaism. Correct belief in the faith once for all delivered in Jesus Christ is essential in waiting faithfully until the glory of Christ is revealed.

Licentious living

False doctrine is not the only predator prowling around to devour the saints. So also is immoral, worldly living. In fact, with Balaam as the model, false teachers often use the pleasures of the flesh as the back-door entrance to denying Christ (Jude 11; see Num 31:16).

James boldly warns the church against temptation and to keep oneself unstained from the world, as friendship with the world is enmity with God (Jas 1:13, 27; 4:4). Peter orders us not return to the passions of our former ignorance or join the flood of debauchery (1 Pet 1:14; 4:4). Having been cleansed from our former sins, we are to be diligent to be found without spot or blemish (2 Pet 1:9; 3:14). John tells the saints not to love the world (1 John 2:15–17), and Jude points out how the false teachers pervert the grace of God into sensuality (Jude 4). Immoral and worldly living can shipwreck the faith and lead one to deny the Lord Jesus.

Suffering

The epistles encourage readers to ready themselves for and to endure sufferings. This departs somewhat from the Old Testament. Under the old covenant, suffering could be a sign of God's displeasure and anger—curses for disobedience (Deut 28). But in the victory of Christ's death, suffering in the New Testament is a participation in Christ and a sign of God's love and favor. Peter clarifies that we should not be surprised by suffering as if it is a strange thing; rather, he pronounces a blessing upon those who suffer for righteousness (1 Peter 4:12; 3:14–15). James reckons it as joyful when various trials test our faith to yield steadfastness (James 1:2–3). Hebrews builds a hall of faith honoring those who chose to be mistreated with God rather than to enjoy the fleeting pleasures of sin (Heb 11:24–25). Second Peter and Jude call out the violence of scoffers and blasphemers and summon the blessing of Christ to keep the saints from stumbling. Suffering is part of the Christian faith, but the kindness of Christ uses this suffering to produce steadfastness as we seek the crown of life.

Relationships in the church

The first churches, like churches today, were made up of individuals from all walks of life. When you put a group of sinners together, there will be friction and drama. Favoritism pushes aside the poor in preference for the rich (Jas 2:1–7). Scoffers draw lines of division and arrogance breaks the unity of love (Jude 17–18). Thus the apostles called for unity of mind (1 Pet 3:8), humility (1 Pet 5:6), tamed tongues (Jas 3:1–12), and the like. Whatever the specific sickness, the authors all applied the same basic remedy: love. God is love, so as his children in Christ, loving one another must characterize all of life in the church. Christ created a strange and diverse community of saints through his gospel; by the magic of his love, Christ preserves the many as one in him.

From these five points of harmony, we can see that the house churches of the first century were not so different from our churches today. The wisdom applied to these issues by the authors has staying power for the ages. These doctrinal and practical topics still face congregations today in the modern world, and so the General Epistles impart grace to build up our faith, pray in the Spirit, and remain in the love of God (Jude 20–21).

REVELATION

We come now to the last book in our journey, Revelation. It is not so much the book's position as the last in Scripture that warrants its detailed coverage, but how it pulls together many themes and motifs from all of Scripture.

On the surface, Revelation is a puzzling, even troubling book. A butchered lamb with seven eyes talks. Horse-like grasshoppers with scorpion tails roam about. A two-headed dragon waits to swallow a newborn baby. It's no surprise that Revelation is so often misunderstood or ignored altogether.

And yet, no other book of Scripture contains right up front an explicit blessing for reading, hearing, and keeping what is in it (Rev 1:3). God wants this book to be read and understood. He enjoins us with his blessing to take and read Revelation. In order to actualize this blessing, then, I will lay out principles for reading the book and then skim its verses to witness the principles in action.

The human author of Revelation is John the apostle. He wrote it after a vision he received on the Lord's Day while in the Spirit and while banished to the island of Patmos (Rev 1:9–11). The date of its composition falls within the reign of Domitian, AD 81–96.[3] John begins the letter, "The revelation of Jesus Christ, which God gave him to show to his servants the things that must soon take place. He made it known by sending his angel to his servant John ..." Revelation is more than anything an account of visions, not unlike Ezekiel or the vision portion of Daniel. Thus, one could read Revelation as Christ's handwriting from heaven.

John's commission to write the things he heard and saw place him firmly within the paradigm of the Old Testament prophets, who were sworn into office within the divine assembly. This means that the biggest help in understanding Revelation is being well versed not in Greco-Roman society (though history is important), but the thought world of the Old Testament prophets. John particularly draws from Daniel and Ezekiel, but the other prophets, including Isaiah and Zechariah, and even the Law and the Psalms, are required reading for truly accessing Revelation's message.

When it comes to any translation project, aspects of the original are lost in translation. This is true for Don Quixote as well as the Gospel of Luke. Yet translation especially hinders the clarity of Revelation. This is due to the style of John's Greek. To begin with, his Greek sounds like it was written by someone who is more familiar with Hebrew, much like Septuagint Greek. Second, John is constantly alluding to the Old Testament but rarely quoting it explicitly. Third, John likes to repeat phrases and then add slight changes or variations, which is part of the apocalypse genre. Such repetition and allusions are very difficult to reproduce in translation.

Besides exotic images, Revelation loves numbers. Numbers dominate the book. As moderns, our instincts favor a literal or mathematical

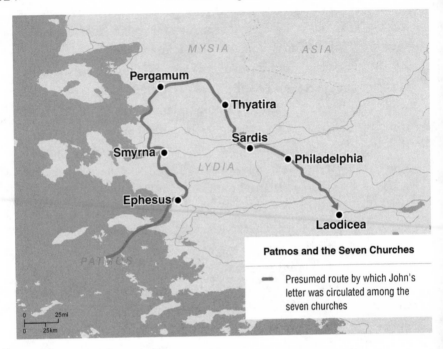

Patmos and the Seven Churches

— Presumed route by which John's letter was circulated among the seven churches

sense to these numbers. Yet in ancient times, numbers were kindred spirits with symbolism and metaphors. And Revelation's use of numbers is thoroughly symbolic. All the numbers in Revelation are symbolic, drawn from the Old Testament and not the first century. For example, in the Old Testament, four symbolizes the whole earth.[4] Twelve is the number of God's people. Three is the divine superlative. Seven can communicate varying shades of holiness, perfection, and completion, depending on context. Ten and its multiples (100, 1,000, etc.) express vastness or large amounts. The symbolic value of numbers can vary some, so each occurrence must be judged by its own context.

The book of Revelation is a vision, and visions in Scripture resemble the world of dreams. As you know from your own dreams, the normal laws of nature rarely operate. In a dream, scrolls can be eaten, creatures can be composites of several, and you can know things without being told. For example, in Revelation 5, when no one can open the scroll, John starts weeping in sadness. Why is this? How does John know that the unopened scroll is sad? He just knows, as one often does in a dream. The how and why questions relevant in other books of the Bible are not as important in Revelation and can even be a distraction.

In the Old Testament, people held the cosmos to have two basic levels of reality, the visible earthly realm and the invisible heavenly realm of the gods. On earth there were economics, families, trees, flowers, rain, and sickness. In heaven there were strange-looking demons, angels, and gods who carried out their business. Yet these two realms were analogically linked. Each king or kingdom had its own divine analogy in heaven. If two nations fought on earth, then their respective deities warred in heaven. If God performed some act in heaven, it would manifest itself on earth, usually as rain or drought. Revelation, therefore, pictures events in heaven, the drama of the last days as it unfolds in the world above. Yet the earthly referent to these heavenly events is not always made explicit. This is why familiarity with the Old Testament, salvation history, and the apocalyptic genre is so important for understanding Revelation.

The final reading principle for Revelation is the Old Testament technique called recapitulation. Recapitulation is the retelling of the same episode, typically from a different perspective or with a different emphasis. For example, a story might be told first from a man's point of view and then from a woman's (see Exodus 14–15 and Judges 4–5). If it is an image, you might see it from the south first, and then from the north. Revelation replays the same image over and over again. This image is the last days, the time between Christ's ascension and second coming. This book is like walking into an art museum and seeing an exhibit where the same farmhouse is painted from three different angles and seasons. The first portrait captures the southern exposure during the spring. You turn ninety degrees to gaze at the western face midsummer. Next, you swivel to eye the northside as the autumn leaves blanket the ground. Each portrait feeds your mind a two-dimensional image, but the several paintings together form a three-dimensional model of a year in the life of the farmhouse.

Similarly, the repeated exposure to the same image in Revelation adds three-dimensional wisdom to God's plan for the last days. This is especially the case with the day of the Lord, which we know from the Old Testament prophets is a complex reality. Therefore, the portraits of Revelation focus more and more on the day of the Lord as the book progresses.

Some of these reading principles may seem difficult, and Revelation itself admits to requiring wisdom (Rev 13:18; 17:9). Yet amid all the details and numbers, Revelation possesses one simple point of inestimable value for the faith: Jesus wins! Christ Jesus has conquered, and he will without fail bring his victory to its blessed conclusion. This is what the book is about. It is not about predicting Christ's second coming or dating events. It is about encouraging the church with the victory of Christ. And why is this victory so important? Because on earth, the saints are suffering and seemingly losing to the forces of evil. On the earthly plane, the church appears to be breaking down, as the saints are being martyred. The vision of Revelation reveals the heavenly realm where the Sovereign Lamb is ruling and protecting his people from their enemies. Within the terrestrial realm, dying in Christ feels like failing, but in reality, blessed are those who die in the Lord, that they may rest from their labors.

With the reading principles and main thesis of Revelation set before us, we can now stroll through its pages to see how Revelation bestows its blessing upon its readers. After the opening greeting, in which we are introduced to the one seated upon the throne (the Father), the seven spirits (the Holy Spirit), and Jesus Christ as the Coming One, John's first vision is to hear and see the glorified Christ. He is told to write to the seven named churches, but this sevenfold imagery represents a picture of the global church. The issues of the seven churches are constant ailments within the visible church throughout the last days. Additionally, the earthly congregations are identified with heavenly stars and lampstands (1:12), forging the link between heaven and earth. Furthermore, the glorious description of the Son of Man in 1:12–18 is used in the headings of each letter. For example, John sees eyes like flames of fire (1:14) and Christ speaks to Thyatira as the one who has eyes like a flame of fire (2:18). Finally, Christ highlights his definitive work in his death and resurrection: "I am the first and the last, and the living one. I died, and behold I am alive forevermore" (1:17–18). And then, the omega glory of Christ promises the blessings of eternal life at the close of each letter: tree of life, crown of life, and so on. The picture opens with the work of Christ on the cross and finishes with the everlasting salvation of his second coming. This completes the first image of Revelation, extending from 1:9 to 3:22. With this image completed, it is time to start over at the beginning.

The second portrait covers Revelation 4:1–8:5, and it opens with John in heaven being thoroughly acquainted with the one seated upon the throne and his unceasing praise as Creator and Lord of all things. Once the Lamb takes the scroll, the creatures and elders laud him with a sevenfold honor (Rev 5:12). A few key points about this scene deserve mention. First, Christ is presented as the Lion of the tribe of Judah who has conquered, and his opening the scroll expresses his royal rule (5:5). The releasing of the scroll's seals that follow in Revelation 6, then, show Christ's victorious royal power. Second, the Lion conquered by being the Lamb who was slain (Rev 5:9). The paradoxical image shocks our sensibilities: the Lion conquered by being a slain Lamb. Third, the effect of the Lamb's blood was to ransom a people of God from every tribe, language, people, and nation as a kingdom of priests (5:10; the fulfillment of Exod 19:4–6). This fourfold reference for God's people becomes John's name for the church throughout the book. The order will alternate, but tribe, language, people, and nation refer together to the church as the fulfillment of the Abrahamic promises.

As the Lamb opens the seals of the scroll, his royal actions bring us to the final day of the Lord (Rev 6:17). The judgments executed by the four horsemen amount to famine, war, and plague, which are classic

Foundation of the altar of Zeus in Pergamum

Old Testament curses. In heaven the Lamb's judgments appear as horsemen; on earth we witness them as disasters of various sorts. In either case, we recognize them as Christ's ruling power. The sixth seal ushers in the great day of wrath, but before the climactic seventh seal, we find an interlude, common in Revelation. This interlude of chapter 7 presents two pictures. The first is the church militant on earth sealed and safely numbered as God's 144,000 (12 x 12 x 1,000 represent the vast total number of the saints; 7:1–8). The second image is the church in the glory of heaven, innumerable, forever praising the one seated on the throne and the Lamb. The precise number on earth displays the Lamb's perfect protection of his earthly struggling saints; he loses not one. The uncountable host in heaven reveals the abundant salvation of God that is beyond human estimation.

Prologue	1:1–8—Alpha and Omega, who is, who was, and who is coming
7 churches	1:9–3:22—Resurrected Son of Man to his churches
7 seals	4:1–8:5—Conquering Lamb
7 trumpets	8:6–11:19—Lord God, who is and who was
Blasphemous Trinity	12:1–15:4—Michael's victory
7 bowls	15:5–16:21—Wrath poured out
Lady Babylon	17:1–19:10—Babylon fallen, supper of the Lamb
Final judgment x3	19:11–21—White Rider 20:1–10—Lake of fire 20:11–15—Books opened
New heaven & earth	21:1–8—God dwells with man
New Jerusalem	21:9–22:5—The light of the Lamb's face
Epilogue	22:6–21—Come, Lord Jesus

Table 7: The Portraits of Revelation

*This gives the basic recapitulatory images of Revelation.
Other thematic structures are present in the book,
so this is not intended as a detailed outline.*

After this interlude on the church, the seventh seal finally opened in 8:1–5 accomplishes two purposes. It closes off the second portrait of the church age and forms a link or hinge with the next portrait. The end of the age is marked by silence, which indicates both the answer of prayer and a stillness before the final judicial verdict. This last wrath is poured out with thunder, rumblings, lightning, and an earthquake. This fourfold superstorm recalls the sounds of God's throne (Rev 4:5) and echoes the theophany of Sinai to seal the end of the age. It also gets repeated in the upcoming portraits (11:19; 16:18). The seventh seal also provides a hinge for the next church age image by introducing the seven trumpets (Rev 8:2). The seven trumpets at the end become the sevenfold structure of the next scene.

The third portrait of the church age reaches from 8:6–11:19. The parallels with the second picture are unmistakable. The first six trumpets inflict curses on the earth; this time the imagery is drawn chiefly from the plagues of Egypt. Between the sixth and seventh trumpets, an interlude is given that focuses on the church (10:1–11:14). The seventh trumpet marks the end of history in three ways. First, the kingdom of the world has become the kingdom of the Lord and Christ (11:15). Second, it finishes with the fourfold superstorm: lightning, rumblings, thunder, and earthquake, adding a fifth, hail (11:19). Third, in 11:17 the elders sing, "We give thanks to you, Lord God Almighty, who is and who was." Something is missing here. In the previous uses, they said "who is, who was, *and who is coming*" (Rev 1:4, 8; 4:8, emphasis mine). The immanent future "is coming" has been dropped, because the Lord has come in the final parousia.

The seventh trumpet vision ends with a hinge verse: "God's temple in heaven was opened" (11:19). Yet this hinge ties in not with the opening of chapter 12, but to 15:5, where another sevenfold portrait is painted (Rev 15:5–16:21). The link between 11:19 and 15:5 brackets off 12:1–15:4 as its own church age portrait. This portrait does not employ a sevenfold pattern, but it does give us snapshots of the time between Christ's first coming and his parousia.

In 12:1–6, the reality depicted in the image takes us back to Christ's earthly ministry, with the drama of the woman giving birth to the Psalm 2 man-child, who is caught up to God (12:5). The cross and ascension victory of Christ is further elaborated as Michael defeats Satan with the cry "the salvation ... and authority of his Christ have come" (12:10). The figure of Michael corresponds to Christ himself, not an angel. Michael means "Who is like God?" and is a declaration of the Lord's incomparability, a name fit for the Lord alone.

Once the dragon is silenced and banished from heaven, we get sketches of three monsters who are a profane imitation of the Trinity. The first is a ten-horned dragon with seven crowned heads. He attempts to copy the one seated upon the throne. The second is the beast, a knock-off of Christ, who is given authority from the dragon. Its mortal wound was healed so that the whole earth would marvel and worship the dragon and the beast (13:2–4). The third monster copies the work of the Spirit by performing signs and deceiving the world to worship the beast, and is later called the false prophet (16:13). Moreover, those who worship the beast are called "those who dwell upon the earth," or "earth-dwellers," which is Revelation's term for non-believers. The visible church is termed "every tribe, people, language, and nation," while the pagans are the earth-dwellers. The number symbolism of the Old Testament is further demonstrated in the number of the beast, which is also said to be the number of man, 666. Humans were created on the sixth day (Gen 1). To repeat a number three times is a divine superlative. The number 666 represents man attempting to become like God; it is self-idolatry.

After outlining the three devilish beasts, the scene again switches its interest to the church, with another image of 144,000 and three angelic calls for the endurance of the saints (14:1–13). Once the earth has been harvested and the winepress of wrath is full, the song of Moses and the Lamb crown the final judgment of the Lord God (15:3–4). These chapters call the church to fidelity to Christ as they await his certain victory. The opening of Revelation 15 both closes off the portrait that began in 12:1 and prepares us for the next sevenfold picture, the seven bowls of wrath (Rev 16:1–21).

The seven bowls are the final seven-step picture of the last days. Thus they are more intense and hasten to the final judgment with more urgency. The first five bowls resemble the previous curse imagery; the sixth draws the battle lines for the three beasts' assault on God Almighty. But before the battle even begins, it is finished with the seventh bowl's "it is done" and the fourfold superstorm (16:17–18). Like the other seventh steps, the seventh bowl adds a hinge to swing us into the next portrait, which is the introduction of Babylon. With the exception of a brief announcement in 14:8, this is the first we have heard about Babylon, and we may feel unacquainted with its identity. Who is Babylon? The next portrait tells us.

The portrait of Babylon, the great prostitute, extends from 17:1–19:10, which includes an interlude on the saints coming to the marriage supper of the Lamb (19:6–10). Often Babylon is simply equated with Rome, but this is not entirely correct. Lady Babylon is pictured not as a single earthly empire, but as an embodiment of the rebellious ways of the city of man who joins forces with the apostate church.[5] Using imagery from Ezekiel's oracle against Tyre (Ezek 27), Jezebel, and Jerusalem, John makes Lady Babylon the ideal merger of the world city and apostate Jerusalem, sired by the antichrist beast. In fact, Lady Babylon is illustrated in ways to contrast with Lady Jerusalem in Revelation 12. Therefore, after her prostitutions are described (Old Testament imagery for idolatry), her fall is mourned in chapter 18.

After Lady Babylon's profile, Revelation closes with three quick vignettes of the final judgment. Like a diamond, the day of the Lord has many facets, so we can approach it from several angles. First, in Revelation 19:11–21, the White Rider summons the birds to feast on all the slain, which is imagery pulled in part from Ezekiel 38–39 that pictures the everlasting curse upon the rebellious. Second, the thousand years end with Satan and his horde imprisoned in the eternal lake of fire (Rev 20:1–10). Third and final is the judgment of humans, as the books of judgment are opened to punish the wicked by works, while the book of life is read for the people of the Lamb (20:11–15).

With judgment sealed for eternity, the glory of God's everlasting salvation can be unfurled in all its sweet majesty (Rev 21–22). This last picture bursts at the seams with its gorgeous climactic blessings. The Immanuel goal, forfeited by Adam, of God's intimate presence living with humans now blossoms into full bloom: "Behold, the dwelling place of God is with man" (21:3). The Alpha creation comes to a finish with the Omega peace, "It is done!" (21:6). The bride of the Lamb is revealed to be the holy city of Jerusalem. The people are the place, with its twelve apostolic foundations and twelve tribal gates. The Lamb's blood has washed and purified his people as pristinely holy without an atom of impurity. The temple building has been replaced with the very presence of the one seated on the throne and the Lamb. Bubbling up from the throne are the healing waters of the river of life, and on either side of the river the tree of life. And in the light of the Lamb's face his people will live as royals forever and ever. From that first gospel promise to crush the serpent until now, the Lamb of God has kept with victorious perfection every promise of God's people, and he did so for the glory of the Father for eternity. The agonizing vicissitudes of the earthly life veil the coming glory, but by the portraits of Revelation, the eyes of faith gaze with unhindered clarity upon face of the Lamb, crying, "Amen. Come, Lord Jesus."

STUDY QUESTIONS

1. What is meant by the name General Epistles?

2. What problem were the audience of the book of Hebrews struggling with?

3. How did the New Testament church stick out compared to the other religions?

4. Discuss the five issues facing the churches in the General Epistles and how they are still current today?

5. What are some of the reading principles for Revelation?

6. What is the one simple message of Revelation?

7. List some of the ways that Revelation 21–22 fulfill so much of what God promised in the Old Testament.

ACKNOWLEDGMENTS

As this book is the fruit of a nearly two-decade project, my gratitude extends to a host of individuals who have impacted and encouraged me along the way. I cannot list them all, but to begin with, my sincere thanks goes out to Dr. Byron Curtis, who took me on as a teaching assistant in his Bible survey class back in college. Dr. Curtis's high standards and fervor for the Bible set me on the right path. I am grateful to the faculty and board of Westminster Seminary California for giving me the opportunity to teach their Bible survey class for the past seventeen years, as this book takes the oral tradition of the class and puts it into writing. Likewise, I am indebted to my students, who asked questions and gave me feedback, allowing me to hone my material and its presentation.

A special thanks goes to Phil Sipe, whose dogged zeal put me in touch with Lexham Press. Without Phil, this book would not be. I am grateful to the folks at Lexham Press for taking on this book, especially to Elliot Ritzema for all his invaluable editing and feedback. The elders of Escondido Orthodox Presbyterian Church, where I serve, are owed a deep debt of gratitude for giving me sabbaticals to write. Their friendship and encouragement were priceless. The editing of Le Ann Trees was extremely helpful and careful, for which I give her my thanks. I am thankful for Dr. John V. Fesko, Dr. David VanDrunen, and Dr. Steve Baugh, whose stirring academic conversation refined my thinking on all things biblical and more. I cannot thank enough Dr. Josh VanEe for his friendship, his reading over parts of the manuscript, and particularly for our hours of dialogue about the ancient Near East and the world of the Bible. Most of the pictures in this book come from Josh, for which I am also very appreciative. I also thank Dr. Bryan Estelle. Our conversations on the way up to Tahquitz or around the campfire have made me a better student of the Bible.

Finally, I cannot thank enough my family for all their support, laughs, and love. My kids, Xander, Bëor and Lúthien, are my joy and delight. Teaching them all the weird wonders of the Bible is what is it all about. I am thankful to my mom for her probing Bible questions and her thoughtful spiritual curiosity. And, most of all, I thank my wife Tovauh, whose love and companionship sustain me like the lotus.

IMAGE ATTRIBUTIONS

The Acropolis in Athens
Photo by Joshua VanEe
Used by permission

Atrahasis
Photo by Jack 1956*
Public Domain
Via Wikimedia Commons

Beit She'an looking west, near Jezreel
Photo by Joshua VanEe
Used by permission

Bethlehem, David's hometown
Photo by Joshua VanEe
Used by permission

En Gedi, where David hid from Saul
Photo by Joshua VanEe
Used by permission

Foundation of the altar of Zeus in Pergamum
Photo by David A. deSilva
Copyright 2020 Faithlife / Logos Bible Software

From the caves of Qumran, looking east to the Dead Sea
    and the Moabite highlands
Photo by Joshua VanEe
Used by permission

Garden of Gethsemane
Photo by David Lenhert
Used by permission

The Golan Heights, with Mount Hermon in the distance
Photo by Joshua VanEe
Used by permission

The Kidron Valley, with Jerusalem on the right and the Mount
    of Olives on the left
Photo by Joshua VanEe
Used by permission

Model of the tabernacle
Photo by Barry J. Beitzel
Copyright 2020 Faithlife / Logos Bible Software

Papyrus 46
Public domain

Ruins of Capernaum
Photo by Joshua VanEe
Used by permission

Ruins of Corinth
Photo by Joshua VanEe
Used by permission

Sea of Galilee
Photo by Joshua VanEe
Used by permission

Semitic traders bringing their wares to Egypt
Public domain

Shechem as seen from Mount Gerizim
Photo by Joshua VanEe
Used by permission

Shiloh
Photo by Joshua VanEe
Used by permission

Terrace house in Ephesus
Photo by Joshua VanEe
Used by permission

The Valley of Elah, where David fought Goliath
Photo by Joshua VanEe
Used by permission

NOTES

Chapter 1

1. Jack M. Sasson, "Time ... To Begin," in *Shar'arei Talmon: Studies in the Bible, Qumran, and the Ancient Near East Presented to Shemaryahu Talmon*, ed. Michael Fisbane et al. (Winona Lake, IN: Eisenbrauns, 1992), 191.

2. Gordon Wenham, *Genesis 1–15*, Word Biblical Commentary 1 (Waco: Word Books, 1987), xlvii.

3. William W. Hallo and K. Lawson Younger, *The Context of Scripture, vol. 1* (New York: Brill, 1997), 400.

4. Hallo and Younger, *Context of Scripture,* 1:516–18.

5. John H. Walton, *Genesis 1 as Ancient Cosmology* (Winona Lake: Eisenbrauns, 2011), 22.

6. Hallo and Younger, *Context of Scripture,* 1:7. See also James B. Pritchard, ed., *The Ancient Near Eastern Texts Relating to the Old Testament,* 3rd ed. (Princeton: Princeton University Press, 1969), 3–4.

7. Walton, *Cosmology,* 27.

8. Hallo and Younger, *Context of Scripture,* 1:23.

9. The presence of rebellion is debated, as the flood comes in *Atrahasis* for humanity's noisiness. The moral connotations of this noisiness are not entirely clear, though rebellion is likely.

10.   Tony W. Cartledge, *Vows in the Hebrew Bible and the Ancient Near East*, JSOT 147 (Sheffield: JSOT Press, 1992), 15.

11.   David P. Wright, "Holiness (OT)," in David Noel Freedman, ed., *The Anchor Yale Bible Dictionary* (New York: Doubleday, 1992), 3:237.

12.   P. P. Jensen, "Holiness in the Priestly Writings of the Old Testament," in *Holiness Past and Present*, ed. B. Z. Kedar and R. J. Z. Werblowsky (London: T&T Clark, 2003), 107.

13.   Job Y. Jindo, *Biblical Metaphor Reconsidered: A Cognitive Approach to Poetic Prophecy in Jeremiah 1–24*, HSM 64 (Winona Lake, IN: Eisenbrauns, 2010), 154.

14.   Jon D. Levenson, *Resurrection and the Restoration of Israel: The Ultimate Victory of the God of Life* (New Haven: Yale, 2006), 86.

15.   Victor A. Hurowitz, "YHWH's Exalted House—Aspects of the Design and Symbolism of Solomon's Temple," in *Temple and Worship in Biblical Israel*, ed. John Day (New York: T&T Clark, 2005), 87.

16.   Daniel C. Timmer, *Creation, Tabernacle and Sabbath: The Sabbath Frame of Exodus 31:12–17; 35:1–3 in Exegetical and Theological Perspective* (Göttingen: Vandenhoeck & Ruprecht, 2009), 86.

17.   Jindo, *Biblical Metaphor*, 160.

Chapter 2

1.   "Sevenfold" here indicates complete or balanced justice, which for murder is a life for a life—that is, capital punishment.

2.   William W. Hallo and K. Lawson Younger, *The Context of Scripture, vol.* 1 (New York: Brill, 1997), 79.

3.   The Sefire treaties are on three basalt stones discovered near Aleppo, Syria. See evidence listed by Nahum M. Sarna in *Genesis: The JPS Torah Commentary* (Jerusalem: Jewish Publication Society, 1989), 114–15. For the whole text of the treaties see William W. Hallo and K. Lawson Younger, *The Context of Scripture, vol.* 2 (Boston: Brill, 2000), 213–17.

4.   Menahem Haran, "The *Berit* 'Covenant': Its Nature and Ceremonial Background," in *Tehillah le-Moshe: Biblical and Judaic Studies in Honor of Moshe Greenberg*, ed. Mordecai Cogan, Barry L. Eichler, and Jeffrey H. Tigay (Winona Lake, IN: Eisenbrauns, 1997), 218.

5.   Bruce K. Waltke, *Genesis: A Commentary* (Grand Rapids: Zondervan, 2001), 467.

6.   Sarna, *Genesis*, 293.

Chapter 3

1. K. A. Kitchen, *On the Reliability of the Old Testament* (Grand Rapids: Eerdmans, 2003), 253.

2. Jack M. Sasson, *Judges 1–12*, Anchor Yale Bible 6D (New Haven: Yale University Press, 2014), 261.

3. Kitchen, *Reliability*, 209.

Chapter 4

1. Paul S. Minear, *To Heal and To Reveal: The Prophetic Vocation According to Luke* (New York: Seabury Press, 1976), 4.

2. Minear, *To Heal*, 3.

3. Howard Eilberg-Schwartz, *The Savage in Judaism: An Anthropology of Israelite Religion and Ancient Judaism* (Indianapolis: Indiana University Press, 1990), 1–21.

4. William W. Hallo and K. Lawson Younger, *The Context of Scripture, vol. 2* (Boston: Brill, 2000), 336.

5. Delbert R. Hillers, *Treaty-Curses and the Old Testament Prophets* (Rome: Pontifical Biblical Institute, 1964), 80.

6. Jon D. Levenson, *Sinai and Zion: An Entry into the Jewish Bible* (New York: HarperCollins, 1985), 28.

7. William L. Moran, "The Ancient Near Eastern Background of the Love of God in Deuteronomy," *Catholic Biblical Quarterly* 25 (1963): 77–87.

8. Hallo and Younger, *Context of Scripture* 2:93.

9. Hallo and Younger, *Context of Scripture* 2:95.

10. James B. Pritchard, ed., *The Ancient Near Eastern Texts Relating to the Old Testament*, 3rd ed. (Princeton: Princeton University Press, 1969), 206.

11. Table reprinted from K. A. Kitchen, *On the Reliability of the Old Testament* (Grand Rapids: Eerdmans, 2003), 284. Used by permission.

12. Moshe Weinfeld, *Deuteronomy 1–11*, Anchor Yale Bible 5 (New York: Doubleday, 1991), 239.

13. Brent A. Strawn, "Keep/Observe/Do—Carefully—Today! The Rhetoric of Repetition in Deuteronomy," in *A God So Near: Essays on Old Testament Theology in Honor of Patrick D. Miller,* ed. Brent A. Strawn and Nancy R. Bowen (Winona Lake, IN: Eisenbrauns, 2003), 226.

14. See Michael B. Hundley, *Keeping Heaven on Earth: Safeguarding the Divine Presence in the Priestly Tabernacle* (Tübingen: Mohr Siebeck, 2011).

15. Jon D. Levenson, *Resurrection and the Restoration of Israel: The Ultimate Victory of the God of Life* (New Haven: Yale, 2006), 90.

16. Victor Avigdor Hurowitz, "Ascending the Mountain of the Lord—A Glimpse into the Solomonic Temple," in *Capital Cities: Urban Planning and Spiritual Dimensions*, ed. Joan Goodnick Westenholz (Jerusalem: Bible Lands Museum Jerusalem, 1998), 220.

17. Daniel C. Timmer, *Creation, Tabernacle, and Sabbath: The Sabbath Frame of Exodus 31:12–17; 35:1–3 in Exegetical and Theological Perspective* (Göttingen: Vandenhoeck & Ruprecht, 2009), 39.

18. Levenson, *Resurrection*, 93.

19. See Menahem Haran, *Temples and Temple Service in Ancient Israel* (Winona Lake, IN: Eisenbrauns, 1985), 164–74.

20. Jacob Milgrom, *Leviticus 1–16*, Anchor Yale Bible 3 (New Haven: Yale University Press, 2008), 615; and so Ezekiel condemns the priests for this very failure (Ezek 22:26).

21. Edmund Leach, "The Logic of Sacrifice," in *Anthropological Approaches to the Old Testament*, ed. B. Lang (Philadelphia: Fortress, 1985), 137.

22. Yitzhaq Feder, *Blood Expiation in Hittite and Biblical Ritual: Origins, Context, and Meaning* (Atlanta: Society of Biblical Literature, 2011), 33.

23. However, they still had to keep the purity laws and go to a priest, since Jesus had not yet been crucified and raised from the dead, finally rendering the sacrificial system obsolete.

Chapter 5

1. In 1 Sam 13:21, the Septuagint (the Greek version of the Old Testament) reads, "But he did not rebuke his son Amnon, for he favored him, since he was his first-born." A version from the Dead Sea Scrolls reads, "for he loved him, for he was his firstborn."

Chapter 6

1. The text labels them as youngsters, but Rehoboam is forty-one years old when he becomes king.

2. Gary N. Knoppers, *Two Nations Under God: The Deuteronomistic History of Solomon and the Dual Monarchies, Vol. 7: The Reign of Jeroboam, the Fall of Israel, and the Reign of Josiah*, HSM 53 (Atlanta: Scholars Press, 1994), 42.

3. Dates in this table follow K. A. Kitchen, *On the Reliability of the Old Testament* (Grand Rapids: Eerdmans, 2003), 30–32.

4. James B. Pritchard, ed., *The Ancient Near Eastern Texts Relating to the Old Testament*, 3rd ed. (Princeton: Princeton University Press, 1969), 320.

5. Mordechai Cogan, *I Kings*, Anchor Yale Bible 10 (New York: Doubleday, 2001), 416, 418.

6. It is debated what Tyrian deity Baal refers to, though a likely answer is Baal-Shamem, "Lord of the Heavens," a weather god, see Cogan, *I Kings*, 421.

7. Athaliah's exact paternity is ambiguous in Scripture; see Reuven Chaim (Rudolph) Klein, "Queen Athaliah: The Daughter of Ahab or Omri?," *Jewish Bible Quarterly* 42, no. 1 (2014): 11–20.

8. Cogan, *I Kings*, 184–85. See also Jacob Milgrom, *Leviticus 23–27*, Anchor Yale Bible 3B (New Haven: Yale University Press, 2008), 2316–18.

9. See Mordechai Cogan and Hayim Tadmor, *II Kings*, Anchor Yale Bible 11 (New Haven: Yale University Press, 2008), 218–22.

Chapter 7

1. A literal translation of Ezekiel's term for idols. To catch his scorn, "shit gods" would not be a bad modern equivalent.

2. K. A. Kitchen, *On the Reliability of the Old Testament* (Grand Rapids: Eerdmans, 2003), 376.

Chapter 8

1. Jack R. Lundbom, *Jeremiah 37–52*, Anchor Yale Bible 21C (New York: Doubleday, 2004), 519–20.

2. Specially, chapters 1–4 are acrostics and chapter 5 is not an acrostic but resembles chapters 1–4 with 22 verses.

3. Or alternatively, "her punishment is accepted."

4. See Meredith G. Kline, "Double Trouble," *Journal of the Evangelical Theological Society* 32, no. 2 (1989): 171–79. See also Jer 16:18 and the discussion by Jack Lundbom, *Jeremiah 1–20*, Anchor Yale Bible 21A (New York: Doubleday, 1999), 771.

5. Jacob Milgrom's translation from *Leviticus 23–27*, Anchor Yale Bible 3B (New York: Doubleday, 2001), 2273.

6. Milgrom, *Leviticus 23–27*, 2323.

7. This discrepancy in numbers reveals how the authors of Scripture could use numbers as general approximations (so in 2 Kings) or to be more precise (so Jeremiah).

8. See Lisbeth S. Fried and David Noel Freedman's appendix, "Was the Jubilee Year Observed in Preexilic Judah?," in Milgrom, *Leviticus 23–27*, 2257–70.

9. This is not a problem for the biblical author, as another clear example of such projection is found in Ezra 6:14, when Artaxerxes (465–424) is given credit for the temple in 520. The unity of the act and purpose can be credited to different agents who share in it at different times or stages. Artaxerxes' help to build the wall aligns with Darius' previous help for the temple.

10. This is further brought out in Ezra 7 in that Artaxerxes' letter is written in Aramaic (vv. 12–26), but the text around it remains in Hebrew (vv. 1–11 and vv. 27–28).

11. They further admit their status as slaves as did Ezra in 9:37.

12. Other Old Testament books may be later than Nehemiah (i.e. Ecclesiastes, Malachi, Chronicles), but in terms of a dateable figure he is the last one.

13. See Meredith G. Kline, "The Covenant of the Seventieth Week," in *The Law and the Prophets: Old Testament Studies in Honor of Oswald T. Allis*, ed. J. H. Skilton (Nutley, NJ: P&R, 1974), 452–69.

14. See Michael V. Fox, *Character and Ideology in the Book of Esther*, 2nd ed. (Grand Rapids: Eerdmans, 2001), 171–211 .

Chapter 9

1. Strictly speaking Psalms is not a wisdom text, even though there are a few wisdom psalms, but it is included here due to its poetic nature. Likewise, Song of Songs is not a wisdom text, but it is love poetry.

2. Michael V. Fox, *Proverbs 1–9*, Anchor Yale Bible 18A (New York: Doubleday, 2000), 17.

3. Roland E. Murphy, *The Tree of Life: An Exploration of Biblical Wisdom Literature*, 2nd ed. (Grand Rapids: Eerdmans, 1996), 119.

4. Murphy, *Tree of Life*, 113.

5. Murphy, *Tree of Life*, 114.

6. Fox, *Proverbs 1–9*, 32.

7. See Fox's excellent survey of wisdom and folly terminology, *Proverbs 1–9*, 28–43.

8. Fox, *Proverbs 1–9*, 34.

9.   James B. Pritchard, ed., *The Ancient Near Eastern Texts Relating to the Old Testament*, 3rd ed. (Princeton: Princeton University Press, 1969), 421.

10. Fox, *Proverbs 1–9*, 19.

11. William W. Hallo and K. Lawson Younger, *The Context of Scripture*, vol. 1 (New York: Brill, 1997), 62.

12. Pritchard, *Ancient Near Eastern Texts*, 412. See Eccl 12.

13. See Prov 3:7; Isa 5:21; Jer 9:23.

14. Hallo and Younger, *Context of Scripture*, 1:115.

15. Fox, *Proverbs 1–9*, 18.

16. Hallo and Younger, *Context of Scripture*, 1:116.

17. Fox, *Proverbs 1–9*, 21.

18. Fox, *Proverbs 1–9*, 73.

19. Hallo and Younger, *Context of Scripture*, 1:569.

20. Fox's reconstruction, *Proverbs 1–9*, 332.

21. Pritchard, *Ancient Near Eastern Texts*, 429; see Prov 27:3; Job 6:2–3.

22. Michael V. Fox, *Proverbs 10–31*, Anchor Yale Bible 18B (New Haven: Yale University Press, 2009), 794.

23. See the discussion of the difficult issues surrounding v. 30 in James Alfred Loader, *Proverbs 1–9* (Leuven: Peeters, 2014), 356–61.

24. See Meredith G. Kline, "Trial by Ordeal," in *Through Christ's Word: A Festschrift for Dr. Philip E. Hughes*, ed. W. Robert Godfrey and Jesse L. Boyd III (Phillipsburg, NJ: P&R, 1985), 81–93.

25. Think of Samson and his riddle contest in Judg 14.

26. C. L. Seow, *Ecclesiastes*, Anchor Yale Bible 18C (New York: Doubleday, 1997), 3.

27. Antoon Schoors, *Ecclesiastes* (Leuven: Peeters, 2013), 30–36.

28. See Seow's extensive evidence in *Ecclesiastes*, 11–36.

29. Michael V. Fox, *Qohelet and His Contradictions*, JSOT 71 (Sheffield: Almond Press, 1989), 31.

30. Fox, *Contradictions*, 32.

31. Brian P. Gault, *Body as Landscape, Love as Intoxication: Conceptual Metaphors in the Song of Songs* (Atlanta: SBL Press, 2019), 31.

32. Sigmund Mowinckel, *The Psalms in Israel's Worship* (Grand Rapids: Eerdmans, 2004), 81.

33. See the discussion in Tony W. Cartledge, *Vows in the Hebrew Bible and the Ancient Near East*, JSOT 147 (Sheffield: JSOT Press, 1992), 150–61.

34. Mowinckel, *The Psalms*, 27.

Chapter 10

1. Everett Ferguson, *Backgrounds of Early Christianity*, 3rd ed. (Grand Rapids: Eerdmans, 2003), 405.

2. The title "the Great" was not used by Herod, nor was it used for him in the first century. See Peter Richardson, *Herod: King of the Jews and Friend of the Romans* (Columbia, SC: University of South Carolina Press, 1996), 12.

3. Ferguson, *Backgrounds*, 412.

4. Richardson, *Herod*, 2.

5. Quoted from *Rome: The Augustan Age*, ed. Kitty Chisholm and John Ferguson (New York: Oxford University Press, 1981), 70.

6. Ferguson, *Backgrounds*, 21–22.

7. Ferguson, *Backgrounds*, 427.

8. Ferguson, *Backgrounds*, 428.

9. Ferguson, *Backgrounds*, 513.

10. Josephus says this to contrast the Sadducees with the Pharisees, but this most likely means the Sadducees disagreed with Pharisaic interpretation in favor of their own. It does not mean the Sadducees had no tradition of interpretation.

11. See Anthony J. Saldarini, *Pharisees, Scribes and Sadducees in Palestinian Society* (Grand Rapids: Eerdmans, 1988), 302–5.

12. Saldarini, *Pharisees*, 34.

13. Following Pearson, I translate Luke 2:2 as "this was the registration prior to (before) Quirinius." See his full discussion in Brook W. R. Pearson, "The Lucan Censuses, Revisited," *Catholic Biblical Quarterly* 61, no. 2 (1999): 262–82.

14. See Josephus, *Antiquities* 18.6–7.

15. S. Talmon, "The Concepts of Messiah and Messianism in Early Judaism," *The Messiah*, ed. James H. Charlesworth (Minneapolis: Fortress Press, 1992), 113. See also his "Types of Messianic Expectation at the Turn of the Era" in *King, Cult and Calendar in Ancient Israel: Collected Studies* (Jerusalem: Magnes Press, 1986), 202–24.

16. The distinction between casting out demons and healing is not to ignore to the complex relationship between demon possession and mental or physical afflictions.

17. See discussion under "The Birth and Kingdom of Jesus" above.

18. See S. Safrai and M. Stern, eds., *The Jewish People in the First Century: Historical Geography, Political History, Social, Cultural and Religious Life and Institutions*, vol 2 (Amsterdam: Van Gorcum, 1976), 903.

19. Joseph A. Fitzmyer, *The Gospel According to Luke X–XXIV*, Anchor Yale Bible 28A (New Haven: Yale University Press, 1985), 1382.

20. Jacob Milgrom, *Leviticus 23–27*, Anchor Yale Bible 3B (New York: Doubleday, 2001), 1968; see his further discussion on pages 1967–70.

21. See Exod 12; 23:15; 34:18–25; Lev 23:4–8; Num 28:16–25; Deut 16:1–8.

22. The dating of this day was not agreed upon as the calendars of Qumran, Jubilees, and the Samaritans locate it elsewhere. See the discussion in Milgrom, *Leviticus 23–27*, 2056–63.

23. Every Gospel notes this same time: Matt 27:45; Mark 15:33; Luke 23:44; John 19:14.

Chapter 11

1. See Exod 23:16; 34:22; Lev 23:15–21; Num 28:26–31; Deut 16:9–12.

2. Cited by Joseph A. Fitzmyer, *The Acts of the Apostles*, Anchor Yale Bible 31 (New York: Doubleday, 1998), 612.

3. See Fitzmyer's excellent discussion in *Acts*, 619–23.

4. See A. N. Sherwin-White, *Roman Law and Roman Society in the New Testament* (Grand Rapids: Baker, 1992), 99–107.

5. It is difficult to value this amount in modern terms. By weight, this number of silver drachmas would total about 215,000 grams or 7,584 oz. At today's prices, you could fetch at market $3,158,350 with a $14.69/oz price. Such conversions, though, do not accurately convey the ancient purchasing power of this amount within the lives of everyday people.

Chapter 12

1. See Peter R. Jones, "1 Corinthians 15:8: Paul The Last Apostle," *Tyndale Bulletin* 36 (1985) 3–34.

2. See S. M. Baugh, *Paul and Ephesus: The Apostle among His Contemporaries* (PhD diss; University of California, Irvine, 1990), 152–64.

3.   See Stephen M. Pogoloff, *LOGOS and SOPHIA: The Rhetorical Situation of 1 Corinthians*, SBL Dissertation 134 (Atlanta: Scholars Press, 1992).

4.   See E. Randolph Richards, *Paul and First-Century Letter Writing: Secretaries, Composition and Collection* (Downers Grove, IL: InterVarsity Press, 2004), 32–46.

5.   Richards, *Letter Writing*, 105.

6.   See the helpful charts in Richards, *Letter Writing*, 226–28.

7.   See the analysis of the style of Ephesians by S. M. Baugh, *Ephesians*, Evangelical Exegetical Commentary (Bellingham, WA: Lexham Press, 2016), 8–25.

8.   Richards, *Letter Writing*, 140.

9.   See especially Bruce W. Winter, *After Paul Left Corinth: The Influence of Secular Ethics and Social Change* (Grand Rapids: Eerdmans, 2001).

10.   Baugh, *Ephesians*, 35.

11.   See Clinton E. Arnold, *The Colossian Syncretism: The Interface between Christianity and Folk Belief at Colossae* (Grand Rapids: Baker, 1996).

Chapter 13

1.   See the thorough discussion in James B. Adamson, *James: The Man and His Message* (Grand Rapids: Eerdmans, 1989), 3–52.

2.   See Abraham J. Malherbe, *Social Aspects of Early Christianity*, 2nd Ed (Philadelphia: Fortress Press, 1983), especially chapter 3: "House Churches and Their Problems," 60–91.

3.   See G. K. Beale, *The Book of Revelation*, New International Greek Testament Commentary (Grand Rapids: Eerdmans, 1999), 4.

4.   This comes from the earth having four corners, four winds, and four cardinal directions (Isa 11:12; Ezek 7:2; Jer 49:36; Dan 7:2; Ps 107:3).

5.   See Paul S. Minear, *I Saw a New Earth: An Introduction to the Visions of the Apocalypse* (Cleveland: Corpus Books, 1968), 146–52.